Host Cities

HOST CITIES

HOW REFUGEES ARE TRANSFORMING THE WORLD'S URBAN SETTINGS

KAREN JACOBSEN

Yale
UNIVERSITY PRESS
New Haven and London

Copyright © 2025 by Karen Jacobsen.
All rights reserved.

This book may not be reproduced, in whole or in part, including illustrations, in any form (beyond that copying permitted by Sections 107 and 108 of the U.S. Copyright Law and except by reviewers for the public press), without written permission from the publishers.

Yale University Press books may be purchased in quantity for educational, business, or promotional use. For information, please e-mail sales .press@yale.edu (U.S. office) or sales@yaleup.co.uk (U.K. office).

Set in Adobe Garamond type by Westchester Publishing Services

Printed and bound by CPI Group (UK) Ltd, Croydon, CR0 4YY

Library of Congress Control Number: 2025932508
ISBN 978-0-300-25469-3 (hardcover)

A catalogue record for this book is available from the British Library.

Authorized Representative in the EU: Easy Access System Europe, Mustamäe tee 50, 10621 Tallinn, Estonia, gpsr.requests@easproject.com

10 9 8 7 6 5 4 3 2 1

For Pippa, who for fifty years has taught me all
I know about friendship, with love and gratitude

A city is more than a place in space, it is a drama in time.

Patrick Geddes

Contents

Preface ix
Acknowledgments xix

ONE
FRAMING THE PROBLEM

1 Cities and Humanitarian Influxes 3
2 The Actors and the Numbers 20
3 Informal Cities: How Cities Are Growing 37

TWO
SECONDARY CITIES: TRIPOLI, LEBANON

4 How Refugees Get Stuck in Cities 57
5 Lebanon: The Refugee Context 63
6 Tripoli and the Changing City Landscape 74
7 The Camp and the City 94
8 Here Comes the Money 110
9 Just Give Them Cash 125

CONTENTS

10 Trash Mountain — 138
11 The Smuggling Economy — 153

THREE
GIANT CITIES: CAIRO, EGYPT

12 Comparing the Experiences of Cairo and Tripoli — 167
13 Egypt: The Refugee Context — 173
14 Drops in the Bucket: Cairo's Refugee Neighborhoods — 189
15 The Bus to 6th of October: The Desert Cities and UNHCR — 205
16 Refugee Entrepreneurs — 220
17 "Money Has Come": Remittances and Informal Money Transfers — 230
18 Ard al-Lewa: Drinking, Women's Work, and Social Cohesion — 244
  Epilogue Strengthening Host Cities — 261
  Postscript Update on Mahmoud and Hassan — 271

Notes — 273
Index — 313

Preface

I grew up in a city where migration was tightly controlled. In the 1970s, Johannesburg was Africa's richest city (it still is), and South Africa's apartheid government restricted the movement of its black citizens and immigrants. South Africa's cities and towns were for whites only—people like me. Black citizens lived in slum areas called "townships," well separated from the city. They commuted into the city by bus and train, then returned to the townships at night. No black people were permitted to be in the cities at night unless they had a special permit called a "pass." The largest township outside Johannesburg was Soweto—it was to become famous in 1976 when the Soweto uprising took place, beginning the long and often violent struggle that culminated in 1990 with Nelson Mandela's release from prison, and the victory in 1994 of the African National Congress (ANC) in South Africa's first truly democratic election. But in 1970, there was no sign of this upheaval to come. The ANC's leadership was in prison or in exile, and the Afrikaner Nationalist Party had the country tightly in hand. The economy was thriving, and whites were doing well. The government allowed immigration into South Africa—but only for whites.

In 1970, my parents purchased land in a new municipality north of Johannesburg called Sandton. What had previously been large (white-owned) farms was being developed into affluent suburbia as the city of Johannesburg expanded. In the modest and still very raw

PREFACE

Sandton suburb of Wendywood, my parents built one of the first houses. My brother and I rode our bikes on the raw dirt roads that had been bulldozed through the wildflowers and soft highveld grass. Wendywood was built next to the highway linking Johannesburg and Pretoria, on the other side of which was the township Alexandra, or "Alex," as everyone called it. On school days, my brother and I would cross the pedestrian bridge over the highway and wait for the Putco bus (for whites only) that ran between Pretoria and Johannesburg. In winter, in that warm bus, we would sail past the crowded bus stops of the coal-smoke-hidden township, where hundreds of black people waited for their own unheated and rattletrap buses to take them into the city.

As a child, I never set foot in Alex, but I knew someone from there—Lena, the maid who worked for us. Lena was one of thousands of people from rural areas of South Africa who began to come to South Africa's cities in the 1960s and 1970s to earn money, which they sent back home. The South African government also permitted thousands of men to come from neighboring countries like Mozambique and Malawi to work in South Africa's mines. All migration was strictly controlled by the apartheid government, sometimes in the form of labor agreements with the governments of the migrants' countries. South Africa's harsh border controls prevented refugees from entering, but many crossed the border anyway. During the war in Mozambique in the 1980s, for example, some 350,000 refugees entered South Africa, despite an electric fence and the Kruger Park and its lions along the eastern border area.

I left South Africa when I turned twenty-one and had finished college. It was 1979, and the townships were burning. All over the country, people were resisting the government's policies and facing the wrath of the state's enforcement apparatus. Police and their weapon dogs and even the army were being sent into the increasingly

PREFACE

ungovernable townships, including Alex. As the resistance grew, more and more people were being arrested, and many were leaving the country. Some whites tried to help the black resistance, some going to prison for it. But though I had been active in politics during my university years, I did not want to stay in South Africa; I was young and wanted to see the world, so I left. I lived in London for a while, worked for two years in Zambia as a journalist, and eventually found my way to Boston and graduate school.

Migration, cities, and exile intrigued me, and graduate school gave me a chance to explore these issues. But in the 1980s, the study of refugee policy was new—and it meant going to refugee camps. So, for my PhD research, in early 1990 I first went to Thailand, where 900,000 Cambodian refugees had fled the Pol Pot regime and the Vietnamese Army invasion of Cambodia, and were in camps on the Thai-Cambodian border. I talked to government officials, to UN officials and NGO aid workers, to Thai villagers and refugees living in Aranyaprathet, and to refugees in the camps. Later in 1990, I went to Zimbabwe's beautiful Eastern Highlands, where 150,000 refugees from Mozambique's civil war lived in remote refugee camps near the border, and conducted similar research there.

In the 1990s, although most refugee research focused on camps (as much of it still does today), it was already clear that many refugees were coming to the cities of host countries. For one thing, not all host countries had encampment policies. For example, Egypt, then as now, does not require the thousands of refugees it hosts to live in camps. Nor did (or does) South Africa, Lebanon, Türkiye, Pakistan, or Colombia. Even in countries that did have encampment policies, a large proportion of refugees left or avoided the camps and came to cities. For people who were internally displaced—that is, they did not cross a border when they fled armed conflict or persecution—almost all of them fled to the towns and cities of their countries. This urban movement led to many questions. What draws refugees and internally displaced people (IDPs) to cities, and where do they go when they get there? Does their experience differ from that of regular migrants? What are the best ways to support them? And if humanitarian support is provided to refugees and IDPs, does this raise issues of fairness and equity for the poor communities in which the refugees live?

Starting about twenty-five years ago, donor governments like the United States and the European Union, along with the nongovernmental organizations (NGOs) and UN agencies they fund, began to invest in urban refugee research. This was lucky for me, as my own work was turning in this direction. In the early 2000s, the US State Department, then and now (as of the end of 2024) the world's biggest funder of refugee programs, funded my team at the Feinstein International Center (Tufts University) to conduct a three-city study of refugees in Aden (Yemen), Mae Sot (Thailand), and Polokwane (South Africa). Around this time, the Norwegian Refugee Council asked me to develop an urban profiling methodology that compared the experiences of displaced and nondisplaced households living in the same neighborhoods. This work took me and/or my research team to Khartoum (Sudan), Abidjan (Côte d'Ivoire), and Santa Marta (Colombia). Gradually, UN agencies and NGOs were beginning to figure out that to support refugees in cities, they could not simply import traditional humanitarian programs designed for refugee camps. I was fortunate to be able to contribute to this line of research. Between 2000 and 2024, I conducted research in more than twenty cities, sometimes working with the UN or an international NGO, but often as an independent Tufts-based researcher working with local teams.

As I explored the experience of urban refugees, another set of questions arose: What did the arrival of very large numbers of refugees and IDPs mean for cities? Are the consequences of their arrival

PREFACE

and ongoing presence different from those of regular migration to cities? These dynamics had not been systematically explored in the host cities of countries where most refugees live (in Africa, Asia, and Latin America). Most research and statistical data tended to treat host countries in the aggregate, as if the experiences of both the refugees and the host country can be boiled down to national averages and statistics. But within any host country, there is significant regional variation in the number of refugees and their experiences and in the local responses to them. Not all refugees live in cities, but given the increasing numbers that do, cities give us a lens through which to understand the internal variations of host countries. A book about the impact of refugees on these cities needed to be written, and I began work on it in 2018. Because most of my experience has been in the cities of Africa and the Middle East, this book focuses on those cities.

My central argument is that both the experiences of displaced people (refugees and IDPs) and their impacts on a city are different from those associated with the regular constant in-migration common to all cities. The reasons for this difference are threefold. First, a humanitarian influx is usually much larger and more concentrated than regular urban migration. Very large numbers of displaced people arrive over a shorter period, which creates a range of economic and social shocks for a city. Second, refugees are perceived and received differently from other migrants by the citizens and governments (both national and city) of a host country, and by the international community. Citizens and governments usually receive refugees with more sympathy—at least initially. Their attitudes and responses manifest in a well-established pattern: citizens tend to respond positively to refugees—at least in the early days of their arrival—then this welcoming response changes over time. The citizens' response is highly contingent on the number of refugee arrivals, how long they stay, what kinds of pressures they place on cities, and what kinds of resources they bring to the city. The citizens' and host government's response, I argue, is also influenced by their own experience and history of displacement and migration, especially with respect to the refugees' sending countries. Third, the response of the international community is also very different. In the past seventy-five years, a body of international refugee law and practice has emerged, but there is no counterpart when it comes to other kinds of migrants. Refugees—but not migrants—are the recipients of international humanitarian assistance and protection. As we shall see, this international response manifests in different ways, including with respect to the creation of refugee camps, but the overall effect is that refugees bring a substantial injection of external resources for the host country—and host cities.

Refugee and migrant populations have different implications for host cities. One difference is that refugees are often more likely to mobilize politically to address the problems they face, perhaps because they include human rights activists, journalists, and other political actors who have been persecuted in their home countries. Political mobilization might also occur because refugees, more than migrants, usually have more local host advocates willing to support them. How these differences play out in cities is explored in this book by focusing on two cities. One is a very large metropolis—Cairo; the other is a secondary city—Tripoli, Lebanon's second-biggest city, close to the border with Syria.

Host cities reveal the within-country variation of a host country's experience with refugees, but each host city is itself not uniform in this experience. One of the most clearly observable urban patterns of displacement is the "neighborhood effect." Refugees do not distribute themselves evenly across a city; rather, they tend to move to specific neighborhoods, usually where their co-nationals are already living. These neighborhoods are where most of the urban impact plays out.

As we discuss in Chapter 3, these neighborhoods are often the rapidly growing slum areas, or informal settlements, that today propel the growth of cities in poor countries.

Related to the neighborhood effect is what we might call the "diaspora effect." The presence of a long-standing population of co-nationals already in the city is an important facilitator for new arrivals. Whether they are family members or simply co-nationals, members of the diaspora support newcomers in many ways, including providing an initial place to stay and help with finding housing and jobs. The presence of a diaspora is one of the main reasons migrants and refugees choose to come to specific cities. This diaspora, along with sympathetic locals, is an important mediator of the impact of a humanitarian influx on a city. Yet, the importance of the diaspora as a factor in urban migration and displacement has not been well integrated into our understanding of the dynamics of urban migration and how both urban refugees and their neighbors can be assisted.

As researchers and advocacy groups share their work with policymakers and donors, humanitarian assistance is beginning to change. Both UN agencies and international NGOs are slowly adapting the programs that used to be aimed at helping people in camps. They recognize that one of the best ways to ease the plight of refugees is to promote good relations with their neighbors. When organizations distribute humanitarian resources so that both refugees and locals benefit, refugees come to be seen as an asset and are welcomed in the neighborhood. Other international actors—with financial clout—are also recognizing the need to address urban displacement. After the Syrian crisis, development agencies like the World Bank and donor countries with development projects in host countries began to see that large flows of refugees into cities could change how their development projects unfolded.

PREFACE

A humanitarian influx brings significant changes to a city. Sometimes the displaced people create new problems for the neighborhoods into which they move, but most of the time the city's problems were already there. The arrival and continuing stay of thousands of displaced people is disruptive and burdensome, and it can be a disturbing, even frightening experience for citizens, displaced people, and city authorities alike. But a humanitarian influx also brings many opportunities for positive change. Whether refugees aggravate a host city's existing problems or contribute to their solutions depends on the responses of the city's authorities and citizens, international actors, and the refugees themselves. As we shall see, the outcomes depend on whether these actors can ride the storm and take advantage of new opportunities, or instead remain bogged down in old unproductive modes that sink the city deeper into its problems. There are many examples of both outcomes in cities across the world today.

The city of Johannesburg, where I grew up, has been transformed by refugees. In 2005 I was in Johannesburg, teaching a course on refugees at the University of Witwatersrand, my alma mater. One day, an Eritrean colleague, Isias, invited me and a Nigerian colleague to lunch in "Little Eritrea," the downtown Johannesburg neighborhood where many Eritrean migrants and refugees lived. My Nigerian colleague and I were a little nervous—Johannesburg's inner city was known for its crime—but Isias assured us that we would be safe, so we piled into his car for the short drive through the city. Along the way, Isias pointed out places of interest: "That's where my brother was mugged," "This corner is where someone was stabbed two days ago," and so forth. My colleague and I shrank deeper into our seats and clutched our wallets. Isias soon pulled into the entrance of an underground parking garage and stopped. "You wait out here while I park," he said. Then, as he noticed our expressions, he added, "Don't worry, you are in Eritrea now, and there is no crime here." As we huddled on the sidewalk waiting, we could see that indeed, everyone around us was Eritrean (or Ethiopian—it is difficult to tell the two nationalities apart, since many Eritreans and Ethiopians are of the same Tigrayan ethnicity; even Ethiopians and Eritreans themselves acknowledge this difficulty). The busy street scene could have been Asmara or Addis Ababa. No one paid us any attention, and we relaxed a bit. Isias joined us and we crossed the street to a multistory, tubular building with a circular gallery of shops leading up five floors. There were Eritrean and Ethiopian food and clothing stores, hair stylists, coffee shops, travel agencies, and cell-phone services. Isias told us that the building was "owned by Chinese" who rented the shops to Eritreans or Ethiopians. On the top floor were several restaurants, and for a few South African rand, we dined magnificently on traditional Eritrean food, accompanied by wonderful avocado milkshakes, and finished up with Eritrean coffee. After lunch, we drove around the Marshalltown neighborhood, and Isias showed us a swathe of city blocks filled with panel-beating and car repair services run by Eritreans. The area had been economically rejuvenated since a few years before, when it had been a deserted and run-down part of town. On our way back to the university, Isias pointed to a tall office building and said it was owned by "one of the richest men in Africa," an Eritrean. Little Eritrea has become a thriving Johannesburg neighborhood, made so by refugees and migrants.

Acknowledgments

I am deeply indebted to my field research assistants (and ex-students): Claire Wilson in Lebanon and Ryan Philip (name changed for anti-doxxing reasons) and Alice Johnson in Cairo. All three were wonderful companions, with excellent interview skills, language and cultural awareness, enthusiasm and commitment, and above all, deep compassion. I am very grateful to my UNHCR colleagues, particularly Ninette Kelley and Joel Boutroue, for their willingness to discuss their experience and review sections of the book. This book would not have been possible without the involvement of my agent and dear friend, Jill Kneerim, whom we lost in 2022. Jill's encouragement and wisdom launched the book, and I never really recovered from losing her halfway through writing it. My thanks to David Sobel for his wise editing advice, and to my Fletcher students who helped me research or format the book over the years. I am deeply appreciative of the time given to me by the many refugees, Cairenes, and Tripolitans we spoke to in Tripoli and Cairo, as well as the staff of UN agencies and NGOs in both cities.

The support of my son and dear friends in Boston, Cape Town, and London has been a salve for me in difficult times during the writing of this book, as has the canine devotion of my beloved Junie.

PART ONE
Framing the Problem

1
Cities and Humanitarian Influxes

All cities, large and small, originated with migrants. The movement of people in and out of cities is so fundamental that it is hard to imagine a city in which no migration occurs. Cities constantly expand and contract as people come and go to find work, safety, education, health care, a new life, to join their families, or to travel on to another location. This book is about a particular type of urban migration, a humanitarian influx, which I define as the arrival in a city of more than 10,000 refugees or internally displaced people—that is, people who are fleeing armed conflict, persecution (such as ethnic cleansing or forced conscription), or disasters (such as floods, fires, or earthquakes). Such an influx can occur suddenly—over the course of a few weeks—or it can be spread over months, varying in pace and intensity but subjecting the city to ever-growing numbers of displaced people, many of whom will need humanitarian protection, assistance, and support. Sometimes migrants have come from other parts of the country and are internally displaced. Sometimes they have come from other countries as refugees. In either case, from the city's perspective, as I shall argue in this book, a humanitarian influx is different from the slower, more regular arrival of migrants from elsewhere in the country or from other countries.

FRAMING THE PROBLEM

Why Focus on Cities in Poor Countries?

Most of the scholarly and practitioner research on refugees and humanitarian situations in poor host countries takes a national perspective, focusing on the actions and policies of the national government or the overall experience of refugees in the country. And yet both the refugee experience and the implementation of host government policies vary considerably, especially between different host cities. We saw this dynamic play out in the United States during the first Trump presidency, when some US cities resisted Trump's antirefugee policies and others implemented them. We continue to see this varied domestic response in the United States today, with border states like Texas and various cities within them taking matters into their own hands when it comes to handling border crossings and the migrants who come across. Without understanding how different cities are affected by and respond to displacement, we cannot really grasp the refugee experience of host countries.

In recent years, a wide array of scholars have called for a focus on cities in order to understand global problems, from climate change to democracy.[1] Similarly, understanding forced migration benefits from a focus on cities rather than camps, and on the local rather than the national. Happily, there is a growing body of scholarship about the experience of refugees in cities, which I have drawn on extensively throughout the book. However, a robust body of research on the impact of displacement on cities has yet to emerge.

Media attention—at least in North America and Europe—tends to focus on humanitarian influxes to European and North American cities, and so does scholarly research. When millions of refugees were fleeing the war in Syria in 2014–16, media stories were mostly about those coming to Europe, even though the four countries bordering Syria together received more than six million Syrian refugees. Since the Russian invasion of Ukraine in February 2022, the countries bordering Ukraine have received millions of refugees, but prior to 2022 Europe had not experienced refugees from European countries since the Balkan wars of the early 1990s. Humanitarian influxes are much more frequent in the cities of the Middle East, Africa, Latin America, and Asia. Except for Ukraine, almost all the world's forced displacement occurs from or within poor and middle-income countries. (These countries are sometimes referred to as the "Global South.")

At the end of 2022, there were sixty-two countries each hosting more than 200,000 displaced people, including refugees and internally displaced people (IDPs), which in total accounted for 96 percent of the 112 million people who were displaced globally.[2] Of these sixty-two host countries, twelve were in North America or Europe (the United States, Germany, France, Sweden, the United Kingdom, Ukraine, Russia, Poland, Spain, Italy, Canada, and the Netherlands). Prior to 2022 and the Ukrainian displacement, just seven of the largest host countries were in North America or Europe. The main regions of the world experiencing displacement are Africa, which has eighteen countries with displaced populations greater than 200,000 and a total of more than thirty-nine million displaced; Asia, including the Middle East (West Asia), which has fourteen countries with displaced populations greater than 200,000 and a total of more than thirty-four million displaced; and Latin America, which has eight countries with displaced populations greater than 200,000 and a total of eighteen million displaced (see Table 1.1).

In these regions—Africa, Asia, Latin America, and the Middle East—many displaced people live in villages and rural areas, especially, in the case of refugees, near the borders of their home countries. In host countries that require refugees to live in camps, many do live in refugee camps, but as we explore in Chapter 7, even in these countries, very large numbers of refugees move to the cities of the host country. We know much less about host cities in these parts of the

Table 1.1. Displaced People from UN Major Regions

Origin (UN major regions)	Total refugees and people in refugee-like situations	Asylum seekers (pending cases)	IDPs of concern to UNHCR	Returned IDPs	Others of concern to UNHCR	Total population of concern
Africa	8,886,005	1,556,386	31,567,222	3,141,354	295,036	46,077,808
Asia	15,491,965	1,648,897	19,784,857	631,916	255,718	37,909,021
Europe	6,165,917	214,734	3,990,013	1,318,794	989,723	13,003,771
Latin America	732,321	3,076,179	7,499,374	–	4,190,473	21,253,715
North America + Caribbean	129,193	254,572	313,901	–	38,059	735,725
Oceania	843	6,837	96,000	–	1,736	105,416
Various/ Stateless	231,164	100,894	–	–	174,805	3,537,393
Total	31,637,408	6,858,499	63,251,367	5,092,064	5,945,550	122,622,849

Source: *Statistical Annex 2023* (Geneva, Switzerland: UNHCR, 2023), table 1.

world than we do about host cities in North America and Europe in terms of the impacts a refugee influx has on the cities and on the lives of the citizens and displaced people living in them. This book seeks to address that gap.

The many ways in which a humanitarian influx affects the cities of the world's poor countries offers insights into urban change in cities everywhere. One thing common to all cities is that as the media glare fades (if it ever existed), many humanitarian arrivals move on to other cities or countries. But many do not move on. They find places to stay away from city centers and parks—or are moved away by city authorities—and fade from the public eye. Over time, a sudden mass influx is often followed by the slower but continuous arrival of refugees over months or years, often with spikes and surges creating new problems or aggravating old ones. Within a few years, the number of refugees in a city can grow to hundreds of thousands. As we explore in Chapter 2, this number is likely to be much larger than official numbers suggest.

The Neighborhood Effect

Anyone who has visited sprawling megalopolises like Istanbul, Nairobi, Cairo, or Johannesburg will probably not have noticed the presence of refugees. Can refugees—who are usually just a small fraction of a city's population—have a significant impact on huge cities? The answer lies in the ways refugees cluster in particular neighborhoods where their presence—and impact—is much more salient. Migrants and displaced people tend not to distribute themselves evenly throughout a city; they move to neighborhoods where their compatriots already live, looking for support and drawing on social capital from their own people. Their people might be co-ethnics (for example, ethnic Somalis in Eastleigh, Nairobi), co-religionists (Christian Iraqis in Beirut), co-nationals (Congolese in Kampala), or all of the above (Eritreans in Johannesburg). Where these numbers become large and people stay long enough, such neighborhoods become associated with particular nationalities, resulting in Chinatowns or neighborhoods called "Little Somalia" or "Little Eritrea."

Refugee or migrant neighborhoods are often the affordable areas of town, where people can find cheaper housing and, importantly, endure less government surveillance. Sometimes these are slum areas within the formal boundaries of cities, but often they are vast areas of unincorporated land on the edges of cities, referred to as "informal settlements." These areas are the main engines of growth for most host cities, and the importance of informal settlements for cities warrants its own chapter. Chapter 3 explores informal settlements and their part in the story of the impact of humanitarian influxes on cities. It is important to recognize, however, that not all refugee neighborhoods are the poorest neighborhoods in a city. Not all refugees are poor, for one thing, and over time, the skills, assets, and investments that refugees bring—along with their transnational connections, entrepreneurial energy, business acumen, and a powerful will to survive—can all transform a neighborhood.

The neighborhood effect was illustrated to me once by a Somali woman in Cairo. She told me how when she first arrived in Cairo, the bus deposited her at the bus station: "I was very afraid, there were so many people, and I couldn't speak Arabic. Then I saw a Somali man coming toward me. He greeted me respectfully and asked if I needed help. He said I should go to Ashr [a Cairo neighborhood], where I would find other Somalis to help me. He called a taxi and paid for me to go there. And it was like he said—when I arrived I found people to help me." Migrants purposely choose their destinations based on whether they have support and assistance there in the form of family or co-national connections—earlier refugee or migrant communities—that will help them settle in or navigate their onward journey. People without family connections also come to a city because they are familiar with it from their community's long migration history with that city. The presence of a long-standing diaspora in a city makes a significant difference for new refugee arrivals when it comes to settling in and becoming part of the social fabric of the city. The diaspora also makes a difference in the kind of impact refugees have on the city.

How a Humanitarian Influx Differs from Other Urban Migration

A humanitarian influx and its consequences for the host city are different from slower, more "regular" urban in-migration and its effects. One important difference is the size and intensity. The acute phase of the humanitarian crisis—when thousands of people fleeing armed conflict or disaster arrive in a relatively short period of time—can unfold over a matter of days or weeks, as was the case in February and March 2022 with the Ukraine refugees, and back in April 1994, when the Rwandan genocide caused some two million Rwandans to flee to neighboring countries within a few weeks. Likewise, a disaster like an earthquake or tsunami displaces hundreds of thousands of people, as with the Haitian earthquake in 2010 (one and a half million Haitians), the Japanese earthquake of 2011 (470,000 Japanese), and the 2004 tsunami (half a million Indonesians)—but disaster victims tend to stay within their own country. Displacement resulting from war and persecution usually begins with an initial surge, then evolves into long-term smaller outflows, interspersed with periodic surges and return movements, as is the case with South Sudan, the Democratic Republic of the Congo, Afghanistan, Somalia, and Syria—and now Ukraine and Sudan. This slowing of movement occurs because those who can travel have mostly departed, or sometimes because neighboring governments close their borders and prevent refugees from entering. For example, the flight of Rohingya refugees from Myanmar (Burma) into Bangladesh began as a sudden surge in August 2017, but since then, the flow of refugees has decreased.[3]

Not all humanitarian displacement begins with an "emergency phase" or a mass influx. Sometimes the refugee flow is similar to that of migrants, with people arriving in smaller numbers over longer periods. In cities like Cairo and Johannesburg, the refugee numbers have been slowly creeping up since the early 2000s. Cairo saw a spike with Syrian arrivals from 2012 through 2013, but then the refugee inflow settled back down again until mid-2023, when the eruption of the civil war in Sudan forced hundreds of thousands of Sudanese across the border into Egypt. Slowly unfolding refugee flows occur when the crisis is drawn out, or when people are forewarned and intuit that things will get worse (as in Nazi Germany in the mid-1930s and in Venezuela after 2016) and begin to leave. Rich and well-resourced people with networks outside the country are the first to leave, in part because they have the means to transfer their assets to safer places and time to relocate family members in a strategic way. As the conflict or crisis takes hold and affects more people, the size of the outflow increases rapidly as a wider variety of people began to seek safe haven in neighboring countries.

A second way in which a humanitarian influx differs from other types of migration, and one that is especially important for poor host countries, is that the arrival of refugees, but not other migrants, is usually followed by international humanitarian resources and aid agencies. The best-funded and dominant UN agency responsible for refugees (and IDPs in some countries) is the Office of the High Commissioner for Refugees, known as UNHCR. Both UNHCR and other humanitarian agencies provide various forms of assistance for refugees, but as we shall see throughout this book, the humanitarian industry has a significant impact on host cities too, providing employment and training for locals, and demand for office space and high-end housing as well as humanitarian programs that sometimes include nonrefugee host populations.

A refugee influx usually brings enhanced international support of all kinds—developmental, financial, even trade related. For example, in February 2016, more than four years after the Syrian war began, by which time there were at least four million refugees in Syria's neighboring countries, the UN organized an international pledging conference in London. Donor countries pledged more than US$10 billion, about half to support humanitarian assistance in Syria and the rest to support neighboring countries, especially Jordan, Lebanon, and Türkiye. Along with these pledges (not all of which materialized) came other financial initiatives intended to support refugee-hosting countries. One joint initiative by the World Bank, the Islamic Development Bank Group, and other partners was the creation of the Global Concessional Financing Facility to provide concessional financing to middle-income countries hosting large refugee populations.[4] Since the late 2000s, the private sector has joined the international humanitarian industry, usually in the form of donations from industry-associated foundations created to meet corporate social responsibility requirements. As discussed in Chapter 8, external funds are aimed at national host governments rather than host cities. It is these governments that control the funds and allocate them to cities as they see fit. Very few international funding arrangements related to refugees are made directly with cities. Increased international interest in funding, perhaps especially by private sector actors, could present an opportunity for city governments, but as we will see, there are many obstacles. (For more on the international actors, see Chapter 2.)

A third difference between a refugee influx and "regular" migration concerns the presence of refugee camps. Formally established camps are not the norm for host countries today; only about a third of the world's refugees and a much smaller proportion of IDPs are in camps. But in countries that do have encampment policies, camps are often situated near towns and cities, and over time, their impact on them is dramatic, as we explore in Chapter 7. This impact stems from the movement of refugees and locals between city and camp and the enhanced presence of humanitarian agencies and the resources they bring.

A fourth difference between refugees and migrants lies in the responses of the city authorities, the citizens, and the refugees themselves. A well-established pattern, historically and geographically, is for citizens to start off welcoming refugees—initially, at least. Refugees are seen as being in desperate straits and in need of help (even though many nonrefugee migrants are often just as badly off). The depth and extent of this initial sympathy is influenced by the city's own history with migration and displacement. This history includes the citizenry's own experience of displacement and the city's historical relationship with refugees. A city's displacement history also partly explains why cities within the same country often differ in the extent to which city authorities and citizens enforce the national government's policies toward refugees. For example, many host governments do not allow refugees to work, but in some cities—or neighborhoods—the police and other authorities turn a blind eye to refugees who do work. A city's response changes over time, however. Part of the well-established pattern is that a city's initial welcome turns sour as the number of refugees increases and their stay becomes prolonged.

There are also some important differences in the composition of the refugee and migrant populations in host cities. As noted in the Preface, urban refugee populations often include human rights activists, journalists, and other political actors who have been persecuted in their home countries. Perhaps because of the presence of these actors, refugees seem to be more likely than other migrants to mobilize politically in response to the problems they face. This increased likelihood might also be because refugees have more host advocates willing to support them than do migrants.

How an Influx Impacts Host Cities

A humanitarian influx has immediate dislocating effects for a host city and its neighborhoods and it has long-term consequences that develop slowly. The immediate effects show up in strains on a city's services, especially its health services (with increased visits to emergency rooms and hospitals) and schools (with increased classroom sizes). A city's infrastructure—its energy grid and its transportation, water, and sanitation systems—can quickly become overburdened, especially if these systems are already fragile, as they often are in poor host countries. New arrivals increase the demand for housing (usually rentals) and for jobs, with consequences for the housing and employment markets. There are political, social, and security impacts too, which play out in the neighborhoods where refugees live. When local people confront rising housing prices and a tighter job market, their initially welcoming attitude toward the refugees changes. These shifts are often leveraged by xenophobic groups and politicians, who, supported by their social media, encourage locals to blame refugees for increased crime and insecurity.

Negative impacts and responses are not inevitable, and much depends on a city's leadership. There are many examples of city (and national) leaders, especially mayors, who have responded positively to the arrival of refugees with warmth and enthusiasm, setting the tone for their cities. Nevertheless, in many cities, the mayor's office and city agencies lack the budget and personnel capacity to address the pressures on housing and city services brought by a humanitarian influx, especially in the short term. To make things more difficult, municipal authorities must deal with these challenges in the glare of media coverage. In the early days of an influx, local and sometimes international media emphasize stories about refugees sleeping in city squares, about increases in street crime, and about how city services are overwhelmed. These kinds of media stories and city scenes were typical of the 2015–16 European crisis, which played out particularly in Greece and Italy and their island cities (especially on Lesvos, Sicily, and Lampedusa), but also in Germany, Serbia, and the Nordic countries. Whether ginned up by media coverage or not, the problems stemming from rapid influxes create anxiety and fear among citizens. In their wake come the political implications, if not immediately, then over time, which is why many city politicians include the issues of refugees and immigration in their platforms and in their political calculations and rhetoric.

Over the longer term, a humanitarian influx can change the character of smaller cities and large city neighborhoods. It can remix a city's ethnic composition, aggravate cultural or religious fault lines, and stir up conflict. As neighborhoods absorb refugees, some locals and refugees are economically and politically empowered, while others are marginalized and impoverished. Refugees might increase competition for jobs in certain sectors, but they often have to accept lower wages and work longer hours than their local counterparts. All of this creates antagonism on the part of locals, many of whom already struggle to find decent work and housing and now face increased competition and price gouging. In low-income neighborhoods there are few workplace or housing protections for either refugees or locals. But refugees are more likely to endure abuse and wage discrimination, especially if they are working illegally (which is common, since in many host countries refugees are not permitted to work) and have no legal redress when employers and landlords exploit them.

These consequences play out most dramatically in refugee neighborhoods, but they have indirect or spillover effects for the wider city, too. As Jane Jacobs explained in *The Death and Life of American Cities* back in 1961, it is impossible to understand a city by looking only at individual neighborhoods or sectors. Cities are interwoven, crosscutting "organic" wholes, where changes in one sector spill over to affect the entire city. In huge cities these ripple effects might dissipate quickly, but in smaller cities they can be transformative.

Take housing, for example. The arrival and ongoing presence of large numbers of refugees in a particular neighborhood sets in motion a competitive scramble for affordable housing. Landlords push the rents up in response to increased demand and often make refugees pay higher rents, so the price of housing rises. New (more expensive) housing is built by developers, and rising prices mean long-term residents can no longer afford the rents and must move to poorer and usually more distant parts of the city. This happened in 2022, when Ukrainian refugees came to Poland's border cities. In cities with very large refugee populations, rising property prices are also caused by the concomitant arrival of aid agency staff who also need housing and office and warehouse space. We explore the impact on housing and property markets further in Chapters 6 and 8.

Another spillover effect concerns the environmental impact on a city. In the low-income and informal areas of most cities, the physical infrastructure (water and sewer pipes, roads, energy and waste plants) and public services (garbage removal and processing, water management) are rickety and poorly maintained at best and nonexistent at worst. Well before an influx occurs, these long-standing problems of city systems are aggravated by increased flooding induced by climate change–related factors like increased precipitation and sea level rise. City flooding is also aggravated by environmental problems, including excessive paving, lack of garbage removal, and plastic pollution, which can cause clogs in drainage systems. Wealthy and formally incorporated areas of cities are also increasingly subject to flooding—one need only look at Houston and Miami. In the cities of poor host countries, flooding in informal settlements exposes people to outbreaks of infectious disease and threats to their livelihood.[5] With these hazards already present, an influx of refugees or migrants can overwhelm a city's ability to cope with environmental and public health threats, even assuming any effort on the part of city governments to do so in poor areas. We return to this issue in Chapter 10.

The arrival and continuing presence of refugees and their children can also affect the security and social cohesion of neighborhoods. Large numbers of refugees who share nationalities and religious beliefs can change the demographic and cultural balance of a city neighborhood. For example, as more religiously conservative Syrians began moving into Tripoli neighborhoods after 2011, their presence made some Lebanese residents uncomfortable and they moved to other neighborhoods. By contrast, in Ard al-Lewa in Cairo, young non-Muslim refugees from Eritrea and Sudan engaged in public drinking and carousing, infuriating local Cairenes, who called the police and started social media campaigns against the refugees, as discussed in Chapter 18.

Many of these problems are not new to cities, nor are they caused by refugees. Most host city problems were there long before the refugees arrived. When host cities are already struggling with decrepit infrastructure and understaffed public services, or with police brutality, an influx can push city systems over the edge and into total breakdown. As cities absorb displaced people, there is more pressure on urban transportation, more demand for energy, more refugee children in already overcrowded schools, and more people waiting for health services in emergency rooms and community health centers. These pressures can lead to heightened social tensions and even street protests, which in turn can aggravate security problems and lead to new problems—and new displacements within and outside the city. Community- and faith-based organizations have not stood by; efforts on the part of civil society to address these problems have also been in place long before the refugees arrived. The refugees themselves organize to address the problems they face, as discussed in Chapter 18. A refugee influx can lead to a boost for these efforts, as the influx brings new volunteers, new funds, and new expertise.

One of the main arguments in this book is that an influx can have positive outcomes for a city, depending on how organizations, governments, and individuals—both citizens and refugees—respond. International and local concern for refugees—what we might call the "humanitarian impulse"—leads to new inflows of resources. Especially when powerful and well-funded external actors like donor governments and the private sector work with humanitarian and development agencies and city governments, they can potentially build and support city infrastructure and services. However, when it comes to Africa, there is still a rural bias on the part of some of the wealthiest donor countries, including the United States, which means they concentrate their funding and programs away from the cities. A good example is Uganda, which hosted more than a million refugees in 2022. Uganda received external funding (from the United States, the European Union, and other donors) to support refugees, in amounts ranging from US$214 million to $332 million every year. These funds supported refugees across a range of sectors, from infrastructure to services, but the funds were almost exclusively aimed at the rural areas in the north and west, where refugees live in agricultural settlements. Much less assistance was available for the 106,000 refugees and asylum seekers registered in Uganda's capital, Kampala.[6] How best to provide humanitarian assistance in cities with multiple actors and political agendas, where refugees live alongside locals who are often as badly off as the refugees, is very much a work in progress, with some success stories and many challenges.

The actions of the refugees themselves transform cities, benefiting them in some ways and aggravating problems in others. In the United States, many smaller towns that have lost population and industries have been rejuvenated by resettled refugees. Studies of US towns like Fargo, North Dakota, Lewiston, Maine, and Burlington, Vermont, demonstrate how, in the process of rebuilding their lives, resettled refugees have helped turn around once-fading manufacturing and rust belt towns.[7] In her book, Susan Hartman explores how the population of Utica, New York, plunged after General Electric, which once provided thousands of jobs, started downsizing its plant and eventually closed it. As people migrated away, the city's economy shrank, and arsonists destroyed many homes and buildings. Then, in the 1990s, resettled refugees started coming to Utica. First came Bosnians who had fled the Balkan conflicts. They arrived with education and building skills, and they purchased and rehabilitated hundreds of run-down houses in East Utica. They were followed in the 2000s by Karen and other refugees from eastern Myanmar. They had fled long-standing conflict with the Burmese military and then were resettled from refugee camps in Thailand to the United States. Then came Somali Bantu resettled refugees, and in 2022, Utica began receiving Ukrainians. As of 2022, resettled refugees and their families made up about a quarter of Utica's population of about 60,000.[8] In many other US towns, refugees have improved the housing stock, provided employment, and created jobs by starting new businesses.

This pattern of urban renewal has also been well documented in Europe, Canada, and Australia but much less documented in host cities in Africa and Asia; notable exceptions include book-length studies of refugee hosting cities in Pakistan, Nairobi, and Dar es Salaam.[9] As we explore throughout this book, refugees bring their assets, skills, and entrepreneurship to city neighborhoods, and by mobilizing to help themselves, they also help their local neighbors. Refugees are often blamed for problems that were there long before they arrived. But do refugees make problems worse? The tradition of scapegoating migrants and refugees for city and national problems is long-standing. President Trump was by no means the first politician to blame crime on refugees; this is a daily occurrence in many host and transit countries. But it cannot be denied that an influx brings new problems. This book explores the experience of displaced people in cities, the changes they bring to cities, both positive and negative, and the efforts made by refugee and nonrefugee actors to address these problems. Together, these changes are transforming large parts of the world's cities.

This Book

Parts II and III focus on two host cities that represent the experience of megalopolis primary cities (usually capitals) and secondary port or border cities. The secondary city is Tripoli, Lebanon's northern port about forty-eight kilometers (thirty miles) from the border with Syria and eighty kilometers (fifty miles) north of Beirut. The megalopolis is Cairo, Egypt's inland capital on the Nile, 136 miles southeast of the Mediterranean port of Alexandria. I selected these cities from among the dozens of African and Middle Eastern cities that have hosted more than 250,000 refugees over the past decade and that are both destination and transit cities for displaced people and other migrants from Africa and the Middle East. My selection of Cairo and Tripoli was based on my own knowledge and on the knowledge of my two research assistants, Ryan Philip in Cairo and Claire Wilson in Tripoli. Both Ryan and Claire were my students and research assistants at the Fletcher School, they had spent many years living and working in Cairo and Lebanon, respectively, and both speak Arabic fluently. The chapters in Parts II and III draw on the experience of two refugees: Mahmoud, a middle-aged Syrian man who came to Tripoli in 2015, and Hassan, a young Somali man who came to Cairo in 2008. (I have changed all the names and identifying features of the people mentioned in the book, to ensure their anonymity.)

2
The Actors and the Numbers

Any city into which refugees come is soon—if not already—populated by a cast of actors whose interactions with each other determine what kinds of impacts the refugees will have on the city. These actors include the displaced people themselves, the host population, city and national authorities, aid agencies, and donors, all of whom interact with varying degrees of creativity, trust, independence, and boldness of leadership. The first half of this chapter briefly describes these actors; the rest of the book explores their interactions in more detail. Because no book about refugees can fail to mention the numbers—indeed, most start with them—the second part of this chapter describes the scope of displacement as it is currently reported and the problems with those numbers. I argue that because the numbers are likely to be underreported, the demographic impact of displaced people on cities is much bigger than we realize.

Refugees, the Internally Displaced, Asylum Seekers, and Migrants

In this book, "displaced people" refers to those who fled their homes because they found themselves in critical situations, confronting threats to their lives and unable to be protected by their government. These threats may arise from persecution, armed conflict, sudden-onset disasters, or the destruction of their homes and livelihoods by some combination of climate change and any of the aforementioned threats. People flee their homes to seek safety and protection elsewhere, either within their own country or across borders.[1] When they move to a safer place within their own country, they are called internally displaced persons (IDPs). If they cross the border to find safety in a neighboring or more distant country, they are referred to as refugees.

The word "refugee" has different meanings and connotations, depending on who is using the term. Although it has a formal legal definition, it is commonly used in a nonlegal, broader sense to describe anyone who is fleeing danger and has crossed a border, even if the person does not legally qualify as a refugee under any applicable legal framework. The formal definition of the term "refugee" in international law is found in the 1951 Convention Relating to the Status of Refugees, as modified by the 1967 Protocol Relating to the Status of Refugees (commonly referred to as the Refugee Convention). Under this treaty regime, a refugee is defined as a person who "owing to well-founded fear of being persecuted for reasons of race, religion, nationality, membership of a particular social group, or political opinion, is outside the country of his nationality and is unable or, owing to such fear, is unwilling to avail himself of the protection of that country; or who, not having a nationality and being outside the country of his former habitual residence, is unable or, owing to such fear, is unwilling to return to it" (Article 1(A) of the Refugee Convention). According to this definition, an individual can potentially qualify as a refugee only if they are outside their country of nationality. Internally displaced persons are entitled to the protections of international human rights law and international humanitarian law, but they are not regarded as having a particular legal status under international law, and no international legal rights attach to IDPs. However, some protections are afforded at the regional level. The African Union

Convention for the Protection and Assistance of Internally Displaced Persons in Africa (the "Kampala Convention") provides a legal definition for IDPs and imposes obligations on states parties concerning their treatment.[2]

The international refugee definition requires that the individual has a "well-founded fear of persecution," although what exactly "well-founded" means is up to the interpretation of the judge making the asylum decision. Notably, the Refugee Convention definition of persecution does not include situations of armed conflict, rampant lawless violence, natural disasters, failed states, or the impact of climate change. However, regional and domestic legal definitions, especially those in Africa and in Latin America, often more broadly define the types of harm that qualify an individual for refugee status.[3]

When it comes to national law—or how countries interpret and implement the Refugee Convention—the definition of a refugee varies. States define the term as they see fit, subject to their international obligations. Sometimes national definitions can be confusing. For example, the US legal system uses the term "refugee" to refer to individuals abroad who have already been determined to be refugees, typically by UNHCR, and who are in the process of being resettled into the United States. These refugees are different from asylum seekers, who apply for asylum either at the US border or from within the United States. If asylum seekers are granted asylum, they are called "asylees." When the United States speaks of a "refugee cap," it is referring only to the number of refugees resettled from abroad through official channels, not to asylum seekers in the United States, for which there is no cap.

I use the term "humanitarian influx" to refer to those who are broadly termed refugees (whether or not they have formal legal status) as well as asylum seekers and IDPs. The term "migrant" has no definition in international law, and it can be understood narrowly, referring to an individual who is voluntarily relocating within their country or to another country, or very broadly, as anyone "on the move." I distinguish between displaced people and migrants, even though I recognize that many people who come as migrants to a city might not feel they had much choice in the matter. There is much debate about the difference or nondifference between migrants and refugees, but for my purposes, I make an analytical distinction between a humanitarian movement of displaced people and more regular movements of migrants.

The Host Population, City Governments, and National Governments

The "host population" refers to the people already living in the place to which refugees or IDPs come. This place could be a rural area, thinly populated by farmers or herders living in small villages, or it could be a neighborhood in a huge capital or a smaller border city. The host population includes both citizens of the country and the long-standing migrant or refugee populations already living in the host area. The latter are often from the same country as the new arrivals, constituting a "near-diaspora." This near-diaspora is an important source of assistance for new arrivals, and members often create community-based organizations to support refugees.

The city government, or municipality, is usually comprised of a mayor, the mayor's executive team, and municipal and other authorities such as enforcement agencies, all of whom are responsible for managing and administering a town or city. Very large cities are usually divided into different municipalities, which together comprise the "Greater" city, as in Greater Cairo or Greater Boston. These municipalities sometimes form unions such as those in Lebanon.

In most countries, the national government is responsible for governance issues pertaining to the entire territory, including immigration and the management of refugees, while provinces, states, and cities govern issues of local concern. A host country's national government plays an important role in mediating the impact of a humanitarian influx on host cities. First, national governments decide whether the border should be open to refugees, whether refugees should live in camps, and whether refugees should be allowed to work, own businesses, or access public services like health care and schools. Second, city budgets are determined by national governments, which have the power to limit the funds available to cities, including international (donor) funds. Cities in marginalized or otherwise neglected or oppositional areas of the country often receive smaller budgets than more favored cities—such as those where political support for the government is high. For example, as we shall see in the case of Lebanon, the relationship between the national government and the city of Tripoli has historically been strained. City governments are expected to enforce national laws and policy, but many city governments have their own views about refugees, and depending on city leadership and politics, some are more lax about enforcing national policy than others.

The Humanitarian and Development Industries

The humanitarian industry is a vast system of organizations ranging from relatively well-resourced United Nations agencies and huge international nongovernmental organizations (INGOs) like the International Rescue Committee (IRC) and Human Rights Watch, to smaller advocacy groups and local NGOs that are much more modestly resourced but often have big megaphones in the form of their media links. Humanitarian agencies are concerned with protecting the rights of people caught up in conflict and disasters and providing assistance to them. Refugee agencies are a subset of humanitarian agencies that are focused on those who are displaced, usually refugees. Several UN agencies provide services to refugees, including the World Food Programme (WFP), which provides food aid and cash assistance, and UNICEF, which provides education for refugee children. There are also migration agencies, such as the International Organization for Migration (IOM), but relatively few INGOs or local NGOs specifically support migrants.

The main UN agency responsible for refugees, however, and one of the most powerful UN agencies, is the Office of the High Commissioner for Refugees, known as UNHCR. Since 1951, soon after the United Nations was established, UNHCR has been mandated by member states to protect and assist refugees in accordance with the 1951 Refugee Convention. Like all UN agencies, UNHCR is a member-state organization, which means it is bound to abide by the wishes of states. Thus, UNHCR must be invited by the host government to enter and operate in that country, and UNHCR remains in the country only as long as the government deems it a useful and cooperative presence. To fulfill its mandate to protect refugees, therefore, UNHCR works closely with the host government. If a UN agency offends the government, it risks being expelled, which has often happened to UNHCR (for example, in Libya in 2010 and Sudan in 2013) and other UN agencies such as UNICEF, whose leader was expelled from the Gambia in 2010.[4]

UNHCR is the conduit through which donor governments like the United States and the European Union channel most of their humanitarian funding to refugees. When UNHCR was first created, its budget was $300,000. Today, with more than 100 million forcibly displaced and stateless people worldwide, UNHCR's budget is more than $10 billion.[5] However, the funding of UNHCR's operations in host countries is entirely dependent on the voluntary contributions of UN member states, which means funding is highly variable and dependent on donor countries' political considerations. Just 2 percent of UNHCR's annual budget comes from the UN regular budget, which is used to fund about 200 administrative posts at headquarters. The rest depends on the funding preferences of individual donor governments, although the private sector—corporations, foundations, and private individuals—also contributes funding. UNHCR's reliance on voluntary funds has resulted in serious funding shortages, given the escalation of refugee crises in recent years. These shortages seriously affect UNHCR's ability to assist the people it is mandated to serve.

UNHCR works in 478 locations across 130 countries. In most host countries, UNHCR usually does not conduct field operations itself but rather subcontracts government ministries and hundreds of nongovernmental agencies to provide assistance and services like education and health care to refugees. A major element of the humanitarian industry is the multitude of INGOs that rush to a host country (if they are not already there) to assist refugees. They include both secular organizations such as the IRC, CARE, and Oxfam, and hundreds of faith-based organizations from every major world religion (see Table 2.1).[6] Many faith-based INGOs such as Catholic Relief Services and the Lutheran World Relief ("the hands and feet of Jesus") are powerful, well-funded entities that have their own programs and agendas. Some INGOs partner with or are subcontracted by UNHCR to carry out programs, but many operate independently.

The international development industry is somewhat different. Its purpose is to help poor and low-income countries "develop"—both in terms of economic growth and socially, by improving schools, health care, the criminal justice systems, and so forth. Development agencies span a wide range. There are huge and powerful "multilat-

Table 2.1. Top Five Largest Humanitarian INGOs (2022)

Name of Organization (year founded; country of registration)	Workforce	Last known annual income
BRAC International (1972; Bangladesh)	107,000	US$1.08 billion
Open Society Foundations (1993; US)	+1,000	US$1.35 billion
MSF (1972; France)	45,000	€1.9 billion
Danish Refugee Council (1956; Denmark)	9,000	€430 million
MercyCorps (1979; Portland, US)	5,300	US$520 million

Source: "Welcome to the World 200 Top SGOs," thedotgood, 2022, https://thedotgood.net/ranking/world-200-sgos/.

eral" development banks, such as the World Bank and the Inter-American Development Bank, with vast sources of funding at their disposal. Then there are smaller UN agencies concerned with development, such as the UN Development Programme and the UN Environmental Programme, which are generally much more modestly funded compared with humanitarian agencies like UNHCR. Many INGOs or nonprofits have both development and humanitarian operations, with budgets approaching those of UN agencies. In addition to these powerful international organizations, there are many host country national organizations involved in humanitarian and development assistance. These tend to be much less resourced, although some are supported by international agencies.

Historically, there has been rivalry and competition between humanitarian and development actors, and their activities have rarely overlapped. Donor governments usually have separate agencies handling humanitarian and development affairs, with separate budgets. For example, the US State Department is concerned with refugee assistance outside of the United States (and is by far the largest funder of refugee operations globally), while (until January 2025) USAID has not been involved with refugees but has supported economic development and food security, among other interests, in developing countries. A recent trend, however, is that development and humanitarian "mandates" are becoming entangled, such that humanitarian agencies now conduct what used to be thought of as development activities in addition to dealing with traditional humanitarian needs. We explore this so-called integrated development approach further in Chapter 8.

This integrated approach means humanitarian agencies are increasingly providing long-term assistance to refugees, such as support for their livelihoods and education. Humanitarian agencies routinely offer vocational training, microcredit, small business development, and other program activities that many consider to be more akin to development than to humanitarian support. Likewise, development agencies are becoming involved with refugees. The World Bank, for example, has since 2017 supported cities confronting mass refugee influxes because it recognizes that a large influx can affect a city's economic development and its political stability and thus disrupt the Bank's five-year plans for cities (and countries).[7]

The Donors

Humanitarian donors are of two types: governments (including European Union and other regional governance institutions) and the private sector (including large multinational corporations, philanthropies, foundations, and private donors). Most humanitarian funding for host countries is provided by the governments of wealthy countries. They do this in two ways. The first is through voluntary contributions to multilateral agencies like UNHCR or international financial organizations like the World Bank. The largest funder of UNHCR is the US government, which gave UNHCR $2.19 billion in 2022, followed by the European Union and Germany. The US State Department's annual budget request for refugees and migrants in 2023 was well over $4 billion.[8] The second way donors provide humanitarian funding is through direct bilateral funding of projects in host countries, usually through government contracts with particular organizations. For example, USAID's Bureau for Humanitarian Assistance (shuttered by President Trump in January 2025) might contract with an INGO like Catholic Relief Services to provide logistical support for IDP operations.

It is difficult for cities to gain access to this external funding, in part because of the so-called architecture of humanitarian funding. Most humanitarian funds come from emergency appeals made by the UN to donor countries for the purpose of supporting refugees. As we explore in Chapter 8, humanitarian funding is usually heavily earmarked, leaving humanitarian agencies little leeway in how they can use the funds—for example, they can only be used to support refugees. For cities, it would be helpful to use some of the funds to support poor host neighborhoods that are affected by the presence of refugees. UNHCR notes that while the United States is their largest funder, most *unearmarked* funds were from Norway, Sweden, the United Kingdom, Netherlands, and Denmark. UNHCR says, "Unearmarked funding provides the backbone of UNHCR's activities on a global scale, allowing us to respond to emergencies as they happen and enabling us to stay and deliver long after the headlines have faded."[9]

The private sector is still a relatively small contributor to humanitarian action, both as a source of funding and in other ways. However, UN agencies, in their constant search for new funding, see the private sector as potentially fertile ground. UNHCR, for example, has set up their Private Sector Partnerships service headquartered in Denmark. A few multinational corporations now have projects in host countries. For example, IKEA supports several refugee projects, usually working in partnership with UNHCR or NGOs such as the International Refugee Committee.[10] Others that UNHCR lists as its "partners" are Uniqlo, Unilever, Toms, Sony, MasterCard Foundation, Vodafone Foundation, Fuji Optical, Qatar Airways, Microsoft, and Bain. The World Bank launched a website in 2018 called PS4R (Private Sector for Refugees) that "builds bridges between the private sector and forcibly displaced people for mutual benefit while generating economic growth for the communities that host [them]."[11] The International Finance Corporation began a joint initiative with UNHCR in 2022 that "aims to mobilize private sector projects over the next five years to demonstrate the viability of investments in forced displacement contexts" and "facilitate the engagement of private sector stakeholders in refugee-hosting areas."[12]

The world's largest international gathering of international actors to discuss support for refugees is the World Refugee Forum, which occurs every four years. At the first one in December 2019, the private sector pledged $250 million in refugee assistance, as reported by UNHCR. However, pledges are nonbinding commitments, and by the time the second WRF took place in December 2023, only a third of the more than 1,400 pledges made in 2019, including by the private sector, had been fulfilled. (At the second WRF, some US$2.2 billion in financial commitments were pledged, of which $250 million again came from the private sector.)[13] It's not clear how much private sector funding finds its way to host cities.

Why the Demographic Impact Is Bigger than We Think—Understanding the Numbers

At the end of 2022, there were more than 108 million forcibly displaced people worldwide. Almost forty-six million had crossed the border into another country and were refugees, asylum seekers, and "people in refugee-like situations"; another 62.5 million remained inside their countries as IDPs.[14] Some of these displaced people live in remote camps and rural villages, but most move to cities and towns, either immediately or eventually. Getting a handle on their numbers, however, is difficult for all kinds of reasons, starting with the data.

The most widely used source of data on the numbers of displaced people is UNHCR, which gathers annual data, mostly at the country level, but sometimes with a few cities included. Each year, UNHCR produces an extensive statistical annex that consists of some twenty-four tables of data related to different aspects of the global refugee and IDP picture, including location, demographics, asylum status, and resettlement. These data are taken either from UNHCR's registration lists or from the host government's official numbers if the government provides them. For example, the Turkish government provides UNHCR with government-issued statistics on the 3.4 million refugees, mostly Syrians, that Türkiye hosts. In some cases, government statistics can be at odds with UNHCR statistics. According to the 2015 Jordanian census, there were 1.26 million Syrians in Jordan, of which 953,000 were recorded as refugees, out of a total population of about 9.5 million people. By contrast, UNHCR had registered 689,053 refugees in Jordan that year, of whom 628,223 were Syrian.[15] Similar discrepancies between UNHCR-registered numbers and government counts exist in several major hosting countries.

When it comes to IDPs, the reported numbers are estimates at best. Except for a few countries, such as Colombia, most countries do not have national registries or other official counts of IDPs. Various international organizations try to count IDPs and monitor their movements, but the way the data are collected tends to be country-specific, which makes the data difficult to compare. For example, IOM gathers data on mobility through their Displacement Tracking Matrix, but they rely on what key informants can provide and then try to fill in with country-level surveys, models, and other sources. The Internal Displacement Monitoring Center (IDMC), established in 1998 by the Norwegian Refugee Council, has worked for twenty-five years to get a handle on the numbers of IDPs. Their complex data model attempts to capture the number of people displaced in a particular situation. But as IDMC acknowledges, "data collected by IDMC's partners almost never accounts for all relevant flows and it is often difficult to map all partners' data onto the corresponding part of the data model."[16]

The statistics used by researchers and the media are thus either estimates (for IDPs) or a reflection of UNHCR- (or government-) registered refugees. The UNHCR data are easily accessible and are routinely part of press releases by UN agencies. Like other scholars of forced migration, I use UNHCR statistics because they are somewhat consistent and allow comparisons across countries and across time. However, these data come with an important caveat: the refugee population statistics reported in most host countries and their cities are inevitably inaccurate—either larger or smaller than what UNHCR reports. This is because of the difficulty of accurately recording a population that is constantly shifting and mobile. And, of course, not everyone comes forward to be registered and counted. Why is this?

In many countries, not all or even most people who might qualify as refugees are registered with UNHCR or the government, either because they choose not to, because they lack information about the process, or because they aren't able to get to a UNHCR office to register. In some cases, people simply don't think of themselves as refugees and choose not to engage with the humanitarian system. They may not want or need the assistance that could come with registration. They might wish to stay off the official radar, away from the "humanitarian gaze." Or they may simply be unaware of the existence of the humanitarian or government bureaucracy.

Then there are documentation and registration challenges. People might not know how to register, or they might be afraid to register, believing that entering an official system could create problems for them. In other cases, there are bureaucratic impediments to registering. In Jordan, for instance, not all Syrian refugees are fully registered with UNHCR or fully documented by the Jordanian government. Since 2014, Syrian refugees who leave a camp without going through the official exit process cannot re-register with UNHCR outside the camp.[17] Since many refugees leave the camps, this is a substantial number. Another problem with the Jordanian numbers is that Palestinians living in Syria are not permitted to seek asylum in Jordan, but an unknown number have entered the country using false documents and are unregistered. Syrians registered with UNHCR must also register with the Ministry of the Interior, but there are costs associated with acquiring the necessary documents, and many Syrians avoid this step, which means they are only partially documented. All in all, many Syrians and recently arrived Palestinians from Syria who might qualify as refugees are not registered. This means that the number and thus the demographic impact of displaced people in Jordan is greater than recognized. Since most refugees live in the capital, Amman, and in large towns or those near camps (such as the town of Mafraq, near Zaatari camp), the demographic impact is concentrated in urban areas. This problem is typical of many host countries, especially those where refugees are supposed to live in camps, as we explore in Chapter 7.

Another problem with counting refugees relates to their children. In many countries, the children of refugees and migrants who are born in the host country are not eligible for citizenship, because citizenship is granted on the basis of descent (jus sanguinis). This means that if the refugee parents are not citizens, their children are at risk of becoming stateless. The presence of these children—and their children, as many refugees live in cities for decades—means the refugee population of a city or country continues to grow, even if no more refugees enter. While UNHCR registers the children of already registered parents, there are uncounted numbers of unregistered refugees and migrants whose children add to the numbers present in the city. Their presence means we don't know the total number of noncitizens in that city.

In addition to undercounts, there is the overcount problem (they do not balance each other out). Even for registered refugees, it is difficult for UNHCR to keep the registries updated. Refugees move on to other countries, some return to their home countries, and their departures are not captured at all or not in a timely way. UNHCR tries to keep track of refugees by recording their mobile numbers, but departing refugees often sell their SIM cards to others—there is a well-established black market in SIM cards in many countries.[18] Unless registration lists are regularly updated and validated, they are inaccurate, reflecting both undercounts and overcounts. The extent of this inaccuracy varies between countries, depending on how faithfully registration lists are updated, but it is a widespread problem.

The problems with counting refugees and their children mean we don't know the full extent of the demographic impact of displaced people on cities. We don't know the size of the displaced population before a new influx arrives, how many stay, and how many move on elsewhere or return home. Unlike in camps, where it is relatively easy to do a census, in cities refugees live among nonregistered refugees and the nonrefugee population—which is also difficult for cities to measure. Government statistics on both citizens *and* migrants are widely inaccurate. (Governments use different methods and terminology, making it difficult to compare countries and aggregate global data.) Many governments simply lack the technical capacity to collect migration data. Very few countries have population registries that record residential movements and can be used to track migration.[19] It is also likely that governments lack the will to collect migration data. These data are politically risky—they can be used by politicians to criticize incumbent governments or to promote antimigrant political agendas, and government officials might simply prefer to avoid such risks.

A potentially useful source of data on refugees and migrants could be a county's national census or inter-census surveys. But both these sources have been of little use. Many major host countries either do not conduct national censuses at all (such as Lebanon, where the last census was in 1933) or have not conducted one for many years (Sudan's last census was in 2008, before the independence of South Sudan).[20] Most national censuses in African and Asian countries do not ask questions that could capture refugee and migrant data, such as whether people are foreign-born and where they come from (South Africa and Uganda are two exceptions). Another problem is that in many large cities, census enumerators do not go into informal ("slum") areas where refugees and migrants tend to live, because these areas are not part of the formally defined city area (cadasters). This mean these areas are often omitted from the census, but it is these areas where the most population growth is happening in cities, as we discuss in Chapter 3.

Even in countries that conduct regular censuses, undercoverage of migrants is a significant problem. Studies in the United States, Canada, and Australia have found that recent immigrants and nonpermanent residents were less likely to respond to both the census and surveys, such as the American Community Survey in the United States, whether they are online or conducted by government or other authorities.[21] This lack of response is even more likely for immigrants who are undocumented. In displacement settings, particularly in conflict zones or unstable countries like Haiti, Afghanistan, and

Somalia, there is very little likelihood that we have accurate estimates of the population, given the high degree of mobility. Other reasons why survey data are inaccurate or incomplete for many population groups, not just refugees, are sampling errors, data input errors, or postsurvey data manipulations such as censoring.

The inaccuracy of population data (likely undercounts) means that we don't fully comprehend the demographic impact of a humanitarian influx on a city. Nevertheless, since the Second World War, refugees have shaped the demographic profiles of countries, especially small ones, in significant ways. Jordan is a good example of where a single refugee population—Palestinians—permanently changed the demographics of the country, beginning in 1947. Since the Syrian refugees began coming to Jordan in 2011, they too have changed the country, probably more than the official statistics indicate. This is certainly the case, as we shall see, with Lebanon, as it is with many small countries, and even medium-sized ones such as Uganda and Bangladesh. Even without accurate data, the number of displaced people in cities is surely growing, which makes it all the more important that we understand the implications for cities.

3

Informal Cities: How Cities Are Growing

When people are displaced—especially by armed conflict—their movement often occurs in a series of stages. Initially, people stay close to home, hiding from marauding militias or shelling during the night or day but staying within range of their homes or farms or businesses. The second stage occurs when this hiding strategy no longer ensures safety. Then people flee further afield, to safer villages or camps or nearby towns, where they might remain for a time, perhaps still hoping to return to their homes. A third stage, we might call it the migration stage, occurs when individuals or households decide to leave the camp or village and move to the city. Households often strategize this migration; for example, they might send one member of working age to the city—either within the same country or in a neighboring country—to act as an anchor for the future migration of the entire household, or to find work and send remittances back to the family. In some cases, the individual or household might eventually return to their rural home, but this return movement is relatively rare—unless people are forced to return because of deportation or eviction. Most of the time, once displaced people move to the city, they tend to stay there.

When refugees move to cities, they generally go either to border and port cities or to the host country's capital or primary city. (Of course, a city could be a border and a port city that is also the capital, such as Athens or Dar es Salaam.) The cities of Africa, the Middle

East, Asia, and Latin America are undergoing particularly rapid growth and change in both their primary and secondary cities. Urban primacy tends to be the norm, in which a single megalopolis, usually but not always the capital, is by far the biggest city, and the one most citizens and migrants are drawn to. But many secondary cities are growing even faster. Secondary cities are those with populations between 10 and 50 percent of the country's largest city, typically between 100,000 and 1,000,000—but some much larger. For refugees, secondary cities near the border are usually the first destinations. Then, depending on what the city has to offer, they either stay or move on to the primary city.

This bimodal pattern of refugee movement to border towns and capitals is long-standing and widespread in countries neighboring conflict zones. A recent example is the flight from Ukraine. After the Russian invasion in 2022, more than six million Ukrainian refugees fled to European countries.[1] The border countries of Poland, Russia, Hungary, Moldova, Romania, and Slovakia received most of the refugees, who arrived first in border cities and then either stayed or moved to other cities in the same country or elsewhere in Europe. Poland is host to more than two million Ukrainians—the highest of any neighboring country. About half have refugee status, and 1.6 million have applied for asylum. In Poland, the pattern of movement through the border cities is clear. Since February 2022, there have been more than seventeen million border crossings between Poland and Ukraine. One border town, Przemyśl (with a population of 60,000), received over 50,000 Ukrainian refugees a day during the first few months of the war, accommodating them for a few days, then transporting them to larger cities such as Warsaw and Krakow, or elsewhere in Europe. By the end of 2022, some 6,000 refugees had opted to stay in Przemyśl, because they wanted to be close to their homes and families in Ukraine.[2]

Similarly, since the Venezuelan crisis began in 2014, the distribution of Venezuelans coming to neighboring Colombia, well documented by the Colombian government, shows the bimodal pattern. By January 2022, Colombia had received almost 2.5 million Venezuelans since 2014. The capital, Bogotá, had the highest number, some 495,000, and Medellín, Colombia's second biggest city had another 191,000, but the town with the next-largest number was the much smaller border city of San José de Cúcuta with 170,000 Venezuelan migrants.[3] Likewise, in Brazil, Venezuelans mainly went to the border cities of Pacaraima, Manaus, and Boa Vista, as well as the primary city, Rio de Janeiro.

Since the war in Syria began in 2011, Syrian refugees have likewise gone to neighboring countries' border towns and primary cities: Türkiye's border towns of Gazientiep and Urfa, and the primary city of Istanbul; Jordan's border cities (Irbid and al-Mafraq) and Amman; Iraq's border cities (Mosul, Erbil) and Baghdad; and the border towns of Lebanon and Beirut. Every African country neighboring a conflict zone has seen its border areas grow in population size. There are thousands of South Sudanese refugees in the border towns of Uganda (Arua, Adjumani) and Kenya (Kakuma, Dadaab). Congolese refugees are in all the border towns and capitals of the Democratic Republic of the Congo's nine neighbors. Ethiopian and Eritrean refugees are in Sudan's eastern border towns (Kassala and Gedaref) and in Khartoum. In Europe, Mediterranean island cities like Mytilene (Lesvos, Greece), Lampedusa (Italy), and Valetta (Malta) have received thousands of migrants and refugees from Africa and the Middle East.

The same pattern occurs when people are internally displaced: they flee to both the capital of their country and to nearby towns. For example, in Sudan's chronically conflict-affected Darfur region, the cities of al-Fashir and Nyala have seen rapid expansion from internal displacement for many years, as has the capital, Khartoum.

Border towns are often secondary cities, although when they are also port cities, they can be very large, even megalopolises. For example, Alexandria, Egypt's second city and a port, has a population of 5.2 million people and a refugee population of about 24,000.[4] Secondary cities are sometimes the capital city of a province or state (for example, Augusta is Maine's capital, but is much smaller than Portland). Back in the 1980s, the major factors affecting the growth and development of secondary cities were physical location and natural resources, along with administrative and political factors that allowed them to grow as service centers.[5] Today, the arrival and continuing stay of displaced people (along with the humanitarian industry) is a major factor in the growth and development of host countries' secondary cities. The displaced join the high and growing rates of rural-urban migration, as more people leave rural areas that can no longer support them (in part because climate change decimates rural livelihoods) or that have become too dangerous, given persistent conflict and instability.

City Growth and Where the Displaced Live

Cities grow spatially by radiating out from the core in concentric zones of habitation. The urban core is the area within administrative (municipality) boundaries, and usually includes the oldest parts of a city and some suburbs. Further out is the "urban agglomeration"—new areas of development. As cities grow, new cities split off to form their own municipalities, which in turn sprout new growth, and thus cities become "Greater Boston," for example. A city's "metropolitan area" refers to the reach of the city—its social and economic links with towns and villages from which people commute to the city for work or for health services, or to shop or renew documents. While they do not live in the city, the city is part of their lives.

Rapid expansion and urban sprawl are features of many growing cities, in poor and wealthy countries alike. The "urban land grab," a result of land commodification and speculation, is transforming cities across the globe, absorbing green space, agricultural land, wetlands, and wild areas alike.[6] Commercial property developers build condo developments, gated housing estates, golf courses, shopping malls, hotels, casinos, and big-box stores—and the giant parking lots and feeder roads that all these developments need. As farmers sell their agricultural land to developers, people move to cities, or, since not everyone is able or willing to move, they remain in rural areas with ever-diminishing resources.

The arrival of people displaced by armed conflict or disaster (or often, both) contributes to a different kind of urban sprawl. Displaced people either head to cities immediately or find their way there over time, especially if the conflict and disaster are prolonged. The new arrivals are often poverty-stricken and traumatized. They have seen their family members die, sometimes including their own children, and many are themselves in extremely fragile health, having traveled long distances with little food, helping others weaker than themselves, and bearing the memories of shocking scenes of violence or disaster. Most arrive with nothing, dependent on the goodwill of those in the city—the authorities, humanitarian agencies, or their own networks. In most cities, unless these new arrivals have family in the city, the only place they can find to live is in undeveloped areas on the edge of town where there is space to erect or rent a makeshift shack, but often no water or services of any kind.

In 2008, I led a study of IDPs in and around Khartoum (Sudan).[7] Our research sites included two official IDP camps on the outskirts of Omdurman, Khartoum's sister city on the western bank where the White Nile meets the Blue Nile. One day, I drove with my friend and colleague Helen Young, a Sudan expert, to the outer edge of

Omdurman. In those days, Omdurman was much smaller than it is now, and it didn't take long to get to where the city met the Sahara desert. We had not yet reached the IDP camp, but the road had petered out, and we thought we might be lost. All around us was an expanse of hot sand, with Omdurman's low buildings just visible in the distance through the dusty haze. The sandy expanse was not empty, however. Unbelievably, to my eyes at least, there were dozens of shacks, separated from each other by twenty or so meters, some large enough to hold a family of five or six people, others only big enough for one person. The shacks were made from scraps of metal and wood or old plastic and cardboard and burlap—the most basic possible shelter against the wind and heat and sand.

I thought back to an earlier visit to Sudan, when we had been caught in a haboob. Driving down a busy road in downtown Khartoum, our driver looked into the rearview mirror and then stood on the gas. When I looked back, a boiling cloud of red sand filled the rear window, barreling down the street toward us with an increasing roar of wind. Luckily, we were close to the Intercontinental Hotel. The driver slammed on the brakes as the hotel doorman held the heavy door against the wind, and we piled out of the car into the calm of the hotel lobby. Outside, nothing of the street could be seen or heard except swirling red sand and the roar of the wind. Within minutes the haboob had passed, leaving a thick layer of red sand on every surface.

Seeing the IDPs sitting in their shacks, their children quiet on the sand outside, it was shocking to think what would happen to them if such a storm should hit their rickety shacks. The IDPs seemed to have no material goods of any kind. A water seller on a donkey cart carrying a large clay pot of water passed through once a day, and people purchased water to fill their plastic bottles. It was not clear where people got food until we saw a woman selling small round loaves of Sudan bread on the side of the track. It was difficult to imagine how people could survive. When we talked to some of the IDPs, they said they had arrived from Darfur the week before. They looked deeply exhausted. Mostly, they said, they were just resting.

In 2008, Sudan had one of the world's largest internally displaced populations, an estimated 5.8 million people, of whom some two million resided within Khartoum state. The government established four official IDP camps: two outside Omdurman and two to the south of Khartoum. As in most displacement settings, however, most IDPs did not live in the camps; they lived wherever they could find a place to set up a shack, usually on the edge of the city. Fifteen years later, what was once desert sand strewn with shacks is now part of the expanding city of Omdurman. Over time, as more people arrived, some with a few more resources, slowly an informal economy began to emerge. Services provided by water sellers and food sellers increased. Humanitarian agencies arrived to provide some assistance, and eventually built a small health unit. A few traders set up stalls, some brought construction wood and scrap metal. The shacks were strengthened and improved. More displaced people came, more buildings were built, and gradually the place took on a more permanent feel, which in turn drew people from the city, bringing more trade and services. Throughout the 1990s, Greater Khartoum saw significant urban in-migration, and informal settlements sprung up around the city. As the city grew, it subsumed the IDP camps that were once outside urban boundaries. As the peri-urban land increased in value, the government's urban planners got involved, along with developers. Evictions began, and people living in areas the government wanted to develop were relocated elsewhere in Omdurman and Khartoum.[8]

What happened to the IDPs who first arrived in 2008? As noted, most displaced people who make it to cities do not return to their rural homes; it is more likely that they will eventually bring their families to live with them, once they have found a foothold in the city. Some of the IDPs we talked to might still be there, having found a way to survive and even thrive, perhaps moving deeper into Omdurman or Khartoum. Others possibly returned to their homes in Darfur or South Sudan, perhaps selling their shacks to newcomers. (Those who did would face recurring violence and displacement over the next fifteen years, both in South Sudan and in Darfur.) Many IDPs moved to other countries, taking the route from Khartoum north along the Nile to the Egyptian border and on to Cairo. Some of the IDP settlements were bulldozed by the Khartoum government in 2008, and others are now part of Omdurman, even if not yet formally incorporated into the city.[9] Since April 2023, the most recent civil war in Sudan has displaced an estimated 10.7 million people (2.1 million families), and Sudan again has the highest number of IDPs in world.[10] There are likely new IDP settlements on the outer edges of Khartoum, as there are in the cities and towns of Darfur. We do not yet know; the violence of the war means there are few observers reporting on what is happening in these areas.

The Omdurman example of how informal IDP settlements eventually become incorporated into the formal city is typical in countries afflicted by conflict and disaster. In Sudan, South Sudan, the Democratic Republic of the Congo, Iraq, and Afghanistan, all of which have seen decades of conflict, the cities are ringed with layers upon layers of informal settlements of internally displaced people. Mogadishu, the capital of Somalia, is famous for its spreading IDP settlements, which have been growing since 1991 and have made it into one of the most densely populated cities in Africa.

These peri-urban areas, called "informal settlements" (or "slums"), are not part of the formal city: they are not included in the national census or city cadastral maps, not provided city services (like water, trash removal, or electricity), and not subject to financial regulation, building inspection, or taxation. But when they are not bulldozed by the government, informal settlements are the driving force of urban growth in developing countries today. These settlements take many different forms, and some are more incorporated into the city than others. It is not only displaced people and refugees who populate informal settlements; migrants from rural areas also settle on the edges of town, and so do local people, who are often displaced from their homes in the city by development and rising prices and seek cheaper or safer living space on the edges of town.

"Urban informality" and "informal urbanism" are widely used and widely contested terms. As Deen Sharp notes, informality is seen as "the major mode of urban design and development over the past fifty years throughout the global south," and more recently in the Global North. Informality has come to mean many things, and some scholars like Sharp reject its usefulness as a concept, "questioning how analytically useful the distinction between informal and formal is."[11] "Informal settlements" is a similarly broad term covering a wide range of low-cost housing arrangements adopted by the very poor, locals and migrants alike. There are two types of informal housing. One type is illustrated by the Omdurman IDPs described above: people construct their own nonpermanent structures like tents and shacks, using found materials like plastic sheeting and scrap timber, on empty land or vacant lots. When these tents and shacks are grouped together, they create settlements. These can range from small "informal tented settlements," as they are called in Lebanon and Jordan, housing refugees in groups as large as several hundred tents, or they can cover huge swathes of land adjacent to cities, as in the Mogadishu case.

A second type of informal housing occurs when people repurpose nonresidential buildings, such as unused storefronts, construction sites, industrial zones, or derelict buildings. This kind of informal housing can be created anywhere in the city as displaced people seek out areas where they can find shelter. On a later visit to Sudan, in 2009, I was conducting some research for IOM in Kalma IDP camp, outside Nyala, the capital of South Darfur.[12] One day, returning to the UN compound from the camp, my driver took a shortcut through an industrial area of the city. I asked him to stop when I noticed a group of people, clearly IDPs, who had made a rudimentary shelter against a factory wall. I introduced myself, and, with my driver interpreting, we started a conversation. They were a family of a mom and dad, five children, and a grandparent, who had been forced to leave their village when it was burnt down by the Janjaweed. Because they were from an ethnic group that was very unpopular in Kalma IDP camp, they felt unsafe there, so they had moved into Nyala town. They had been camping outside the factory for a week, trying to stay out of the factory workers' way and using the factory's water when the workers went home. They had a few vegetables and some bread. They knew they would be evicted soon and were hoping the UN would help them.

Informal settlements are different from official refugee camps run by the UN and the government. In host countries such as Lebanon that don't have encampment policies for refugees, gatherings of refugees can look like camps, but they lack any kind of formal humanitarian assistance. Some countries, like Uganda, do not have refugee camps per se. Instead, refugees are required to live in large agricultural settlements in designated areas. These are also different from informal settlements. Refugees and migrants sometimes join or form their own informal settlements, which have sprung up around cities, especially ports, across the world, including in Europe. One example of the latter is the migrant camps outside Calais and Dunkirk in northern France.[13]

How Informal Settlements Transform Cities

Rapid city growth in Africa, Asia, and Latin America mainly takes the form of unplanned or informal settlements that are growing faster than other parts of cities both in terms of horizontal spread and population. One possible cause of their growth is high birth rates. Although there is relatively little research on birth rates in informal settlements, some studies suggest that women's fertility rates are typically higher in informal settlements.[14] Another cause of rapid growth is in-migration from two directions: from other (gentrifying) parts of the city, and from outside the city. As housing prices, especially rents, increase in city centers, long-term residents are priced out and poorer families can only afford dwellings on the edges of town. Most migrants and IDPs from rural areas or other cities in the same country, as well as refugees and labor migrants from other countries, can usually only afford to live in informal settlements. As in the Omdurman example, new arrivals often start from scratch, erecting temporary dwellings from found materials like plastic sheeting and construction waste. Over time, these dwellings become more permanent as people add to or reinforce their shacks, then rent or sell those shacks to newcomers and build more permanent dwellings within the settlement. As new arrivals expand informal settlements, markets emerge. Residents start micro businesses, and over time, commercial activities such as trading, small-scale manufacturing, and the provision of various services become widespread. Small businesses that do well attract the interest of local investors from the city, who see business opportunities and get involved. More people move in and build more shacks, and more babies are born and grow up. Slowly, the settlements become established; some eventually become incorporated into the formal city, while others do not. This pattern of organic city growth is greatly enhanced in countries with massive internal displacement or refugee inflows.

Table 3.1. Border Cities and Capitals in Selected Host Countries

Country	City (types of migrants) C = capital; B = border city
Somalia	(C) Mogadishu (IDPs)
Uganda	(C) Kampala (refugees and IDPs) (B) Mbarara, Arua, Adjumani, Yumbe (refugees from South Sudan and DR Congo)
Sudan	(B) Nyala, Zalingei (Darfur—IDPs); (B) Kassala (east Sudan—Ethiopian refugees) (C) Khartoum (IDPs and refugees)
DR Congo	(B) Goma (eastern DRC—IDPs) (C) Kinshasa (IDPs and refugees)
Ethiopia	(B) Jijiga, Dolo Addo (Somali refugees) (C) Addis Ababa (IDPs)
South Sudan	(C) Juba (IDPs)
Jordan	(B) Irbid, Mafraq (Syrian refugees) (C) Amman (Syrian refugees)
Northern Iraq (Kurdistan)	(B) Mosul (Syrian refugees, Iraqi IDPs) (C) Erbil (Syrian refugees, Iraqi IDPs)
Colombia	(B) Cucuta (Venezuelan refugees) (C) Bogotá (Venezuelan refugees and IDPs)
Bangladesh	(B) Cox's Bazar (refugees from Myanmar) (C) Dhaka (refugees from Myanmar)
Thailand	(B) Chiang Mai (refugees from Myanmar) (C) Bangkok (refugees from Myanmar)

Source: Author.

Border cities are particularly affected in the case of refugees, but both IDPs and refugees move to secondary cities and capitals. Table 3.1 shows some examples of border or secondary cities and capitals in countries that have experienced major refugee or IDP influxes in the past ten years.

The growth of informal settlements increases the physical footprint and population density of a city, but there are other consequences for cities, as discussed throughout this book. Evidence from wealthy or industrialized countries like the United States and China indicates that urban sprawl has negative effects on public health and the environment as a result of traffic congestion, air pollution, increased urban temperatures, land encroachment, and destruction of ecological habitats.[15] In the cities and especially the informal settlements of poor host countries, these consequences are even more serious, because there are few attempts at managing urban growth (and nothing resembling "smart growth"). City and national governments have for the most part ignored informal settlements—when they haven't tried to eliminate them and/or relocate their residents. In some cases, municipal authorities such as building inspectors are bought off by speculators and developers (as in Cairo). In other cases, municipalities simply don't have the funds or capacity to extend infrastructure and services into the sprawl of settlements surrounding (or sometimes within) the formal city. City governments often simply regard informal settlements as slums that don't have enough of a tax base—or powerful enough advocates—to be worth worrying about. City and national authorities are more likely to concern themselves with informal settlements when they become locales for crime, gangs, and security problems. The case of the favelas in Brazilian cities is a good example of this kind of involvement—the Brazilian government has regularly sent police and even military troops into the favelas.[16]

In many cities, political mobilization in informal settlements is transforming city politics. Confrontations regularly occur between the residents, often supported by advocacy groups, and the city or national government, particularly when city governments try to eliminate informal settlements by relocating residents further away or bulldozing the settlements.[17] Governments increasingly find it difficult to act in these ways, because poor people and their advocates mobilize to protect their urban spaces. Protests, regular media and social media, and the work of advocacy and legal support groups help people hold on to their living space and resist relocation or razing of their neighborhoods—not always successfully, of course. In some cases, governments buy people off (often at below market prices). A recent example is the case of Cairo, where for years the Egyptian authorities have been demolishing residential neighborhoods under the pretext that they were illegally acquired. In February 2022, the authorities evacuated residents from al-Jayara, Hosh al-Ghajar, al-Sukar, and al-Lemon neighborhoods in Old Cairo to build a tourism, culture, and entertainment project. Later that year, in August, Egyptian police arrested twenty-three protesters as they demonstrated against the destruction of their homes on al-Warraq Island in Cairo.[18]

In cities across Latin America, Africa, and Asia, there are dozens of examples of residents protesting eviction and destruction of their housing when the government, often backed by the military or police, has cleared informal settlements to make way for luxury housing and other developments. In many cases, advocacy groups such as Slumdwellers International fight the government in court. Efforts by governments to clear slum areas often fail. For example, back in 2012, the Nigerian government tried to clear Makoko, the huge floating slum abutting Lagos (Nigeria's largest city, with a population of twenty million).[19] Since then, there have been other attempts to clear the slum, and dozens of communities on the island have been evicted, but today, Makoko is larger than ever, and many protests and rallies support its continuation. Akinrolabu Samuel, a campaigner with the Nigeria Slum / Informal Settlement Federation, said at a rally in 2020 that the reason for the evictions was real estate development. In response, the Nigerian government, like many other governments, defended the evictions and demolitions, saying that the targeted settlements were homes to criminal gangs, making them a security threat, and that "the government will not allow indiscriminate erection of shanties on the right of way for roads and other projects."[20]

These kinds of actions against informal settlements and confrontations between the residents with their supporters and city authorities are widespread—and well captured by the media. They are also increasingly well studied, under the rubric of urbanization processes. For example, "popular urbanization" is a concept used to analyze the collective initiatives and self-organization of poor or low-income people in many cities.[21] In most cases, the government is able to destroy smaller settlements, especially if the raid is unexpected. The bulldozers come at night when people are asleep and unprepared. But the people who are then displaced have nowhere else to go, so they start new settlements or move into larger ones.

PART TWO
Secondary Cities: Tripoli, Lebanon

The Syrian civil war began in late 2011 and has not ended as of this writing, in mid-2024. Well over fourteen million Syrians have fled their homes to escape armed conflict, forced recruitment of men into the Syrian army, and persecution by militia groups and the Syrian government. Some seven million Syrians are internally displaced, and another 6.3 million are refugees, mostly in neighboring countries: over 3.5 million Syrian refugees in Türkiye, 800,000 in Lebanon, 660,000 in Jordan, and over 100,000 each in Egypt and Iraq. More than a million Syrians have headed to European countries, often via Türkiye and Greece. Their arrival led to what became known as the 2016–18 European "migration crisis"—a political and governance crisis for European governments. In 2024, Syrians comprised one-fifth of the world's 31.6 million refugees.

Syrian refugees began coming to Lebanon when the war started, but the major influx occurred after 2012 as the war intensified (see the map in Figure II.1). From Lebanon, many moved on to other countries, and some returned to Syria, but a very large number, probably well over a million, remained in Lebanon. As discussed in Chapter 2, it's difficult to know exactly how many, given continuing refugee arrivals from and returns to Syria.

The chapters in this part explore the experiences of Tripoli and other Lebanese cities between 2012 and 2019. After that, events in

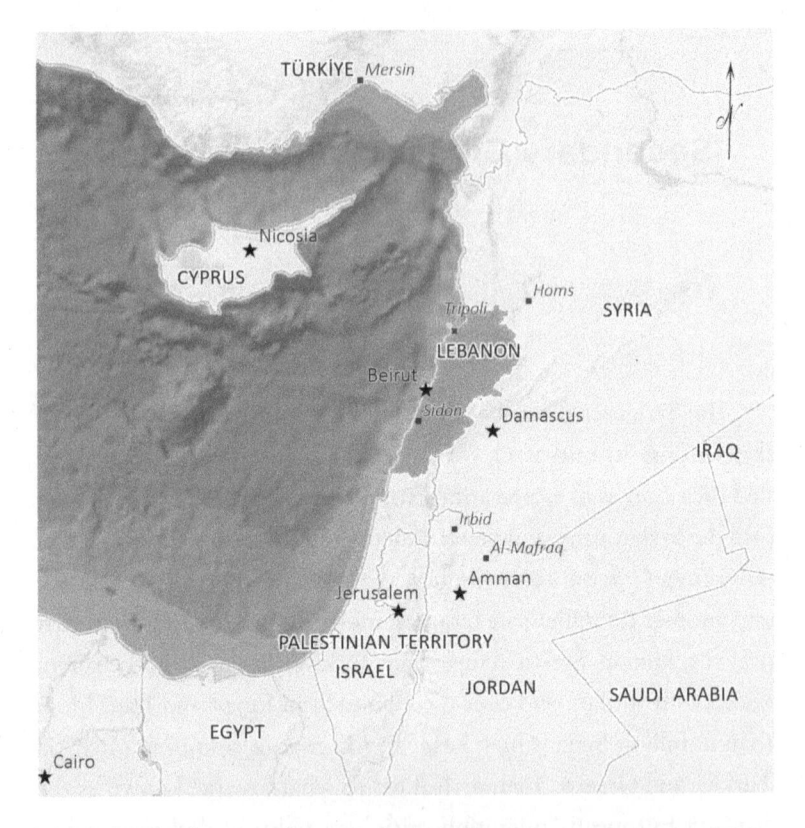

Figure II.1. Lebanon and surrounding countries. Source: ESRI, GEBCO, USGS, NaturalVue, and Natural Earth (with thanks to Marcia Moreno-Baez).

Lebanon—including the crash of the economy and financial system, the Beirut explosions of August 2020, and the COVID-19 pandemic—brought about significant changes for both refugees and hosts. Each chapter focuses on a different aspect of how Tripoli was affected by the arrival and ongoing presence of Syrian refugees (and before them, Palestinian refugees) and the humanitarian industry. We begin with what it means for a refugee to be stuck in what they thought would be a transit city but which over time has become their home. This was the case with Mahmoud, who in 2016 was one of the more than five million Syrian refugees who had fled to neighboring countries.

Field Research for the Tripoli Chapters

In October 2018, I visited Tripoli with Claire, who was then living in Beirut and working with UN Women. Claire is fluent in Levantine Arabic and had visited Tripoli several times, making connections, setting up meetings for our visit, and conducting interviews. During our visit, we were invited to the homes of both refugees and locals and taken for walking tours and a boat excursion to different parts of the city. We talked to refugees, restaurant owners, municipal officials (including the mayor), academics, politicians, and humanitarian workers, both expatriates and locals. After our trip, Claire continued to visit Tripoli and talk to people, sending me her notes and observations for the next six months.

4

How Refugees Get Stuck in Cities

Like thousands of Syrian refugees, Mahmoud moved to Tripoli hoping to transit to Türkiye and thence to Europe (see Box 4.1). But as border and visa regimes have become more stringent, it is increasingly difficult for refugees—and all migrants—to find legal ways to continue their journeys once they have entered a neighboring country. From the perspective of the host government and UNHCR, refugees are usually permitted to stay in the country, at least temporarily. Some may apply for asylum, and if they are found during the "refugee determination process" to meet the legal definition of a refugee, they are eligible to remain in the country as formally recognized refugees. But many refugees do not want to stay in their neighboring countries, where they are usually not permitted to work, and where they, like many locals, struggle to find housing, schools, and decent health care. Like other migrants, refugees prefer to move to western countries.

Finding asylum in European or North American countries is difficult, however, because it requires one first to get there, and many obstacles lie in the way. Let's say you are fleeing persecution by al-Shabaab in Somalia and have found a smuggler to get you to neighboring Kenya, and from there you plan to travel to France to apply for asylum. The Kenyan government requires Somali refugees to stay in a refugee camp near the border, but the smuggler helps you avoid the camp and you get to Nairobi. (This journey from Somalia to Nairobi is not an easy one, as we shall see when we follow Hassan in

Box 4.1. Al-Mina Port, Tripoli, Lebanon, January 2016

Mahmoud stood looking through the locked gates to the port and knew he had come to the end of the road. At the wharf, the docked ferry to Türkiye was being loaded with freight, but the passenger service was now closed to Syrian refugees like him. Only a week earlier, he could have bought a ticket and boarded the ferry for the eleven-hour, 175-mile journey from Lebanon across the eastern Mediterranean to Türkiye's southern port of Mersin. At that time, Türkiye was still allowing Syrians fleeing the civil war to enter the country. From Mersin, Mahmoud, like thousands of other migrants, had planned to head northwest to a Turkish city such as Izmir on the Aegean Sea. There he could easily find a smuggler to get him to one of the nearby Greek islands; then he would be in Europe.

By mid-2015, the Lebanese ferry group Med Star was taking 800 people a day, almost all of them Syrian, compared to its normal load of 700 a week. The fare was $160 per person, more for a cabin in the VIP section. Thousands of Syrian refugees had made this journey, as had Lebanese and Palestinians who took advantage of this opportunity by passing themselves off as Syrians. Then in January 2016, Türkiye reversed a six-year agreement that had allowed free entry to Syrian citizens and started requiring visas that were expensive and difficult to get. For Mahmoud, the window of escape that had seemed so near had closed. Now he was stuck, along with thousands of other Syrians who had hoped to pass through Tripoli. Mahmoud turned away from the gate and looked for a taxi to take him back to the apartment he'd hoped he'd left forever.

later chapters.) Now you have to purchase a plane ticket to France, which you do using Expedia. But when you get to the airport you find out that to board the plane you will need a Schengen visa for Europe. Obtaining such a visa takes many months and requires all kinds of affidavits and proof that you will not remain in Europe. For Somalis, the likelihood of being given a Schengen visa is almost zero. If you have gone to a travel agent or talked to fellow Somalis, they will have told you this and you won't have purchased the ticket. But if you arrive at the airport with your ticket in hand, you will have lost the money. One way or another, you will be stuck in Nairobi.

For refugees who are stuck, like Mahmoud, there are three possible ways forward. The least likely to succeed, but the one most desired by refugees, is to be officially resettled in a third, usually western country, with the help of UNHCR. The more feasible but much riskier way forward is to hire a smuggler to try get to Europe. This option may or may not be successful, will probably be more dangerous, and will definitely be much more expensive. The third option, and the one most refugees end up adopting, is to remain in the city, try to gather funds and explore options, wait to see what happens, and perhaps eventually return to their home country. It's worth understanding each of these options in more detail, as every refugee who comes to a transit city eventually faces them.

Resettlement to a European or North American country is the most desired outcome for most refugees, especially young adults, but it is available only to a lucky few, because relatively few countries resettle refugees at all, and most take only small numbers. In 2023, only twenty-three countries worldwide resettled refugees, and most take only a few thousand refugees each year (nine countries each took fewer than 300). Less than 1 percent—just 158,591—of the world's thirty-eight million refugees and asylum seekers were resettled in countries where they could become citizens.[1] For the majority of the world's refugees, legal resettlement is a dream, not a prospect. For IDPs, resettlement is not possible at all.

The resettlement process begins when a refugee registers with UNHCR and then, some time later, gets an appointment for a refugee status determination (RSD) interview, usually conducted by UNHCR. The purpose of the RSD interview is to determine whether the refugee meets the legal criteria to be defined as a refugee, by asking about the refugee's reasons for leaving their home country. If UNHCR deems the criteria to have been met, the agency assesses which country would be most likely to accept the refugee for resettlement and puts their name forward. Not everyone who qualifies is accepted—acceptance depends on the resettlement country's security and other requirements and on the quota that country is accepting. Refugees who are not accepted for resettlement must remain where they are.

For most migrants and refugees stuck in cities, the only realistic way to get to one's destination of choice is to find a trustworthy and affordable smuggler, pay a hefty sum, and hope that all goes according to plan. Being smuggled is dangerous and expensive, and not at all guaranteed to succeed. Between 2014 and 2018, at least 30,000 refugees and migrants are known to have died trying to reach Europe—we will never know how many died in mountains, deserts, and oceans, their deaths unrecorded. Many more go into significant debt to pay smugglers, often only to be turned back at border entry points or blocked by fences and walls. For those who are successfully smuggled into Europe or the United States, different fates await them. If their smuggling package did not include fake identity documents, they will live in undocumented limbo. Some will try to legalize themselves by applying for asylum when they're already in the destination country (in the United States, this is known as "defensive asylum"), while others will stay under the official radar by working informally and being paid under the table. This is not as desperate a prospect as it sounds, given the number of businesses (especially in the hospitality industry—restaurants, hotels, and country clubs) that regularly employ undocumented workers. Most refugees, like Mahmoud, are reluctant to take the smuggling option because it is both risky and illegal, or they cannot afford the smugglers' fees.

A third possibility is to return to their home country (or home area in the case of IDPs). But the reasons not to return are the same reasons that drove them out in the first place: active armed conflict in their home areas, ongoing persecution by the state or other actors, ruined landscapes, and bombed-out cities with no functioning schools and hospitals, all of which make life dangerous and any kind of livelihood impossible. Today, return to the countries with the highest numbers of refugees and IDPs—Syria, Sudan, Ukraine, Afghanistan, Yemen, South Sudan, Myanmar, and the eastern Democratic Republic of the Congo—is highly risky, especially in some areas of these countries. Nonetheless, return movements do take place. Some refugees feel that being stuck is worse than the prospects of life back home, and they take their chances. Some simply want to return home. Sometimes those who return to their home areas manage as well as their neighbors and family who never left. It is important to remember that in any displacement situation there are always at least some people—sometimes even a majority—who do not leave. Those who stay do so either because they choose to, or because they are unable to leave for various reasons: lack of resources, commitment to family members, place attachment ("This is my home").[2] In some cases, returnees are displaced again when new conflict occurs.

Increasingly, as destination countries harden their borders and the possibilities of resettlement, onward movement, or return become ever more remote, displaced people in cities simply remain where they are. They might move to areas of the city or other cities within the host country where their co-nationals or co-ethnics are already living. City authorities often relocate refugees and migrants (sometimes forcibly) to detention centers or shelters outside town. The refugees wait and weigh their migration options while doing their best to find a decent place to live, get their children into school, find health care, and figure out a way to earn a living—along with thousands of others trying to do the same thing.

5

Lebanon: The Refugee Context

When Mahmoud first realized he was not going to be able to take the ferry, he was devastated. He felt trapped and hopeless, but then, like many migrants who spend time in a place where they never intended to stay for long, he was drawn into the city. It helped that he focused on other people rather than on his own misery. As a teacher, it bothered him that Syrian students had to pay high tuition fees and got a poor education, so in 2013 he set up a school for Syrian children. The school prospered, and as more students applied, he started a second school. The schools absorbed his attention. He planned to leave at some point, but his schools were growing—and even attracting Lebanese students as an alternative to the poor public schools. Mahmoud began to put down roots in Tripoli. He felt more at home. He got married. Like thousands of others, he planned to stay for a while.

In early 2016, when Mahmoud and thousands of others were blocked at the port, Lebanon, a small country with a population of about six million, had been receiving refugees from Syria's civil war for over four years and was hosting well over a million Syrian refugees and asylum seekers. Most of the refugees were Syrian, but they were not the only group fleeing Syria or the only refugee nationality in Lebanon. Most of the 29,000 Lebanese citizens who had been living in Syria before the crisis returned to Lebanon. Many Iraqi refugees who had found safety in Syria after 2008 also came to Lebanon and joined the existing Iraqi refugee population of about 6,000. Some

27,000 Palestinian refugees fled Syria, joining the 174,000 Palestinians already living in Lebanon.[1] By 2016, the main movement from Syria had stabilized, although small numbers continued to move back and forth across the borders. By 2018, Lebanon was hosting close to 1.5 million refugees, including small numbers from African countries.

Lebanon did not require refugees to live in camps, so they settled in and around Lebanon's main cities and towns. Many Syrians also moved to the villages of the Beqaa Valley (where eventually refugees outnumbered the Lebanese by three to one) and the North (where the numbers of Syrians and Lebanese were almost equal).[2] This uneven settlement pattern meant the refugees' impact was highly variable across Lebanon.

As noted in Chapter 2, refugee populations are only estimates, because UNHCR and government registrations do not capture all the people who might qualify as refugees, and the lists are not updated to reflect return or onward movements. After 2015, the number of Syrians in Lebanon was even more of a guess, for two reasons. First, well before 2011, there was a large population of Syrians living in Lebanon, particularly in the North. Estimates range between 450,000 and one million Syrians, but there are no solid numbers or any kind of registration.[3] (The last census in Lebanon was in 1932.) They included mixed Syrian-Lebanese families as well as Syrian workers who came to Lebanon on a seasonal basis or had remained after the Syrian occupation ended in 2005. Prior to 2015, the border between Syria and Lebanon was open, and Lebanese and Syrians crossed at will. This changed after January 2015, when Lebanon began implementing its new policy on Syrians in Lebanon, which stipulated new criteria for entering Lebanon, limited opportunities for employment of Syrians, and regularization of their residency in Lebanon. After that, it became more difficult to cross the border, but not impossible, thanks to smugglers, and many Syrians continued to do so.

A second reason why the actual number of Syrians in Lebanon is unknown is that the Lebanese government told UNHCR to stop registering Syrian refugees in May 2015. The government had become increasingly worried about the growing number of Syrians in Lebanon. Since registration entitled refugees to humanitarian assistance from UNHCR, the government hoped that stopping registration would dissuade refugees from entering the country. Although UNHCR tried to talk the government out of this move, UNHCR could not go against the government's wishes.[4] Like all UN agencies, UNHCR is a member-state organization, governed by the UN General Assembly, and it cannot act in opposition to the government of the country that hosts it. So, from May 2015 onward there was no official registration of Syrian refugees. UNHCR continued to "record" Syrians but did not release these new numbers as of April 2015. The official number of refugees in Lebanon remained frozen, but this did not mean that refugees stopped entering Lebanon. As in all host countries, not all refugees in Lebanon approach UNHCR—some are hesitant to be registered, others prefer to manage on their own. All told, it is likely that thousands of Syrians went unrecorded in Lebanon. At the same time, Syrians continued to leave Lebanon to move elsewhere or return to Syria without informing UNHCR. These movements mean the true population of Syrians in Lebanon is in flux, and unknown.

Any small country would struggle with the arrival of a million refugees, but Lebanon was in a particularly weak position after decades of armed conflict and political turmoil, including a civil war (1975–90), Syrian military intervention and occupation by Syrian forces (1976–2005), the assassination of Prime Minister Rafiq al-Hariri in 2005, a short war with Israel (2006), and ongoing sectarian conflict. South Lebanon was largely under the control of Hezbollah, a Lebanese Shi'ite radical movement sponsored by Iran, which led to frequent border clashes and air strikes with Israel. Politically, at the beginning of the refugee influx in 2012, Lebanon was in a mess. There had been no functioning government for many years, and the Syrian refugees threatened the sectarian balance in Lebanon's multiconfessional political system. Lebanon has the highest percentage of Christians among Middle Eastern countries, and at the end of the civil war in 1990, the different religious sects devised a power-sharing formula. Prior to 2012, the Palestinians had already added to the Sunni Muslim population. Now Christian, Shi'ite, and Druze groups feared the Syrian refugees could increase the Sunni Muslim proportion of Lebanon's population.

Prior to the arrival of the Syrian refugees, Lebanon's economic growth had averaged 9 percent between 2007 and 2010, but there was significant poverty, especially in the North. In 2011, Lebanon was classified as an upper-middle-income country, although nearly 27 percent of the population, 1.2 million people, lived below the poverty threshold of $3.84 per capita per day, and 10 percent were extremely poor (below $2.40 per day). After 2012, the war in Syria began to undermine the economy. The incidence of poverty rose by 6 percent; by 2015, a third of Lebanese lived below the poverty threshold—that is, they could not afford the minimum standards of living. Half of the heads of these households were unemployed. Extremely poor Lebanese households lived in the North, Beqaa, and Mount Lebanon, as did most of the Lebanese returnee households—and most of the Syrian refugees.[5]

In 2017, the World Bank announced that the financial and economic costs of the Syrian refugees amounted to $4.5 billion per year, and that the economic decline had hurt the poor most. The Syrian conflict had cut real GDP growth by 2.85 percentage points each year from 2012 to 2014, entailing large losses in wages, profits, taxes, and investment. An additional 170,000 Lebanese had been pushed below the poverty line (adding to 1.2 million already there) and the unemployment rate had doubled to above 20 percent, impacting unskilled youth in particular. Government revenue collection dropped by US$1.5 billion, and government expenditures increased by US$1.1 billion due to the surge in demand from the refugees for public services. This surge led to a decline in access to and quality of services, and the World Bank estimated an additional US$2.5 billion was needed to return the quality of services to their pre-Syrian conflict level.[6]

Lebanon's high unemployment meant a growing number of citizens sought to leave the country to find work. But even before Türkiye implemented new visa restrictions, not everyone who wanted to leave could do so. Without passports, money, or assets such as houses that they could sell to finance their journey, many could not go, including most Lebanese and refugees. For the Syrians, the only options were to wait for the war in their country to end and then return home, or to hope for resettlement through UNHCR—a distant hope at best.

The arrival of large numbers of refugees aggravated Lebanon's existing problems and created new ones. Given this situation, one might think that the Lebanon government would have sought to manage the Syrian refugees—perhaps requiring that they stay in camps near the border, where UNHCR could take care of them. This was the response of other neighboring countries, notably Jordan, but also Türkiye and Iraq, both of which initially established camps for Syrians. Lebanon did close the border and restrict entry for Syrians, but it did not create camps. Why not? Possible reasons relate to Lebanon's own history of displacement and migration and their troubled experience with Palestinian refugees in camps. In Chapter 7 we explore why Lebanon did not set up camps for Syrians.

As is true of all countries, Lebanon's history is a patchwork of many subregional histories that have played out in different ways, depending on the ethnic and political differences at work. The historical experience and political context of South Lebanon are different from those of North Lebanon. Different cities in Lebanon embody these regional histories. One such city is Tripoli, Lebanon's second-biggest city, situated in the North. The chapters in this part of the book explore Tripoli's experience with displacement and migration, its refugee camps and its history with Syria and how these factors have influenced the city's response to the refugees. One of the main arguments I make is that a city's history of displacement influences both the citizens' and the city government's responses to a humanitarian influx, and it is these responses, along with the actions of the refugees themselves, that transform the city. The rest of this chapter describes the broader displacement context of Lebanon on the eve of the arrival of the Syrian refugees in 2011 and how the policies of the Lebanon government have evolved since then.

Lebanon's History of Migration and Displacement

Lebanon's history of conflict meant the Syrian refugees came into a country whose citizens were very familiar with the experience of displacement and migration. The civil war (1975–90) displaced between 600,000 and 900,000 Lebanese within the country, to neighboring countries, and further abroad. After 1990, Lebanese citizens continued to leave the country, as they still do today. The Lebanese have been emigrating since the late nineteenth century, and the global Lebanese diaspora (including first-generation Lebanese nationals and their descendants) is estimated to be as large as fifteen million. After the civil war ended, internal sectarian conflict and invasions by Israel continued to kill or displace Lebanese citizens. Israel's conflict with Hezbollah in 2006 forced nearly a million Lebanese from their homes. Half of them fled to Lebanon's mountain villages, where they were sheltered in schools or local homes, and 180,000 Lebanese found refuge in Syria. UNHCR reported that prior to the ceasefire with Israel in August 2006, as many as 10,000 Lebanese people arrived at the Syrian border each day. The Syrian government supported Lebanon and provided shelter and relief to the Lebanese refugees, working with humanitarian organizations like UNHCR and the Syrian Arab Red Crescent. Many Syrians accepted refugees into their homes and donated food and goods.[7]

The historical experience of national displacement can incline a government and its citizens to view incoming refugees more favorably, especially when the displacement experience was recent. In this case, just six years before the Syrian refugees began to arrive in Lebanon, Syrians had been supporting displaced Lebanese. But Lebanon's history with Syria is long and complicated, and Lebanese relations with Syrians varied between North and South Lebanon. This history with Syrians, together with Lebanon's experience with Palestinian refugees and the Palestine Liberation Organization (PLO), complicated the responses of both the Lebanese people and the authorities to the arrival of Syrian refugees after 2011.

When Mahmoud arrived in Tripoli in 2012, he entered a city that had a long history with Syria. During the Ottoman Empire, Syria and Lebanon were part of the same country, and they remained so after France took control of the Levant after the First World War. Lebanon became independent from France in 1944, but Syria had always seen Lebanon as part of its historic territory and did not recognize Lebanon's independence until 2008, when the two countries established diplomatic ties for the first time. In 1976, a year into Lebanon's civil war, Syrian troops entered Lebanon and stayed until 2005, when street protests and international pressures forced the troops to leave after Syria was suspected of playing a role in the assassination of former Lebanese prime minister Rafiq al-Hariri. Since then, the Assad regime and Hezbollah, which now has seats in Lebanon's government, have grown closer.[8]

As noted above, prior to the arrival of Syrian refugees in 2012, there was a large population of Syrian nationals living in Lebanon. Many had lived and worked there for thirty years, taking advantage of their privileged migrant status to make lives for themselves. (A 1993 agreement gave preferential treatment to Syrian migrant workers, allowing them to reside and work in Lebanon without a work permit and to cross the border with only their personal IDs.) When the war in Syria broke out, the varying political allegiances of the long-term Syrian population created hotspots of insecurity throughout Lebanon. In the Shia-dominated South, Hezbollah had its power base. The North was Sunni dominated and Tripoli was home to several militant Sunni groups, some supported by the Assad regime and others opposed to it. On several occasions, the tensions between these groups broke out into active armed conflict within the city.

The Lebanon Government's Response to the Syrian Refugees

Lebanon's history of displacement and its relations with Syria likely influenced the government's rather laissez-faire response to the Syrian arrivals in 2012. Lebanon is similar to other Middle East countries (except Egypt) in that it has not signed the 1951 Refugee Convention or the 1967 Protocol relating to the Status of Refugees. As noted, until January 2015, the Syrians benefited from open borders between Lebanon and Syria, and because the government did not see the refugees as a security threat, its response was essentially one of inaction and no policy. No camps were created and refugees found their own accommodations. The government left UNHCR and other humanitarian agencies to manage the refugees, including their registration. As noted, in early 2015, the government ordered UNHCR to stop registering "refugees" (Arabic: *lajiun*) from Syria (UNHCR even deregistered some in compliance with the decree), and henceforth labeled them "displaced people" (*nazihun*) or "de facto refugees," which has no legal relevance and means the government does not treat Syrian refugees differently from migrants.[9] UNHCR continued to provide Syrian refugees with protection, services, and sometimes resettlement, but no longer issued documents proving their refugee status to the international community.

As the Syrian war intensified and the number of refugees increased, the state's inaction shifted toward policies intended to deter the arrival of Syrians. In October 2014, the government drafted a new decree for refugees: after 2015, there would be border restrictions and strict entry regulations, costly visa and residency permit renewal fees, and barriers to work and services. Syrian nationals could no longer enter Lebanon for humanitarian reasons; they could enter only for purposes of business and trade, or as tourists if they held US$1,000 and a hotel reservation, or if they owned assets in Lebanon or were sponsored by a Lebanese employer (through the *kafala* system, a legal sponsorship system in all Middle Eastern countries except Iraq that gives employers control over migrant workers' employment and immigration status).[10] Syrian refugees could work only in agriculture, cleaning, and construction.[11]

These new restrictions changed what Syrians were permitted to do, as well as their rights and protections. Before 2015, registered Syrian refugees were allowed to work for the first six months after their arrival. Although they were supposed to obtain a work permit, few such permits had been issued to Syrians, and there was lax enforcement of labor regulations and a lenient working environment. Nonregistered refugees, refugees without work permits, and refugees operating businesses without a license could usually work; the authorities turned a blind eye. After 2015, this working environment became much more restrictive. The temporary residency permit, a prerequisite to obtaining a work permit, became difficult to obtain. Registered refugees who tried to renew their residency permit using their UNHCR registration certificate were required to sign a pledge not to work. As a result, most Syrian refugees could work only informally. Outside the protection of the law, many faced harmful working conditions and exploitation. They were paid less, were required to work longer hours, and could do little if employers withheld wages, as they seldom had formal contracts.[12] The high unemployment levels in cities like Tripoli meant some Lebanese resented the fact that any refugees were being employed. As Figure 5.1 shows, some neighborhoods expressed their feelings with banners.

Figure 5.1. Tripoli banner, January 2017. The banner was hung in two different locations in al-Qoubeh, Tripoli. The sign says, "Dear Syrian refugee, I deserve work in my country more than you do." Source: Khaled Ismail, Claire Wilson, and Nathan Cohen-Fournier, "Community Tensions in a Fragile Urban Economy" (Refugees in Towns Project, Tufts University, 2017), https://refugeesintowns.net/all-reports/tripoli.

Beginning in 2019, the situation in Lebanon deteriorated for everyone as the country experienced one crisis after another. In 2019 the government defaulted on its foreign debts and Lebanon's currency collapsed, and then there were mass protests in October 2019, the COVID pandemic began in early 2020, and the Beirut port explosion occurred in August 2020.[13] As the economy spiraled downward, poverty increased and many Syrians and Lebanese alike became destitute.

For years, the Lebanese government had been talking about the need for the Syrian refugees to return to Syria, but little had been done. In 2018, Lebanon organized "voluntary return" trips to Syria. Syrians who wished to go back would register, then the list was checked by Syrian security officials to see if anyone on it was wanted for arrest or deemed a security threat to Damascus, and if so, Lebanese authorities removed them from the list. These return trips were halted in 2020 with the COVID pandemic border closures. By then, some 21,000 refugees had returned to Syria this way, according to Lebanese officials. UNHCR said at least 76,500 Syrian refugees had returned voluntarily from Lebanon since 2016, some via government-organized trips and some on their own. There have also been refugee deportations to Syria. In 2019 a regulation stated that all unauthorized refugees who entered Lebanon after April 2019 would be deported. Human Rights Watch says that between April 25, 2019, and September 19, 2021, some 6,345 Syrians were deported under that regulation. Since 2021, Lebanon's government has periodically announced plans to deport or repatriate Syrians, sometimes without the involvement of UNHCR, which would be a breach of international obligations.[14]

6

Tripoli and the Changing City Landscape

Lebanon's North is a region of about 2,070 square kilometers (800 square miles), divided into North governorate (capital: Tripoli) and Akkar governorate (capital: Halba). The rolling landscape, dotted with villages and small towns, lies between the mountainous Syrian border and the Mediterranean Sea. It is an impoverished region, historically neglected by the national government. Tripoli is Lebanon's second-largest city and one of the world's oldest port cities. The port, al-Mina, began as a Phoenician trading hub (Lebanon was known as Phoenicia in classical times), and in the thirteenth century the Crusaders built the Citadel fort a few kilometers inland. Today Greater Tripoli consists of three municipalities (Jabal Beddawi, Tripoli, and al-Qalamoun) together with the port of al-Mina.

Between Syria and the North there is a long history of cross-border movement. Tripoli is 100 kilometers from the Syrian city of Homs and forty-eight kilometers across the sea from the Syrian port of Tartus (see the map in Figure II.1). Many Lebanese and Syrians have family and friends or trade connections in both countries. During Lebanon's civil war, thousands of Lebanese fled across the border into Syria; some stayed, and others returned with Syrian spouses. In 2012, Homs, a major rebel stronghold, was besieged by Assad's forces, and Syria's western region was caught up in heavy conflict. Refugees fled into North Lebanon, with some coming directly to Tripoli and, like

Mahmoud, heading for the port to continue their journey, and others settling in the towns and mountain villages of North Lebanon. Many are within Tripoli's metropolitan reach, and both refugees and Lebanese citizens commute to Tripoli for work, trade, and health services.

The Syrians found shelters anywhere they could. Away from Tripoli, land was much cheaper. In Halba, just twenty-five kilometers from Tripoli and less than sixteen kilometers from the Syrian border, Syrians could rent a ten-square-meter plot of land that cost twice as much in Tripoli. Many preferred to live in Tripoli, however, despite its higher prices, because there were more opportunities for onward movement and for employment, and because their families and networks were there. Tripolitans were mostly sympathetic toward the new arrivals—perhaps partly motivated by gratitude for the Syrians' earlier help. But not all Lebanese citizens felt this way—and the reception changed over time, as we shall see.

When Mahmoud first came to Tripoli as a single man, he lived in the Christian suburb of al-Koura, where he worked for an NGO as a teacher. Then in 2015, his sister's husband was killed in the fighting in Syria, and she and her seven children came to live with Mahmoud, along with his widowed mother. In 2017 he met and married Nour, a fellow Syrian refugee, and they had a baby son, Anwar. His family now needed more living space, so Mahmoud looked in Jabal Beddawi, one of Greater Tripoli's three municipalities, where many Syrians already lived. Jabal Beddawi is a dense sprawl of high-rise apartment buildings sprinkled with dusty palm trees on the patches of bare ground among the gray concrete. Mahmoud found two apartments in a newly built four-story building on the edge of town. The Lebanese landlord was expecting his brother to return from Dubai to live in one of the apartments, which meant Mahmoud and his family might have to leave at short notice, but the uncertainty meant

Mahmoud was able to negotiate a good deal on the rent. He did not sign a lease, however. Formal leases are rare in Tripoli, especially for refugees, and landlords often hike the rent unexpectedly or evict refugee renters with little warning. But Mahmoud took the risk because even though he struggled to pay for both apartments—the rent for each was about $300 per month without utilities—the apartments were close to the school Mahmoud was setting up, and large enough for his family. Mahmoud, Nour, and Anwar moved into one apartment with his mother, and his sister and her children took the one above them. The apartments were roomy and sunny, each with two bedrooms and a living room opening to a veranda overlooking a construction site and the hills beyond. They arranged the living room in traditional Arab style, with sofa cushions along three walls and bare floor in the middle, where Nour served meals on a wax cloth. It was the kind of comfortable apartment that only those who were somewhat better-off could afford, not typical of the kind of housing most Syrian refugees could find or afford.

As in most host cities, Tripoli's refugee arrivals did not distribute themselves evenly across the city. They moved to specific neighborhoods where their co-nationals were already living, or where they could find affordable housing. They moved into high-end suburbs like Maarad, middle-class suburbs like Abou Samra, working-class neighborhoods in Jabal Beddawi, and older, run-down areas like the neighborhood around the Old Souk. They lived in new developments like Mahmoud's apartment building in Jabal Beddawi, in very poor informal settlements ("shantytowns"), or in the Palestinian camp in Beddawi. Their arrival reshaped the city landscape in at least four ways: spatially, economically, socially, and in terms of the security of neighborhoods. This chapter discusses the spatial impact on the landscape and the economic impact on housing markets in Tripoli and Halba. Subsequent chapter explore the social and security impacts.

The Spatial Landscape

Increased demand for housing in places like Tripoli and Halba spurred new development and housing construction. Much of the city of Tripoli is built on a rounded cape jutting out into the Mediterranean, which blocks expansion to the west and north, so new construction, like Mahmoud's apartment building, occurred on the edge of Beddawi, wiping out farmland and extending the city's footprint into the rocky hills around Tripoli. New construction also occurred within the city, densifying the housing by adding floors or extensions to existing apartment buildings. In smaller host towns like Halba, new construction boomed along the main road. In Tripoli, the spatial landscape also changed because of the presence of the humanitarian industry.

In host cities, humanitarian agencies set up offices and warehouses, and their international staff generally want upscale housing, all of which put upward pressure on prices in land and housing markets. International aid workers' taste for luxury goods and services, such as high-end groceries and restaurants, creates new demand in these markets.[1] Tripoli was no exception. In the Mina area, at least a dozen bars, coffee shops, and restaurants are frequented by expatriate NGO and UN aid workers. (One particular seafood restaurant, run by "The Captain," is very popular. The Captain and his staff appreciate their frequent patronage because most of them tip well.)

The UN compound buildings are a feature of a host city's landscape. In Mogadishu (Somalia), for example, the UNHCR compound alone takes up 10,000 square meters (one hectare), part of the much larger UN physical presence in Mogadishu. Generally, UNHCR tries to keep a low profile in cities. In Tripoli the UNHCR compound sits at the edge of the Rachid Karame Fairground near al-Mina (see Box 6.1).

UNHCR located its compound here because few Tripolitans visit or use the abandoned fairground. A service road gives easy access, and

> ### Box 6.1. The Rachid Karame Fairground and UNHCR's Compound
>
> The seventy-hectare Rachid Karame Fairground was originally conceived and designed as the setting for a world's fair by the Brazilian architect Oscar Niemeyer, after he visited Tripoli in 1962. Several of his neofuturistic structures were built on the site during the early 1970s, including a helipad and a columned outdoor theater surrounded by a moatlike reflective pool. When Lebanon's civil war broke out in 1975, construction stopped and never resumed. The fairground was used as a barracks and staging ground for the occupying Syrian Armed Forces until 1990. Today the fairground is largely abandoned, although when we visited in October 2018, the gardens with their rosebushes, oleanders, and palm trees were being maintained by a team of gardeners, some of whom were Syrian refugees. The contrast between Niemeyer's flamboyant structures and UNHCR's huddled, temporary-looking arrangement of trailers and Quonset huts is stark. (Perhaps UNHCR deliberately allowed the compound to assume a temporary appearance, to assuage the Lebanese government's concerns that the refugees were here to stay?) In January 2023, UNESCO added the site to the List of World Heritage in Danger.

the compound doesn't aggravate the city's traffic congestion.[2] The UNHCR buildings are separated by a stretch of empty land. A barricaded security gate controls vehicle access to the compound, with guards checking visitor documents and phoning the main office for visitor clearance. The refugees use a guarded separate entrance to the reception center where they wait for services (in 2018 the waiting time was one to three hours).

The Housing Market

The arrival of thousands of Syrian refugees created a demand shock across Lebanon's urban housing market, especially for low-cost rentals. Refugees are generally more likely to be renters than buyers; in Tripoli about 70 percent of refugees rented accommodations. Landlords discovered they could charge refugees more and provide less. This happened in poor and wealthy neighborhoods alike, a common pattern in cities experiencing a humanitarian influx. After the Russian invasion of Ukraine in February 2022 and the flight of Ukrainians into neighboring countries, rents in many cities increased. In Poland, the population grew by 15 percent in Warsaw and by 23 percent in Krakow. By March–April of 2022, rents had increased by 16.5 percent in Krakow and 14 percent in Warsaw (house purchase prices rose less—by 4 percent and 1 percent, respectively).[3]

As UN and other international agencies arrived in Tripoli after 2012, hundreds of expatriate staff needed housing and office space, usually in upscale areas like Maarad and al-Mina, leading to further inflation of rents and gentrification. Many Lebanese families had to move out when their landlords discovered they could rent their apartments for much more to an aid agency. Between 2011 and 2015, rents in Tripoli increased 200 percent.[4] In low-income neighborhoods, poor people, including Lebanese, Palestinians, and refugees, struggled to afford the new rents, and many had to leave—or were evicted—often moving further out to the town's periphery, and sometimes to informal settlements. How the Syrian refugees affected the urban housing market in North Lebanon is worth understanding in detail. Market dynamics reveal how difficult it is for external actors like aid agencies to have a positive impact on something as complex as housing in cities. The case of Halba points to the importance of understanding how urban markets work before making any external intervention.

In 2017, Akkar governorate (North Lebanon) had the densest population of refugees in Lebanon—some 250,000 Syrian registered refugees out of Akkar's total population of 350,000. Halba, the governorate's capital, had a population of 13,812 inhabitants, of which almost 8,000 were Syrian.[5] In their study of Halba's housing market and urban landscape, Fawaz et al. describe how the Syrians' arrival prompted developers to expand existing apartment stock, adding floors or even entire new buildings, often shoddily and rapidly built, and sometimes rented out to Syrian families before they were completed. As prices rose, many Lebanese residents moved out of their apartments and rented them to Syrians, using the rent to pay off their mortgages, while they moved back to their family villages, where housing costs were much lower. Within five years, large-scale "Syrian compounds" (as the locals called them) crowded along the main road through Halba. These compounds consisted of "12–16 buildings, each four to five floors high with six to eight apartments per floor, almost all inhabited by Syrian refugees." Fawaz et al. call these compounds "one of the most imposing urbanization patterns of the Syrian refugee crisis in Lebanon," visibly reflecting how refugees have contributed to the sprawling urbanization of the region.[6]

This pattern of sprawling urbanization is a common feature of border towns in countries as diverse as Brazil, Sudan, and Bangladesh. With regard to the Halba compounds, Fawaz et al. suggest the kinds of development practices that enable such patterns: "While apparently legal in their permitting processes, these compounds often exploit the blurred boundaries of state law and weak inspections to intensify development. Their financing relies on a convergence of sources that are not typically studied together, such as subsidized public loans and humanitarian aid . . . distributed to Syrian refugees. . . . The flows of capital and people that sustain this spatial production are distinguished by the historically highly informal governance practices as well as laissez-faire characterizing this border city." Patching together support from UNHCR and daily work, the Syrians struggled to pay the rent, and the poor quality of the buildings meant they often had to repair them. Sometimes neighbors came together to fix buildings or formed WhatsApp groups to discuss how to manage noise, dirt, and other challenges, either through self-help or by appealing to the municipality or UNHCR.[7]

In Halba and Tripoli, as in many host cities, as housing demand booms, households and developers add new units or extra floors to existing buildings that are not designed or built to carry extra loads, jeopardizing the safety of residents. Increased density of neighborhoods puts intense pressure on urban services, especially the water supply, sanitation, garbage collection, and the electricity supply, as we will explore later. Tripoli could not keep up with the rapid expansion. Some new roads were built, at least in the more high-income developments, but the city's transportation and energy infrastructure shouldered the new burden without additional funds or capacity.[8]

Long before 2012, finding affordable and secure housing in Tripoli was a challenge for migrants and Lebanese alike. After 2012, the situation got much worse. A 2014 report noted the "predatory relationship emerging between property owners, realtors, and slum lords on the one hand and tenants on the other."[9] Landlords' ability to hike rents and evict people was helped by Lebanon's lax regulation of land and real estate markets and by the fact that few people could afford housing loans. Housing policies that favored property owners had emerged after Lebanon's civil war, when the government began to promote mortgage-based homeownership. At the same time, providing affordable and adequate housing disappeared from the policy agenda. Poorly controlled urban growth and unequal access to housing, services, and economic opportunities are problems that occur in cities across the world. The inequalities are rooted in deficient or biased policy decisions—or the absence of any urban policy. In Lebanon, the 1965 Housing Law recognized housing as a human right, but the government made no effort to ensure reasonably priced and adequate housing. This national housing situation meant that the arrival of over a million Syrian refugees amplified (but did not cause) Tripoli's housing problems, especially in low-income and informal areas.

Neighborhood Social Transformation

The Syrian refugees also transformed the social landscape of the neighborhoods into which they moved. Like other cities in Lebanon, notably Beirut, Greater Tripoli was already home to many Syrians, but the new arrivals tended to be more socially and religiously conservative—or at least they were perceived to be by the Lebanese. In some neighborhoods, Lebanese families moved out because they didn't like the conservative religious values of the Syrian newcomers. For example, the souk area in Tripoli's old city took on a Syrian character as refugees occupied the aging buildings and Lebanese families, many of whom had lived there for generations, moved away. By 2018, many Lebanese said the suburb of Abou Samra had become a Syrian neighborhood.

Similar processes of neighborhood transformation were occurring in other cities. In Beirut, the neighborhood of al-Naba'a was transformed by Syrian refugees. One study found that Syrian refugees occupied 70 percent of the area's housing, with the rest distributed among Lebanese citizens and other migrants. On some streets near the mosque and in the center of the neighborhood, Syrian occupancy was almost 100 percent. Syrian households tended to be much larger than Lebanese ones, with an average of 6.3 individuals sharing a one- or two-room unit, compared with two to four individuals per apartment for Lebanese families. The study describes two kinds of neighborhood transformation in Naba'a. On the one hand, the neighborhood has become more congested and the aging physical infrastructure is unable to handle the population pressure: "Garbage is piled high on street corners, children play in the middle of the street, and cars move slowly allowing for pedestrians to share the pavements. Potholes, water, and sewage are frequently observed on the streets." On the other hand, the makeup of the population has improved. Previously there had been a heavy concentration of single males, many of them Syrian migrant workers, but now "many long-term residents expressed relief at the reduction in the number of single males, lower incidences of street violence, and the return of . . . 'family life and patterns' . . . and healthier neighborhood life."[10] The Naba'a study notes that the settlement's transformation came about through Syrian migrant social networks that helped find housing for new arrivals or those who had been evicted.

Like Halba, Naba'a replicated widespread slum patterns of informal construction in which multistory apartment buildings are built incrementally, starting as ground-floor buildings and then expanding upward as property owners add floors over the years. These buildings, which often include roof dwellings, are structurally unsound and potentially hazardous to their occupants. Building permits are easily obtained through bribes to local officials, or from the local police force, militias, or other informal actors, rather than through formal planning agencies. The profits from the demand for cheap housing mean practices like adding new floors and splitting single-family apartments into multifamily ones have intensified since the arrival of the Syrians. Both of these housing trends are widespread in cities across Africa and Asia, as we explore in the case of Cairo.

Informal Settlements

For many Syrians and Lebanese seeking a place to live, the only option was to move into informal housing. As discussed in Chapter 3, "informal housing" is a broad term covering a wide range of low-cost housing arrangements adopted by the very poor—locals and migrants alike—around the world. Both types described earlier are present in Tripoli: nonresidential buildings such as unused storefronts or derelict buildings like the shopping mall (see Box 6.2), as well as buildings under construction; and nonpermanent structures like tents and shacks, which are often grouped into what is known in Lebanon as "informal tented settlements." The latter are usually constructed by the refugees, who put up temporary huts or tents made of plastic sheeting on empty land or vacant lots usually outside the formal city boundaries or in nonresidential zones. Informal tented settlements range in size from a few to several hundred tents. By 2014 there were more than 450 such settlements across Lebanon, and by March 2018 the number had climbed to more than 5,000, housing about 230,300 people. About two-thirds were in the Beqaa Valley and about a quarter were in the North. Between 2018 and 2022, more refugee families, especially female-headed households, moved into nonresidential or nonpermanent housing. About a third of female-headed households were living in informal settlements.[11]

Rent increases, predatory landlords, and competition with refugees for housing also affected Lebanese citizens, more of whom began moving into temporary housing and informal settlements. In 2014 Lebanese observers and UN agencies already worried that "the growth of informal settlements . . . represents a major concern, both in terms of the quality of shelter and living conditions as well as from a longer-term land-use and sustainability perspective."[12] Ten years later, this growth has become even more rapid in terms of both population and space taken up, not just in Lebanon but also in cities across Africa, South America, and Asia, as displaced and local people alike increasingly are able to find and afford accommodations only in these informal settlements.

Box 6.2. The Derelict Shopping Mall

About ten miles outside Tripoli, along a little-used road, is a partially built shopping mall, long abandoned by its developers, with no electricity, running water, sewerage, or other services of any kind. In 2018 this derelict mall was home to a community of about fifty Syrian refugee families. Claire and I visited it in October 2018, after we got permission from the community leaders. We took a taxi from Tripoli, but our driver had never heard of the mall or even the nearby village, and we struggled to find it, asking directions many times. When we got there, an elderly community leader and the woman who was his deputy met us and gave us a tour. We climbed the stairs to the top of the building, which was designed so that the wide balconies of its five floors encircled an open-air courtyard. Off the balconies were storerooms, now occupied by refugee families, most of which consisted of one parent, usually the mother, a grandparent, and three to five children. Sometimes the storeroom was divided by a curtain, and two families shared the space. There was a small window at the back of the room, concrete floors, and a door leading to the balcony. The refugees had furnished the bare rooms with whatever they could find to make shared beds and sometimes a chair or two, and some had carpets they'd brought from Syria. Although there was no running water or electricity, the Syrians managed by pirating electricity and buying water from water sellers who passed by the building. Most families, especially the mothers and children, spent their time on the balcony. There were few men—those who came with their families from Syria were away looking for work in Tripoli or on farms. On the balconies, a few people sold fruit and vegetables that they had purchased from markets near Tripoli. Otherwise, there was little activity—except for the children playing up and down the balconies.

Informal settlements seldom have city services, so residents mobilize to work out a solution. Some services are pirated by residents tapping into the city's electricity grid or someone's internet service. It is more difficult to pirate or jerry-rig services like water and sanitation, but some informal settlements organize to do this. An example of such organizing is Palestinian gatherings. Many Palestinians have chosen to live outside the twelve official camps around Lebanon, in what are called "gatherings." A study in 2009 counted forty-two such gatherings, which consist of groups of at least twenty-five Palestinian refugee households living in an area with no official UNRWA camp status. Without access to government services, the inhabitants take matters into their own hands. For example, the Palestinian gathering of Maashouk in South Lebanon has organized itself to access electricity and water and to handle waste management and shelter maintenance. In North Lebanon, there are nine such gatherings within or near Greater Tripoli. Some share the same urban facilities as the Lebanese population, but others such as Mankoubeen, Mouhajjareen, and the one near the official UNRWA Beddawi camp are in much worse condition.[13]

On its outskirts and within the city itself, Greater Tripoli has a number of informal settlements—some new, others long-standing. Some were settled years before by Lebanese and over time have become impoverished. After 2011, these settlements grew as both Lebanese and refugees from Palestine and Syria moved in. One of the oldest such settlements is Hay al-Tanak.

Hay al-Tanak is an informal settlement on the edge of al-Mina, across the road from the long narrow strip of rocky beach bordering most of the port area. One side of the settlement borders the wealthy neighborhood of Maarad and the other side edges up to al-Mina's popular "Corniche," with its many restaurants and bars. The settlement began in the 1930s as a working-class neighborhood of Tripoli known as Haret al-Jdideh, with houses built with ceilings and concrete walls. Hay al-Tanak, which means "place of tin" (*tanak*), earned its name after the civil war when Lebanese needing affordable housing built makeshift houses with tin roofs and found materials such as cardboard, sandbags, tires, and concrete blocks. No population count has ever been done, but NGO workers estimate the settlement has about 200 households, or about 1,000 people, including a longstanding population of Syrians and Palestinians who had been living in Lebanon before 2012. After 2012, Syrian refugees moved in, and the settlement became predominantly Syrian as Lebanese families rented their homes to Syrians, then moved to other areas further outside Tripoli. Living conditions in Hay al-Tanak were and still are difficult. Residents are not legally permitted to undertake new construction, but they add to their dwellings slowly and unobtrusively, often building at night. Many children are stateless because residents cannot afford to register their marriages or their children. (The fee for marriage or birth registration is L£400,000, about US$4.40).[14]

As the situation in Lebanon has deteriorated, things have become much worse in Hay al-Tanak. One news report said that "fights have commonly broken out over food rations and aid for years now, but the area is too neglected and cast aside for these disputes to be reported on in local media."[15] For destitute Syrians and Lebanese who cannot afford even a place like Hay al-Tanak, the only option is to move further out of town, but still within the city's metropolitan reach, to informal tented settlements and derelict sites such as the abandoned shopping mall. One study found that by 2022, rents in Lebanon had increased by 176 percent compared to 2021, and more than half (58 percent) of Syrian refugee families were living in shelters that are dangerous, substandard, or overcrowded.[16] Of course, Lebanese families too are affected by such rent increases.

Housing and Humanitarian Programs

Humanitarian agencies increasingly recognize that in cities, housing and rent are the biggest challenges for refugees and host populations alike. Throughout the Middle East, UN agencies and INGOs have sought to improve the housing conditions of refugees and local populations living in the most insecure dwellings. They have rehabilitated unfinished homes, repaired residential buildings in bad condition, and installed sanitation facilities. In informal tented settlements, the agencies have provided shelter materials and improved fire prevention. Such activities tend to be constrained by limited donor funding. As we will discuss in Chapter 8, funding is usually heavily earmarked by donors, and informal settlements are not a priority. In Lebanon, as elsewhere, this means that the number of people UNHCR and its partners reach is only a fraction of those who need help—both refugees and Lebanese.[17]

Many housing programs are short-term interventions aimed at helping refugees by helping host populations. Some show promise for longer-term impact. In Lebanon, some aid agencies work directly with landlords to help refugees with rent, and in doing so, improve relations between refugees and hosts. One such program implemented by the Norwegian Refugee Council (NRC) focused on Syrians, Palestinians, and Lebanese citizens who had returned from Syria, as well as "extremely vulnerable" Lebanese households. NRC recognized that the host population viewed refugees as a source of economic and social problems and that "both tangible and symbolic" supports were needed to encourage the host population to accommodate the displaced.[18] Accordingly, they designed the Occupancy Free of Charge (OFC) program complemented by community support projects.

The OFC program offered Lebanese landlords a package of building upgrades for unfinished buildings in exchange for rent-free hosting of displaced households for a twelve-month period. The idea was that by easing their rent burden, refugees would have a chance to become established and financially stable, and they could begin paying rent when the period was up. The program also provided tangible support to Lebanese hosts by improving their buildings and adding housing units to the rental stock, and it sought to provide symbolic support by demonstrating that the Lebanese were not bearing the burden alone. From April 2016 to December 2017 (Phase 1 of the OFC program), NRC upgraded a total of 3,454 houses, affecting 2,763 households (some 12,638 individuals), who also received materials and awareness sessions on safe hygiene practices and legal assistance. NRC also implemented three community support projects (CSPs) for some eight municipalities in the North and Beqaa. These infrastructure projects included the provision of solid waste dumpsters, the construction of a borehole, and the rehabilitation of rainwater drainage canals.

An evaluation in 2018 found that the OFC intervention had mixed results. On the one hand, the program provided immediate financial and mental relief to displaced families and contributed to strengthening relations between the displaced and hosts. On the other hand, the program did not really enable refugees to find longer-term solutions or sustainable "coping strategies." The infrastructure investments made by the CSPs were useful to the communities that were directly targeted, but the impact was small-scale and did "little to affect the tensions arising from overcrowding, competition for jobs and the annoyance caused by litter, and lack of water or sewage."[19]

Given the housing situation in towns like Halba and in informal settlements, and the limited scale of humanitarian housing programs like the OFC, what are the ways to address the housing impact of refugees on towns? Could the refugee influx present a window of opportunity? One of the clearest messages coming from Fawaz et al.'s study of Halba concerns the complexity of actors, funding, and market transactions underpinning the housing market and the livelihoods derived from it. Different institutions—religious, humanitarian, and state—are involved in disbursing and managing housing funds. As they note, the range of actors include sheikhs who manage fundraising campaigns in Saudi Arabia to support Sunni Syrian refugees in Lebanon; the Lebanese state that provides housing loans to members of the Lebanese Armed Forces; and humanitarian agencies that support refugees with housing assistance. Meanwhile, the labor of Syrian refugees (with long experience in the construction industry in Lebanon) is used to build or rehabilitate housing for Syrians. All this activity is mediated through informal market transactions that "rest on social institutions such as kinship, religious belonging, shared histories, or common memories," but which render both parties exposed in a transaction: landlords are vulnerable to default by tenants, and tenants are powerless when rents increase.[20] Both landlords and tenants are at risk when donors change their minds about their funding priorities and pull the funds.

In protracted humanitarian crises like those resulting from the conflicts in Syria, Ukraine, Sudan, Gaza, and Myanmar, the housing economies of host cities undergo dramatic shifts. Usually, these shifts most affect the poor, whether displaced or local. The complexity of Halba's housing market seven years after the refugee influx suggests that a deep look is warranted before development or humanitarian agencies—or governments, for that matter—design interventions that try to stabilize affected urban communities. Halba's complexity is typical of many border cities and towns, but each will have its own dynamics. Still, there might be common threads that are worth incorporating into humanitarian housing planning and program design.

First, it's clear that traditional short-term, one-off humanitarian responses to refugees' immediate needs have little effect; what is needed is long-term interventions that address housing in neighborhoods where refugees and locals live. Despite its small scale, the NRC's OFC program points to how it could become a model for the future if it were scaled up and if locals were adequately consulted. As noted by the NRC evaluation, interventions like the OFC program and community support projects can potentially reduce community tensions if they are planned and implemented with "a high degree of involvement of community members, refugees, mayors and mukhtars." There is plenty of evidence from host countries that participatory joint planning can strengthen refugee-host relations and increase communities' sense of ownership of new interventions. The NRC evaluation indicated there were many Lebanese who want to participate in solving their communities' infrastructure, housing, and coexistence problems: "Landlords made their properties available for refugee households; sometimes out of profit motives, sometimes out of moral and family concerns [that] were turned into a humanitarian wish to 'help,' as landlords got to know the refugee families living next door."[21]

New ways of thinking about how to support both refugees and locals in city neighborhoods have emerged in recent years. So-called area-based approaches are premised on the idea that mutual benefits come from addressing the needs of the neighborhoods or communities in which refugees live, rather than refugees' needs alone. This approach has a long history that began in the 1960s and 1970s with urban and regional planners working on community renewal through "area-based initiatives" in poor neighborhoods. Today the approach is gaining traction with humanitarian and development agencies but has yet to reach scale. Community support projects using an area-based approach engage locals and refugees living in the same neighborhood to work together to identify urgent neighborhood needs (such as sanitation or clean water provision), develop proposals, apply for funding, and take responsibility for the contracting and monitoring of the project. The idea is to address neighborhood needs and build relationships between refugees and hosts, while strengthening their ability to plan, implement, and "own" projects. The hope is that eventually, communities can lead such processes after humanitarian or development agencies have departed. There are now dozens of area-based projects around the world, at city-level scale, at borough scale or a neighborhood scale.[22]

Two such projects in Tripoli target poor neighborhoods with high concentrations of refugees. The first, implemented by CARE and their local partner Akkarouna, was funded by the US State Department. It focused on five Tripoli neighborhoods with high concentrations of refugees (Abou Samra, Mankoubin, Shalfeh, Shok, and Wadi Nahle) and rehabilitated "whole streets and specific buildings as well as individual household support, to serve Syrian and host communities alike." The other project took place in Hay al-Tanak and was implemented by the French NGO Solidarités International and coordinated by the Tripoli municipality and UN-Habitat.[23] The NGO gathered neighborhood-level data about priorities, managed tensions, and negotiated compromises. By the end of the one-year project, they had rehabilitated 203 housing units (providing privacy and weatherproofing, and access to water, sanitation, and electricity); upgraded thirty buildings with 135 households (upgrading common areas like staircases and the roof); and rehabilitated three public spaces, including constructing a small basketball field and completing a range of other accomplishments that benefited the entire community, such as creating wall murals, asphalting roads, upgrading streetlights to LED lights, solar panels, or batteries for blackouts, installing bins and dumpsters for waste collection, and much more. After the end of the project the NGO noted that residents had organized their own mini "cleaning campaigns" and were doing more to maintain public spaces.

These kinds of area-based projects, which focus on urban neighborhoods rather than a sector or target group, are still relatively new, but they show much promise for host cities. If they could be multiplied and scaled up across cities, and if humanitarian and development agencies could work together to fund them, they could go a long way to rehabilitating neighborhoods, easing tensions between refugees and hosts, and increasing and improving housing stock. One promising recent example is the Shirika Plan in Kenya, which seeks to open Kenya's refugee camps and link them to the nearby towns of Kakuma and Dadaab, treating the whole area as a target of development. We discuss this plan in Chapter 7.

7

The Camp and the City

A few kilometers from Mahmoud's place, in the middle of Jabal Beddawi, northeast of downtown Tripoli, is Beddawi Palestinian camp. When the camp was established in 1955, it was well outside Tripoli, but as Jabal Beddawi grew and eventually became its own municipality, it engulfed the camp. Today the city surrounds the camp, but where the camp begins is immediately obvious because conditions become much worse at the boundary. Beddawi camp is now a crowded slum with dilapidated buildings lining rutted, unpaved streets crisscrossed by open drains. The streets are filled with street sellers, pedestrians, motorbikes, and donkey carts, as described in Box 7.1.

Encampment policies—the government's requirement that refugees live in camps—are not the norm for host countries today. In 2022, out of 203 countries hosting refugees, just thirty-six required refugees to live in camps, and twenty-three of these were in Africa.[1] In most of those countries, host governments struggle to enforce encampment policies and as many or more refugees live outside the camps as inside them. The situation for Syrian refugees in neighboring countries is typical. Jordan and Iraq have refugee camps, but most refugees do not live in them. By 2018, only a third of the 283,000 Syrian refugees in Iraq lived in camps, as did only 16 percent of the 715,000 Syrian refugees in Jordan. Türkiye began with a few camps, but by 2018, 96 percent of the 3.6 million Syrian refugees living in

Box 7.1. A Stroll through Beddawi Camp

Some of Mahmoud's pupils lived in Beddawi camp, and he often went there to visit and check on them and their families. Claire and I joined him one afternoon in October 2018. We walked from his school, crossing the busy intersection bordering the camp. A small booth at the camp's entrance flew the flag of Fatah al-Islam, one of the Palestinian factions that tries to control the camp. The booth was manned by three tough-looking men with a military mien, sunglasses, and full beards. Two sat on motorcycles, another talked on his phone. They watched the people, Lebanese, Palestinian, and Syrians, coming and going. We walked down the camp's main market street past open-fronted stalls selling groceries, vegetables, hardware, cheap clothes, and plastic goods.

Mahmoud greeted ten-year-old twins sitting on the steps outside their father's fabric stall. The father was a tall, thin man who was perhaps forty but looked seventy, clean-shaven with a beaklike nose and thinning gray hair. He had left Syria with his family two years earlier. He wanted to restart his fabric business in downtown Tripoli, but the only place he could afford to rent store space was in the camp. His stall was typical of those in urban street markets in the Middle East: a three-walled room open to two front steps the width of the store that led directly onto the street. Rolls of fabric were piled on the shelves and floor—gaudy upholstery material with silver and gold polyester thread, most of it made in China. While the adults talked, the twins sat on the steps and watched passersby try to avoid a deep rut in the road, trickling dark sludge. A man talking on his phone and not paying attention walked into the rut, and as he stepped out cursing, the twins ran up and offered him a rag to wipe his shoes and were rewarded with a few coins.

Türkiye were in towns and cities, and by 2022, Türkiye no longer had camps. Lebanon did not require Syrians to move into camps, but it did have a long history of Palestinian camps, with significant implications for nearby cities.

Refugee and IDP camps can be in remote locations near the border with the sending country, or they can be near or even within urban areas. Greater Tripoli is typical of many cities that have engulfed nearby refugee camps as city and camp expand toward each other. The presence of refugee camps in or near a city has significant economic, social, and security consequences for the city, both positive and negative. Measuring the economic impact of refugee camps on the host population has received some attention by economists, but their work mostly focuses on the refugee camps themselves and host communities surrounding camps. There is little such econometric research on urban centers, likely because in cities it is much more difficult to separate out the impact of refugees from that of other migrants and their neighbors. An exception is the work of economists like Jennifer Alix-Garcia and her colleagues. Their work on the impact of Darfur IDP camps on the town of Nyala (Sudan) and on the effects of refugee camps on the town of Kakuma (Kenya) is impressively nuanced.[2]

When the Syrians began coming to Lebanon, the government did not require them to live in refugee camps, whereas neighboring countries, notably Jordan but also Iraq and Türkiye, initially created camps for Syrian refugees. Lebanon's decision was curious, as it did have long-standing camps for Palestinian refugees. As we explore in this chapter, the history of those Palestinian camps partly explains why the government did not require camps for the Syrians. We begin with a short discussion of why host countries do and do not create camps, then explore how camps impact cities.

Why Host Governments Create Camps

During or soon after a humanitarian influx, the host government must decide whether to create official camps or settlements for the displaced or require them to live in existing camps. Official refugee (and some IDP) camps and settlements are different from informal settlements in that they are supported by UNHCR and other international humanitarian agencies. However, although UNHCR is often blamed for creating refugee camps, it is the host government that decides whether or not to pursue an encampment policy.

There are many reasons why a host government might want some or all refugees to live in camps. Governments can better monitor and manage refugees when they're in camps, and by locating camps in remote areas near borders, governments can segregate refugees so they don't compete with nationals for jobs or other resources such as schools and health care. (Refugees often prefer to stay close to the border in order to monitor the situation back home—and cross back over when the conflict eases.) For example, Tanzania's 1998 Refugees Act curtailed refugee mobility beyond four kilometers from the camps on its western border with Burundi and the Democratic Republic of the Congo and prohibited refugees from receiving wages outside of the camp.[3]

Security concerns also push a government to require refugees to live in camps. However, although international refugee law requires that refugee camps are for civilians and noncombatants only, it's difficult for host governments to enforce this requirement, as combatants can enter the camps simply by shedding their military gear and hiding among the refugees.[4] In 1990, when I was conducting my dissertation research in Site 2 camp for Cambodian refugees on Thailand's northeastern border with Cambodia, an aid worker told me that Khmer Rouge fighters regularly used the camps for "R and R" (rest and recuperation) and to visit their families, first hiding their weapons outside the camp.

Strategic considerations might also influence the government's decision to opt for camps. One view is that host governments use refugee camps instrumentally to raise the profile of refugees in their territory and thus bring in additional financial aid. This would explain why Jordan created refugee camps for Syrian refugees—it perceived the error of not having created camps for the inflow of Iraqi refugees that had occurred several years earlier.[5] Governments shed some of their responsibilities for refugees when camps become the responsibility of UNHCR and NGOs, who take care of refugees' shelter and protection needs. These international duties are part of the broad and long-standing "burden-sharing" responsibility of the international community to help refugees and their hosts. UNHCR usually tries to discourage host governments from creating camps, but if the government insists, UNHCR is obliged to assist the government, while doing its best to protect and support the refugees. In some countries, UNHCR manages the camps, although the person officially in charge of the camps is usually a government official (the "camp commandant").

Despite these considerations, most host governments do not create camps. Why not? One set of factors is a host country's own history of war and displacement and its historical experience with camps. Many citizens of host countries have been refugees or internally displaced themselves, and their governments give ideological and historical reasons for not requiring refugees to live in camps, claiming solidarity and "brotherhood" with the refugees. For example, many members of South Africa's ruling African National Congress (ANC) had been refugees for years in neighboring countries like Zambia and Namibia. After the ANC came to power in 1994, President Mandela declared that African refugees arriving in South Africa were their brothers and would be treated with the hospitality they had once offered South Africans. This meant not putting refugees in camps. South Africa's Refugees Act, created in 1998 and coming into force in 2000, was one of the most progressive pieces of refugee legislation in the world. Sadly, the hospitality did not last, and today this legislation has been significantly eroded, with several amendments to the Refugees Act and high levels of xenophobia toward African refugees, including by some South African politicians. There has been talk of creating camps near the border with Zimbabwe, but so far this hasn't happened.

Lebanon's Decision Not to Create Camps for Syrians

Lebanon is an interesting case of a host country that has not created camps despite strong countervailing forces to do so, and especially because it already had camps for the long-standing population of Palestinian refugees. When the Syrian refugees started to arrive in 2012, UNHCR advocated against camps, asking that Lebanon instead support local populations "so that refugees could live with as much dignity, independence, and normality as possible." However, UNHCR also discussed with the government the possibility of establishing temporary shelter sites to relieve the refugees' situation. Some Lebanese politicians supported this suggestion "as a humanitarian necessity," but—as was so often the case in Lebanon—there was no political consensus to move in this direction, and no action was taken.[6] Instead, the refugees moved into cities or set up informal settlements, and as the housing supply shrank, many moved into the existing Palestinian camps. Creating camps for the Syrians seemed to make sense, at least from the government's point of view. Why did this not happen?

There is much debate about the decision, but an important factor was the government's desire not to repeat Lebanon's sixty-year experience with Palestinian refugees in camps, which had been a major source of insecurity and conflict. When the Palestinians first came to Lebanon in 1948, they were required to live in camps at a distance from Lebanon's towns because the government wanted to prevent the integration of a large new Muslim population into Lebanon's religiously fragmented society. However, in those days as is still the case today, in host countries where governments try to keep refugees in remote border areas, there is a well-established pattern of refugees leaving the camps and moving closer to job opportunities—usually in or near towns. Sometimes they might create their own settlements in these new locations. In Lebanon, one such camp was Shatila, established in 1949 by Palestinian refugees who left the distant village where they had initially been settled and secured land about twelve kilometers outside Beirut. The settlement was later made an official camp by the International Committee of the Red Cross.

At first, the Lebanon government did not allow the Palestinians to expand their camps, then in 1969 it signed the Cairo Agreement with the Palestine Liberation Organization (PLO), which gave the Palestinians the right to train in Lebanon for the liberation of their homeland—"to join the Palestinian revolution through armed struggle"—and permitted them to self-administer their camps, although the camps remained under Lebanese sovereignty. The Palestinians began constructing concrete buildings and expanding the camps. At the same time, Lebanon's cities were growing, and some camps, once distant from the city, were engulfed by what Diana Martin calls the ever-expanding "misery belt" of Lebanon's cities. Since then, non-Palestinians, including Lebanese citizens as well as Syrian, Egyptian, and other migrants, have also moved into the camps. Prior to 2009, Martin estimates, 30 percent of the population of the twelve official Palestinian camps in Lebanon was non-Palestinian. Most Palestinian camps were near towns, and two of them were close to Tripoli.[7]

The Palestinian Camps of Tripoli

Tripoli's history offers an example of how the presence of nearby camps—and the loss of them—can affect a city. In 1949, Nahr al-Bared Palestinian camp was established some sixteen kilometers north of Tripoli, followed by Beddawi camp in 1955. Until 2007, Nahr al-Bared was one of the most economically successful Palestinian camps in Lebanon. Its position on the main road, halfway to the Syrian city of Homs, made the camp's souk (market) the largest in northern Lebanon, and a commercial hub. Both Lebanese and non-Lebanese shopped in the souk because of the tax-free goods and low (black-market) prices. But by 2007, tensions were brewing in the camp. Under the 1969 Cairo Agreement, the Lebanese Army was not permitted to enter the Palestinian camps, and internal security was provided by Palestinian factions such as Fatah al-Islam.[8]

In May 2007, a crisis occurred. It began with a bank robbery in Tripoli by a group of Fatah al-Islam militants. Lebanese Internal Security Forces (ISF) surrounded and then attacked a building in which the militants were hiding, unleashing a day-long battle. In response, Fatah al-Islam attacked an ISF checkpoint, killing several soldiers in their sleep. The Lebanese Army then began shelling Nahr al-Bared camp, and a three-month long siege ensued, during which the camp sustained heavy damage. Most inhabitants fled to Beddawi camp, which at that time was still outside the boundaries of Tripoli proper, and to other parts of Lebanon, including Beirut and Sidon. The last civilians (the families of Fatah al-Islam members) were evacuated from Nahr al-Bared before the conflict ended on September 2, 2007, when the Lebanese Army took control of the camp and most of the militants were killed or captured. Some of the defeated Fatah al-Islam moved to Ain al-Hilweh refugee camp near Lebanon's southern city of Sidon.

The destruction of Nahr al-Bared was a devastating blow to the local economy and to the lives of the refugees and Lebanese citizens living in or near the camp. All 6,000 Palestinian refugee families (some 27,000 residents) and over 1,600 Lebanese living in the camp were forced to leave, and only a fraction of the infrastructure survived. Since then, UNRWA has slowly reconstructed the camp, while displaced families live in temporary housing or metal containers as they wait for their homes to be rebuilt. After 2011, 504 Palestinian refugees from Syria and a few dozen Syrian families arrived in Nahr al-Bared, adding pressure on the camp's overstretched infrastructure and resources. As of the early 2020s, most of Nahr al-Bared camp had been reconstructed and 3,550 families who had previously lived there had returned.[9]

The demise of Nahr al-Bared camp had implications for Jabal Beddawi and Greater Tripoli. Beddawi camp's population increased from 15,000 to 30,000 almost overnight, seriously straining camp services. The pressure increased after 2012 as Syrian refugees moved in, along with Palestinians fleeing Syria, and Lebanese Tripolitans also moved in as other parts of Tripoli became too expensive.[10] Nobody knows how many people live in Beddawi camp today. UNRWA registered 21,252 persons as of June 2018, but it acknowledges this figure is not an accurate indication of actual numbers. Palestinians move in and out of camp, as do Syrians and Lebanese. It is an ungoverned space, and its population growth has placed significant strain on its already decrepit infrastructure and on UNRWA services. As in other Palestinian camps in Lebanon, Beddawi's inhabitants are very poor and have few job prospects, as Palestinians are not permitted to work in most sectors.

Like many long-standing refugee camps near to or engulfed by a city, Beddawi camp both serves certain functions and creates problems for the city. On the one hand, camp residents are a source of cheap (undocumented) labor for the city, whose local employers benefit from paying less for security guards, house cleaners, office workers, and the like. The camp also serves as a last resort for people who can't find housing elsewhere in the city. On the other hand, there are negative implications for the city, especially security problems. Historically, the Palestinian camps have been a serious security concern for Tripoli and other cities, in part because of an earlier decision made by the national government. The 1969 Cairo Agreement enabled the Palestinian camps to become bases for armed movements. In the South, the camps were used as launch sites for attacks against Israel, which, beginning in 1968, led to Israeli military interventions for the next forty years (in 1978, 1982, 1993, 1996, and 2006). After the "Black September" crisis in Jordan in 1970 and the expulsion of the PLO from Jordan, the Lebanese government allowed a new wave of Palestinian refugees to come to Lebanon. Continuing Palestinian attacks and retaliation from Israel, together with increased tensions between Christians and Muslims, threw Lebanon into civil war in 1975, with military intervention and occupation by Syria. In June 1987, Lebanese president Amine Gemayel signed a law that annulled the Cairo Agreement with the PLO. But control of the Palestinian camps—and large swathes of towns and areas around the camps—by radical groups like Hezbollah (Shi'ite) and Fatah al-Islam (Sunni) continues, with periodic clashes with the Lebanese military.[11]

The concerns Lebanon's cities had about the Palestinian camps grew after 2012. Beirut now surrounds two Palestinian camps, Shatila and Bourj al-Barajneh. The southern city of Sidon is adjacent to Ain al-Hilweh, the largest Palestinian refugee camp in Lebanon, whose population of 70,000 swelled to nearly 120,000 with the arrival of refugees from Syria. These security concerns surely explain why creating more camps for Syrian refugees held little appeal. Additionally, Lebanon continues to struggle with a fragile peace (made more fragile by the ongoing situation in Gaza as of 2024), and many Lebanese fear old conflicts will be stirred up by both the Palestinian and Syrian refugees.

This history suggests that in 2012, the Lebanese government feared that putting Syrian refugees into camps would create greater problems than not having them in camps. Plus, the government was struggling to impose order and provide services for its own citizens and was in no position to create functioning camps for the refugees. Lebanon's no-camp policy may be lauded as both cheaper for the host country and more humane for the refugees, but it was likely less a humanitarian gesture and more the result of deep political fears.

How a Nearby Camp Affects a City

In most host countries, refugee camps are not prisons; they seldom restrict fully the movements of refugees, and people come and go quite freely. Sometimes refugees require a permit to leave the camps, but these are generally easily obtained, or the requirement is simply ignored by the gatekeepers, perhaps with the help of a small bribe. This means there is constant movement between towns and camps. Refugees and locals alike move back and forth to trade and conduct business or to visit family living in and outside the camps. This movement is especially noticeable in border towns near camps, but even distant camps are connected to cities. In host countries like Kenya and Bangladesh, both of which have large refugee camp complexes, there is plenty of movement between the camps, their nearby towns (Dadaab and Kakuma in Kenya, and Cox's Bazar in Bangladesh), and the distant capitals (Nairobi and Dhaka). These towns and cities acquire large permanent refugee populations, some of whom moved from the camps, while others skipped the camps entirely and traveled straight to the city. Table 7.1 lists a few examples of host countries with camps and their affected towns.

Table 7.1. Some Host Countries with Camps near Towns and Cities

Host country	Camps (main refugee nationalities; no. camps)	Nearest town (distance from camp(s))	Distance from capital and border	Date of camp inception
Kenya	Dadaab complex (Somalis; three camps)	Dadaab (7 km)	500 km from Nairobi; 80 km from Kenya-Somalia border	1991
	Kakuma and Kalobeyei complex (South Sudanese; four camps)	Kakuma (5 km)	1,000 km from Nairobi; 95 km from Kenya-Sudan border	1992
Uganda	Northwest (South Sudanese; multiple settlements)	Yumbe (16 km)	553 km from Kampala; 50 km from South Sudan border	2016
	Rhino camp (South Sudanese)	Arua (63 km)	460 km from Kampala; 70 km from South Sudan border	1980
	Nakivale settlement (Congolese)	Mbarara (25 km)	300 km from Kampala; 250 km from DRC border	1958
Tanzania	Nyarugusu camp (Congolese)	Kasulu (60 km)	1,212 km from Dar es Salaam	1996
Sudan (western)	Darfur: Kalma and ZamZam camps (IDPs)	Nyala (14 km) Al-Fashir (17 km)	1,200 km from Khartoum	
Sudan (eastern)	Shagarab camps (Eritreans, Ethiopians; three camps)	Kassala (114 km), Gedaref (160 km)	500 km from Khartoum	1980s?
Bangladesh	Kutupalong complex (Rohingya; thirty-three camps)	Cox's Bazar (30 km)	400 km from Dhaka	1991

(continued)

Table 7.1. (*continued*)

Host country	Camps (main refugee nationalities; no. camps)	Nearest town (distance from camp(s))	Distance from capital and border	Date of camp inception
Jordan	Zaatari (Syrians)	Mafraq (15 km)	68 km from Amman	2012
Algeria	Tindouf camps (Sahrawis; five camps)	Tindouf (< 10 km)	1812 km from Algiers	1976
Ghana	Buduburam camp (Liberians)	Accra (34 km)	Accra	1990

Source: Author's calculations.

This movement means camp populations are part of the surrounding host economy and society. Refugees incorporate camp resources like food aid and camp schools into their household survival strategies, and when camps are near towns, their livelihood strategies bridge the camp and the town. It is common for refugee families to organize themselves so that some family members stay in a camp where they can get humanitarian assistance, while others work in nearby towns. Splitting family members between the camp and the town ensures access to resources in both settings. For example, a family's mother and young children might stay in the camp so they can access food and other humanitarian assistance and so the children can go to the camp school, while other family members move to the town to find jobs or conduct trade. In some cases, families register in the camps but then move out, and a family member returns for the monthly food distribution to obtain the ration (for example, a bag of corn or rice). The family members might then consume the ration if it is needed (which it often is) or they might sell part of it to purchase goods they need.

Camps also provide resources and jobs for the local host population, regional traders, and humanitarian staff. In some cases, locals use the camp schools or health facilities. For example, the vast Kakuma camp and Kalobeyei settlement complex in northwestern Kenya has been in place since 1992, mainly for refugees from South Sudan, but there are also Somalis, Congolese, Burundians, Eritreans, and other nationalities. Kakuma camp is divided into four areas (Kakuma 1, 2, 3, and 4) and Kalobeyei Integrated Settlement comprises three villages.[12] The camps and settlements, about five kilometers from the town of Kakuma, provide all kinds of services for both refugees and locals. Health services are free for refugees as well as for Kenyans, who comprise 10 to 15 percent of the clients. Camp schools are also available to Kenyans, but school utilization by locals is relatively low compared to that of the refugees. Kenyans come from around the region to trade and conduct other business in the camp-based economy that extends to the town. Many locals find housing and employment in the camps, too. As is often the case, the relationship between a nearby camp and a town can yield economic benefits for the host population.[13]

These benefits do not always mean that the town population appreciates either the camp or the refugees, especially when the situation becomes protracted. The longer camps are in place, the stronger their social and economic linkages with the cities near them become, and often the refugees become more politically empowered, too. As the boundaries between camp and city become blurred, refugees come to be seen as competitors or threats, especially if they become politically active. A good example of this unfolding dynamic is the political activism that developed in Buduburam camp outside Accra, Ghana, which eventually led the government to reject the refugees and demolish the camp (see Box 7.2).

There is another way to deal with long-standing camps: host governments can decide not to demolish them, but rather to embrace

Box 7.2. Political Action in Buduburam Camp

Buduburam camp for Liberian refugees was established in 1990 about twenty-one miles from Ghana's capital, Accra, to accommodate refugees fleeing the First Liberian Civil War (1989–96). In the years after the camp opened, its population fluctuated as people returned to Liberia and newcomers from ongoing conflict in Liberia arrived. The camp economy grew and became a profitable trading area, and refugees and locals shifted from farming to trading. Some of the Liberians moved into the nearby suburbs of Accra such as Kasoa and Awutu, whose residents did not welcome this development. In January 2012, UNHCR invoked Article 1C of the 1951 Convention, known as the cessation clause, with respect to Liberian refugees. Simply put, this clause is invoked when UNHCR determines (through a lengthy process) that refugee protection is no longer needed for a particular nationality because conditions in their home country are safe for their return. UNHCR advised the remaining Liberian refugees in Buduburam to return to Liberia. About 1,000 refugees did return, but some 7,000 remained in the camp, and the Ghanaian government began referring to them as "Economic Community of West African States (ECOWAS) migrants" rather than refugees. In 2021, the government announced its intention to demolish the camp because it believed the camp had become a hideout for criminals, and because the peace in Liberia meant the refugees could safely return. The refugees reacted strongly, and tensions grew with the Ghanaian authorities. As in many such confrontations, however, the refugees lost. In early March 2024, Reuters reported that "under the orders of traditional authorities who own the land," the camp had been demolished, and "the once bustling Liberia Camp that had stood for 34 years was reduced to concrete rubble."

Sources: Note on the Cessation Clauses, EC/47/SC/CRP.30, UNHCR, May 30, 1997, and "Surge in Returns This Year as End of Refugee Status for Liberians Nears," UNHCR, June 26, 2012, https://www.refworld.org/docid/4fec44002.html; Isaac Yeboah Addo and Augustine Tanle, "Rethinking Solutions for Protracted Refugee Situation: A Case Study of the Buduburam Refugee Camp Closure in Ghana," *Scientific African* 21, no. 3 (2023): e01746; Elizabeth Holzer, "A Case Study of Political Failure in a Refugee Camp," *Journal of Refugee Studies* 25, no. 2 (2012): 257–281; Naohiko Omata, "Unwelcome Participation, Undesirable Agency? Paradoxes of De-politicisation in a Refugee Camp," *Refugee Survey Quarterly* 36, no. 3 (2017): 108–131.

them and turn them into urban settlements. This is what happened in the case of Kenya, which launched the Shirika Plan in 2023. The five-year transition plan seeks to turn the decades-old Kakuma camps and the Dadaab camp complex (in northeastern Kenya on the border with Somalia) into more open urban settlements that enable freedom of movement and economic activity by refugees in the Turkana and Garissa districts. The plan complements another progressive move on Kenya's part: the new 2021 Refugee Act, which replaced the 2006 Refugee Act that required refugees to live in camps. The new act promises refugees greater access to the labor market and more freedoms and rights, but still requires most refugees to live in "designated areas." How the act will be implemented (that is, the government regulations that will be announced) will determine how much the new law changes the situation for refugees; it is still early days. If it is successful, the Shirika Plan, which was designed by UNHCR working with the government, could mean that the towns of Kakuma and Dadaab benefit from the development investment funds that UNHCR has mobilized—as of mid-2023, about Ksh28 billion ($199.71 million), possibly supplemented by funding pledged by the World Bank.[14] The plan could be a significant step forward both for the refugees in the camps and for the towns nearby. But a lot depends on the funding. and as Chapter 8 explains, this is seldom a straightforward undertaking.

8

Here Comes the Money

For host countries, one of the most dramatic consequences of a refugee influx is the humanitarian and development funds that follow it. During the initial "emergency" period when large refugee flows occur, a surge of funding arrives, and as refugees' stay becomes protracted, that funding often increases for a few years before it decreases. This is a well-established pattern. The most recent example pertains to the funds received by the countries bordering Ukraine after the Russian invasion in February 2022. Soon after the invasion, governments and many other donors, not least individuals contributing private donations and participating in crowdfunding, began sending funds to support Ukrainian refugees in neighboring countries. Poland, which registered nearly 1.5 million refugees after February 2022, was one of the main recipients. In 2022, Poland received over $328 million in humanitarian contributions, compared with less than $58,000 in 2021.[1] These funds, however, do not necessarily find their way to the host cities that are most affected by humanitarian flows.

City governments typically have three sources of revenue. The most desirable from a city government's point of view is the revenue generated from their own residents through taxes and fees. These funds, known as own-source revenues (OSRs), are desirable because the municipality can allocate them according to city priorities. In wealthy countries, OSRs usually comprise the largest share of a city's budget, but in the cities of poor countries—especially secondary cities—

this share is much smaller.[2] This is in part because the informal sector comprises a large part of poorer cities' economies, and also because most municipalities lack the capacity to enforce tax and fee collection in the formal sector, let alone the informal sector. In many host countries, citizens refuse to pay taxes because of government corruption. This was illustrated in Kenya in 2024, when the anger of the public, especially young people, exploded in massive street protests against President Ruto's plan to boost revenue by introducing new taxes on essential goods. One Kenyan writer said that Kenyan citizens believe "the new taxes would be used to line the pockets of Mr. Ruto's allies."[3] Likewise, in Tripoli, for the same reasons, both the public and the business sector are unwilling to pay new taxes. A 2021 study of economic development in Greater Tripoli asked firms about local public spending priorities. About half (54 percent) of surveyed firms said that even if their firm had sufficient funds, they would not be willing to pay higher local taxes in return for better local services.[4] In many host cities, low levels of trust and confidence in government service provision make it difficult for the city to collect taxes and fees.

Cities' meager tax bases mean they are dependent on a second domestic revenue stream: fiscal transfers from the national government. In poor countries, these generally make up 80 to 90 percent of municipal revenues. Government allocations, however, are heavily earmarked, so cities are constrained in their ability to use them for expenditures on local priorities. The political and fiscal autonomy of cities vis-à-vis the national government is highly variable; even within countries, some cities have more autonomy than others. Lebanon has 1,113 municipalities and some fifty unions of municipalities, and their autonomy and budgets vary greatly: "Some municipalities [and Unions] have considerable resources and hundreds of employees while others are practically broke and without employees."[5] The Independent Municipal Fund, Lebanon's intergovernmental transfer system, has not been able to properly support municipalities and municipal unions in their budgeting and local development planning efforts. This is in part because disbursement from the central government depends on an allocation formula that is linked to the registered population.[6] Given the size of the refugee and other unregistered populations, the actual resident population is much higher than the registered population. Intergovernmental funding is also often highly politicized. Cities that are supportive of the parties or individuals in power get more, and those who are in opposition get less.

A third revenue stream for cities is external, in the form of foreign aid and international private donor funding. Most humanitarian assistance comes from national (donor) governments and goes either to national (host) governments ("bilateral funding") or to organizations like the UN or World Bank ("multilateral funding"). Because multilateral organizations are controlled by member states, they also tend to work with national governments rather than cities. Much less donor funding goes directly to cities or to civil society organizations. There are many reasons for this, including that donor governments believe that national governments are less risky prospects when it comes to the appropriate use of their funds and accountability. But this global humanitarian funding architecture is changing. Since 2015, aid organizations and donors have looked for ways to get funds to cities directly, bypassing national governments.

One small but impressive example of such an organization is the Mayors Migration Council (MMC), which was created by mayors around the world in 2020 in response to the COVID pandemic and has continued to grow. The MMC is a mayor-led coalition that seeks "to use the power of city-led diplomacy and action to create a world where urban migrants, displaced people, and receiving communities can thrive." Today its leadership board includes the mayors of Amman, Bristol, Dhaka North, Freetown, Kampala, Milan, Montevideo,

Montreal, and Zurich. The MMC has mobilized the Global Cities Fund for Migrants and Refugees (GCF), which helps cities implement programs of their own design that seek to include refugees and migrants. As the GCF website notes, "By directly funding cities . . . the GCF builds precedents of fiscal feasibility in city governments that are often disregarded by donors with low risk tolerance." By the end of 2023, the GCF had mobilized $8 million in funding and was assisting twenty-eight cities. Its vision was to "scale up to support more cities and deepen its impact through larger multi-year grants and more predictable funding rounds."[7]

At present, international financing meets only a small portion of cities' increased budget needs resulting from a refugee influx, but the number of potential sources is growing. The MMC lists nineteen funds that now support cities directly.[8] They are a mix of governments (mostly in the European Union), philanthropies, and UN trust funds. Not all have an explicit refugee or migration focus, but many do. In addition to the GCF, these sources range from the EU Asylum and Migration Fund (AMF), which made €9.9 billion available for 2021–27, to the Neighborhood, Development and International Cooperation Instrument—Global Europe, which has a fund of €79.5 billion, of which 10 percent is allocated to migration-related activities.

One way to think about how host governments approach the issue of humanitarian funds is to see host governments as rent seekers, who "commodify" or instrumentalize refugees to secure additional funds from donors. (Rent seeking is the act of growing one's wealth by manipulating the social or political environment without making any reciprocal contribution.)[9] The idea is that host governments instrumentalize their geopolitical position and willingness to host refugees as leverage to extract revenue or other concessions from donor states. For example, Türkiye is widely seen as having successfully coerced the European Union into an unprecedented €6 billion aid package (the EU Facility for Refugees in Türkiye) to tackle the influx of Syrian refugees. Jordan too has extracted donor concessions, ensuring that Jordanians benefit from refugee assistance (see Box 8.1). This view sees national governments as wily actors who take advantage of western governments' desire to keep refugees in their regions of origin instead of allowing them to move on to Europe or the United States. According to this perspective, even if host governments are not actively rent seeking or engaging in "refugee commodification," they are instrumentalizing refugees as part of a foreign policy strategy aimed at attracting foreign aid.[10]

Box 8.1. How Host Governments Extract Concessions: Jordan

Jordan provides a good example of how host governments extract donor concessions in return for hosting large numbers of refugees. In negotiating the Jordan Compact in 2016 (and three years later, the London Initiative), the Jordanian government obtained from donors a range of financing and trade concessions in exchange for allowing Syrian refugees to work in certain sectors and pursue livelihoods. Jordan required that refugee aid provided by donors also benefit Jordanians. For example, social transfer programs for Syrian refugees had to include a 30–50 percent share for Jordanian recipients. These programs included unconditional cash transfers and winterization, education, vocational training, employment. and empowerment schemes.

Sources: Cindy Huang and Kate Gough, "The Jordan Compact: Three Years on, Where Do We Stand?," Center for Global Development, March 12, 2019, https://reliefweb.int/report/jordan/jordan-compact-three-years-where-do-we-stand; Tina Zintl and Markus Loewe, "More than the Sum of Its Parts: Donor-Sponsored Cash-for-Work Programmes and Social Cohesion in Jordanian Communities Hosting Syrian Refugees," *European Journal of Development Research* 34, no. 3 (2022).

The foreign policy actions of national governments don't help us understand what happens at the city level. Do city governments also instrumentalize refugees by engaging in this kind of rent-seeking behavior? There is very little fine-grained research, especially in Africa and the Middle East, on whether and how city governments instrumentalize refugees to attract foreign aid. An interesting study by the Turkish scholar Zeynep Balcioglu explored the views of officials in different municipalities of Greater Istanbul and could not find much evidence of active rent seeking.[11] For one thing, Balcioglu argues, it is difficult for municipalities to obtain direct funding from international organizations like UNHCR because of the extensive bureaucratic requirements involved. There are seldom application portals or other direct ways for municipalities to submit funding applications, and organizations like UNHCR target the municipalities they want to work with, rather than the other way round.[12] When it comes to funding city projects, external funds are closely tied to specific refugee-related projects and closely monitored by the funding agency, making it difficult for municipalities to use funds for their own priorities. In addition, donor funding often requires in-kind or even matching contributions from the municipalities. Few municipalities have the capacity and expertise to commit this much effort to collaborative projects that require constant scrutinization by international organizations. In Sultanbeyli, one of Istanbul's districts with the densest population of Syrian refugees, one municipality official told Balcioglu, "We call [these] collaborations 'burden sharing,' yet I am not sure if it is the case. It takes so much effort to integrate their work into ours. They come here with their projects and pre-set goals. . . . We are open to collaborations, but we have not made any funding applications so far. The management insists that we should, but we already have got so much on our plate that we just cannot make the time for it. Also, frankly speaking, we do not know how to do them."[13]

As the Turkish official suggests, applying for international funding requires time, staff capacity, and awareness of international administrative requirements, all of which are in short supply in host city municipalities. These requirements put obstacles in the way of rent seeking, if that is construed as "getting something for doing nothing."

Balcioglu found that in addition to believing that the funding was not worth the effort of meeting the donors' bureaucratic requirements, Turkish municipality officials considered working with foreign agencies to be political risky. One municipal official used a Turkish idiom that translates as "the bird you frighten is not worth the stone you throw"—that is, it is more trouble than it is worth. He went on to say, "We considered collaborating with [international organizations], but we gave up on the idea pretty quickly as we think it could be politically problematic. Those organizations will come here and make themselves present. They will put up logos and banners and stuff, which we do not like. The public will see it and get suspicious for all the possible reasons. They will bring their own staff; and you know, they will cause trouble."[14] Whether the views of these Turkish officials are widespread is difficult to know, because there is little research about the attitudes of municipal officials toward external aid in African and Asian host cities. While national governments might be able to engage in rent seeking, this kind of behavior is much more difficult for city governments, given their low capacity and political wariness.

Donors also experience difficulties engaging with city governments. The European Union's humanitarian wing, the European Civil Protection and Humanitarian Aid Operations (ECHO), says of urban areas that "engagement with local authorities may prove more challenging. Urban local governments tend to be under greater pressure with multiple priorities. . . . Legal and administrative environments [have] unclear roles and responsibilities of authorities (e.g.

municipalities not assuming responsibilities for the development of peri-urban areas); and a lack, or overlap, of administrative and legal boundaries, [which] make it difficult to identify key interlocutors to engage with for programming and exit strategies, as well as requiring multi-layered engagement with local authorities. Moreover, compared to rural areas, local urban environments may be more prone to politicisation (e.g. Syria; Iraq)."[15] The ECHO report goes on to say that while local authorities and local NGOs are best at understanding and adapting the humanitarian response to local specificities, they lack the structure, the resources, and sometimes the absorption capacity to fulfil their role.[16] These structural and political obstacles for both city governments and donors mean that while national governments might benefit from increased humanitarian funding, direct donor funding of cities is fraught with difficulties.

There is a different view of humanitarian funding and the impact of the humanitarian industry more broadly. A small but growing contingent of aid workers, activists, and humanitarian observers portrays the humanitarian industry as a new colonizing force, and these groups have begun to argue for the decolonization of humanitarian assistance.[17] The argument is that the humanitarian aid system is based on a well-established architecture of power in which donors—largely European countries and the United States—provide funds mainly to a small group of United Nations agencies: UNHCR, the World Food Programme, and the UN children's fund (UNICEF). These agencies then subcontract international NGOs and sometimes local or national agencies in host countries to carry out their programming agendas. These NGOs and agencies are known as the UN's "implementing partners." Donor funds tend to go mainly to large, institutionally sophisticated NGOs that are able to meet the donors' complex banking, reporting and auditing requirements. Smaller, local agencies, including city government agencies, which are usually better known to the communities they serve and more aware of their problems, rarely get direct funding. The funding power of donors and their associated UN agencies means it is they who set the humanitarian agendas, including which agencies receive funds, which beneficiaries receive assistance, and what kinds of programs are implemented. In particular, when the UN agencies make decisions about how funds are used, they act at the behest of the donors.

Is this a fair assessment of the humanitarian industry? And what would such a power architecture mean for cities? Given Lebanon's large share of humanitarian funds and the presence of so many humanitarian agencies in the country, Tripoli is a good place to explore the experience of cities in terms of where the funds came from, who controlled them, who benefited from them, and what kinds of programs were put in place. As noted, I focus on the period 2012–19.

Lebanon and Tripoli: Sources and Control of Humanitarian Funds

When the Syrian refugee influx began, the Lebanese government was in no position to mount a solid national response. The political stalemate that had paralyzed the country for years meant the national government and city municipalities were weak and unable to provide adequate services to their own citizens, let alone a million refugees. The humanitarian needs of the refugees required an urgent response, but there was no national strategy and few mechanisms for coordinating a response. The UN agencies already in the country had relatively small programs; until 2012, UNHCR's operation in Lebanon was one of the smallest in the region. Ninette Kelley, UNHCR's Country Representative, had been there since 2010, when, as she says, "it was a small program mainly aimed at supporting the Iraqi refugees." Since UN agencies and a few international NGOs were the only organizations in the country with any experience managing a large refugee influx, UNHCR took the lead. At first, it struggled. Lebanon has not signed the 1951 Refugee Convention or the 1967 Protocol, which meant UNHCR had to work with informal agreements with the government. There were no camps, so Syrian refugees began settling all over the country. The initial scramble to mount a humanitarian response resulted in an unequal distribution of regional and social aid.

As the humanitarian funds began to arrive, Lebanon's aid profile was transformed. In 2011, on the eve of the arrival of the Syrian refugees, total humanitarian funding in Lebanon was $43.8 million. Most of this funding (65 percent) came from three donors—Saudi Arabia, Norway, and the European Commission—and more than half (51 percent) went to UNRWA to support the Palestinian refugees. By 2015, the amount had leapt to over a billion dollars (US$1.286 million) annually. The United States had become Lebanon's largest humanitarian funder (22 percent), and the European Commission was second (18 percent).[18] The total was a giant sum for a small country, but it was under half of what the government of Lebanon and the UN agencies had requested. Until 2012, UNHCR's operation in Lebanon was one of the smallest in the region; then, for a few years between 2012 and 2016, it became one of the world's biggest. Where did all this money come from, where did it go, who controlled it, and what did it mean for the cities hosting most of the Syrian and other refugees?

The pattern of humanitarian funds coming from a few western donors and being controlled by UN agencies was clearly in place in Lebanon. In 2019, almost 80 percent of Lebanon's $1.11 billion in funding came from the United States, Germany, the European Commission, and the United Kingdom. Three-quarters of these funds were received and controlled by three UN agencies: the World Food Programme (WFP), UNHCR, and UNICEF. Only 18 percent of the funds was directly allocated to NGOs, and just 4 percent went to national NGOs.[19] UNHCR's country budget in 2011 had been under a million dollars, and in 2015 its funded budget had climbed to $303 million. The WFP had not been present in Lebanon before 2012, but its budget was $248.5 million in 2015, by which time two UN agencies, UNHCR and WFP, received 42 percent of all humanitarian funding. Another UN agency, UNICEF, was in third place at $246.2 million, and UNRWA was fourth with $60 million (just 4 percent of Lebanon's humanitarian budget).[20]

In addition to this humanitarian funding, development aid from donor countries also grew. In 2014, the World Bank deemed Lebanon eligible for its assistance because the situation could be characterized as both a man-made crisis (the arrival of a large refugee population) and the result of conflict (taking place in Syria). There is some overlap in the reporting of humanitarian and development funding, but the UN's Financial Tracking Service reported that by the end of 2017, around $1.68 billion in development funds from external sources had been disbursed in Lebanon. Even with the overlap in reported humanitarian and development funding, Lebanon received in the region of $1.3 billion annually between 2013 and 2018 because of the influx. This figure continued to grow as more funding came on stream. The Concessional Financing Facility (CFF) that was first set up to benefit Jordan was extended to Lebanon, and as of the end of 2020, the CFF had approved $330 million, with an additional $295 million pledged to Lebanon. (Humanitarian funding increased to $1.59 billion in 2020 because of COVID and the Beirut explosion, then sank below $1 billion in 2021.)[21]

Who controlled this huge amount of incoming funds? Since 1995, the aspirational goal of donors, aid agencies, and national governments has been that the government and UN agencies should come up with joint plans of action that recognize local governments as the main actors in aid coordination and effectiveness.[22] The government of Lebanon began to coordinate relief efforts in March 2012, establishing an interministerial committee headed by the Lebanese High Relief Commission and including the Ministry of Social Affairs and UNHCR. However, the government response was weak, hampered by political divisions and a lack of funds, and civil society organizations, including political parties and Islamic charities, stepped in to fill the gap. Relief efforts were concentrated in the border areas rather than in the towns and cities. As more funds poured into Lebanon, donors and aid agencies worked with the government to create mechanisms of coordination and collaboration. The Lebanon Crisis Response Plan (LCRP) emerged in 2015. Its authors hailed this plan as "innovative," in part because its "humanitarian and stabilization approach" sought both to address humanitarian needs and to strengthen the national capacity to address long-term poverty and social tensions. The Ministry of Social Affairs led the LCRP, and line ministries worked with aid agencies to coordinate the response. By early 2023 the LCRP consisted of 118 partner organizations, which assisted more than 3.2 million crisis-affected people in Lebanon, including 1.5 million displaced Syrians, 1.5 million vulnerable Lebanese, 31,400 Palestinian refugees from Syria, and 180,000 of the existing population of Palestine refugees. Between 2015 and 2023, Lebanon received over US$9.3 billion in donor contributions to support these people. The LCRP also seeks to "mitigate the impacts of the Syria crisis on Lebanon's infrastructure, economy and public institutions."[23]

An important aspect of the humanitarian agenda concerns which "beneficiaries" are targeted for assistance. When it comes to displacement settings, humanitarian assistance has traditionally been aimed only at refugees or IDPs, and sometimes earmarked for specific refugee groups. Between 2012 and 2020 the bulk of international humanitarian funding worldwide was focused on Syrian refugees in neighboring host countries, with much less funding going to Palestinians and other refugee nationalities in those countries. Because humanitarian funding is a zero-sum game, this focus on Syrian refugees meant there was less funding for non-Syrian refugees in other host countries. In 2022–23, the humanitarian funding focus was on Ukrainian refugees. In 2024, global public attention (and funding) switched to Gaza. And so it goes: the bulk of humanitarian funding lurches from one emergency to another, with "older" or protracted displacement settings usually the first to be cut back.

The focus on displaced people also means that the host population gets little benefit from humanitarian assistance. While this is less of a problem in camp settings, in cities refugees and locals live in the same neighborhoods and struggle with the same issues. The Syrian refugee crisis, which played out largely in cities, brought attention to how local people—and cities—were being affected by displacement. By 2018, an integrated approach was emerging in Lebanon. In their rhetoric and their targeted funding, humanitarian and development agencies were talking and acting in terms of support for the struggling Lebanese population and the host cities. Funding for Lebanese municipalities increased in 2019 to $33.7 million, compared with $26 million in 2018. These funds supported assistance to Lebanese community projects and municipal projects such as solid waste management, wastewater and water management, flood risk management, and provision of recreational spaces, road infrastructure, and community infrastructure. Technical, operational, and financial assistance was also provided.

However, aid agencies' collaboration with local authorities and municipalities was contingent on donor agendas. Unions of city municipalities like those of Greater Tripoli struggled to obtain funding from national authorities and aid agencies alike. Long-term relationships between humanitarian organizations and local municipalities were few and far between. Some aid agencies developed solid relationships with local authorities and used them as entry points to areas where they operated, while others ignored or bypassed local authorities to avoid their bureaucracies or their messy internal politics. Some agencies made a "reconnaissance" visit to local authorities when they first arrived, but then failed to coordinate further with them, even when the agency's interventions fell directly within the municipality's jurisdiction.[24]

Some cities saw their OSR increase because of rents from UN agencies and NGOs for land and office space. In Tripoli, the UNHCR compound in the Rachid Karame Fairground (described in Chapter 6) is partly on public land owned by the Fair, which is a public entity with a board managing the Fair overseen by the Lebanese Ministry of Economy and Trade. According to a UNHCR official who was actively involved in negotiations with the government about UNHCR's sites in Lebanon in 2012, then prime minister Najib Mikati helped UNHCR find the Rachid Karame site and offered it free to UNHCR in the initial months of the Syrian influx in 2011–12 and then charged rent of US$136,620 for 2013. When UNHCR needed to expand the site to 3,675 square meters in 2014, the rent was raised to US$291,060—a substantial injection of foreign currency for the city. In total, UNHCR's rent payments in Lebanon amounted to more than US$500,000 a year.[25] Except for the rent on the Tripoli site, all these payments go directly to private owners. These funds are then either moved out of the country, taxed, or used for consumption in local economies. Whether the landlords pay taxes on these funds, thereby contributing to cities' own-source revenues, is an open question. It would be useful to know how much cities are able to garner from international humanitarian and development agencies by way of rents, fees, and services, but that calculation is beyond the purview of this book.

As it became clear that the humanitarian influx had made life more difficult for poor people in Lebanon, development-oriented organizations like the World Bank stepped in. Humanitarian agencies like the World Food Programme also began providing assistance to poor Lebanese. After the COVID pandemic and lockdown struck in March 2020, this assistance increased substantially. The LCRP funds were split into two categories: support for Lebanese infrastructure and cities, and program support for the affected population, which initially meant only refugees but later included Lebanese. We discuss one form of programming—cash assistance—in Chapter 9. Once the LCRP got going, funds in the form of UNHCR's Institutional and Community Support flowed to the Lebanese public sector and to cities.[26] Development agencies like the World Bank also sought to prop up Tripoli's failing physical infrastructure, and they soon confronted even more challenges, as discussed in Chapter 10.

9

Just Give Them Cash

Imagine that you live in a poor neighborhood, where you struggle to pay the rent for a dingy apartment with heat and plumbing that don't work. The teachers don't show up at the local school and your kids are not getting any kind of decent education. One day, your neighborhood starts receiving refugees from, say, Canada, where a terrible civil war has begun. At first, you sympathize with the Canadians and try to help them. After all, you know them; they speak your language and share your culture and religion, and you have often visited Canada and love the food. Maybe you even take one or two Canadians into your home until they can find somewhere to stay. Then more and more refugees start coming to your neighborhood, and they are joined by their extended families. They move into nearby apartments. After a while, your landlord tells you he is increasing the rent because he can get more from the refugees. The refugee children are in school with your children, who report that class sizes have doubled, and there are more discipline problems. Your husband loses his job when his employer replaces him with a Canadian who is paid much less. Now you are really struggling with the rent, and it seems your family might have to move to a cheaper area. But the only such areas are further out of town, where job prospects are even worse. You borrow money from your brother and start running a tab at the corner grocery store where the shopkeeper knows you.

Then one day, your Canadian refugee neighbor who lives next door, and whose family is in the same desperate economic situation as yours, tells you that she is getting help from a European NGO. The NGO is going to pay your neighbor's rent for a year and will work with the landlord to ensure that the heating works and that they don't get evicted. As your jaw drops, she tells you that her family will also be receiving cash assistance from WFP, as their family has met the criteria for being sufficiently "vulnerable." Your neighbor shows you the ATM card she received, which she can use at the grocery store to buy food and household supplies. Every month, the card will be topped up. "But what about my family?" you shout at your neighbor. A deep sense of injustice settles on you. The next day, when you see a protest march on the street calling for the return of the refugees to Canada, you step into the street and join them.

When refugees or IDPs move to cities, they move into the neighborhoods they can afford, usually where others like themselves are living. Sometimes these are very poor areas—informal settlements or slums—and sometimes they are working-class or middle-class neighborhoods. Always, they live among the host population, which often includes other immigrants, and confront the same problems. In poor neighborhoods, everyone confronts crime and insecurity, lack of decent work, weak or nonexistent public services, and decrepit infrastructure. This does not mean that refugees are in the same situation as nationals, who do not have to struggle with requirements for work permits, or the experience of having lost their homes and family members, or xenophobia. But in poor neighborhoods locals are also struggling, and they are sometimes worse off than refugees because they don't have access to humanitarian aid. This situation was illustrated in the 2018 movie *Capernaum,* a Lebanese drama directed by Nadine Labaki about Zain El Hajj, a twelve-year-old Syrian refugee boy living in the slums of Beirut among Lebanese families who are as destitute as his own family. One scene in the movie shows refugees receiving humanitarian assistance while equally poor Lebanese citizens are turned away.

When refugees live alongside locals who are equally needful, giving assistance only to refugees can lead to deep resentment, as the scenario that opens this chapter illustrates. This resentment increases when the economic situation worsens and locals come to see refugees as the cause of their problems. As local resentment grows, refugees' lives become much harder. Conversely, when neighbors are supportive, refugees can go about their daily business without being harassed or reported or targeted by protests, and local support tamps down interference by city authorities. Importantly, neighborhood support can sustain refugees when humanitarian programs are insufficient or nonexistent, or when aid agencies depart the country. Sustaining this local support—or not undermining it—is or should be a goal of international aid agencies.

There is plenty of evidence that the best way to help refugees is to promote good relations with their neighbors by spreading humanitarian resources so that both refugees and locals benefit. This is both effective and fair. When resources flow into a neighborhood, refugees are seen as an asset, and tensions between refugees and hosts are reduced. It is fair because large numbers of refugees impose strains on neighborhoods. Some aid agencies recognize the problems they create in providing aid only to refugees when locals have equal needs, and in recent years there have been efforts to target the host population as well as refugees through area-based approaches. But this kind of broad-based approach is still not widespread. In many host cities, the humanitarian focus continues to be on refugees rather than on the neighborhoods and communities in which they live. Area-based approaches that include both displaced people and locals living in the same neighborhood of the city are still quite rare.

Humanitarian programs in cities increasingly use cash programming as an alternative to traditional kinds of humanitarian assistance. This chapter explores cash programming in Tripoli and in other host cities in Africa and Asia, the impact it has on those cities, and how city governments might lobby donors to ensure cash programs improve the lot of everyone living in poor city neighborhoods.

Cash as Humanitarian Assistance

Humanitarian agencies began using cash transfers in disaster situations as early as 2001, but until the mid-2000s, most humanitarian assistance was food, often alongside other commodities like household goods (so-called in-kind assistance). By 2010, humanitarian assistance increasingly took the form of cash, given especially to refugees in cities, in addition to or in place of food aid. Cash assistance now supports people in humanitarian situations all over the world. It takes the form of vouchers or funds digitally loaded onto ATM cards. These interventions really took hold with the Syrian refugee crisis after 2012. In 2016 UNHCR began ramping up its cash assistance, and by 2019 it had distributed around $2.4 billion to twenty million people in more than one hundred countries. Cash-based transfers have risen from $10 million in 2009 to $2.1 billion in 2019, and now represent over a third of all WFP assistance, supporting almost twenty-eight million people in sixty-four countries. In 2022, cash and vouchers accounted for an estimated 20 percent of total humanitarian assistance.[1]

Most cash is disbursed without restrictions, meaning that refugees spend it as they see fit, and the local economy benefits from the injection of cash spent in local stores and on local services. Providing cash instead of food and in-kind assistance is widely seen by aid agencies as giving people more choice and flexibility in the assistance they receive and helping them maintain their dignity, while at the same time stimulating local economies and markets. Former UNHCR representative Ninette Kelley said, "Getting cash means the refugees determine their own needs and priorities, and they can find the best deals. [Cash] gives them more autonomy. It would be the same for you or me—would you prefer to have money to decide what you or your family want to eat or spend on, or have somebody decide for you and plop it on your doorstep?" Ninette Kelley pointed to other advantages of cash:

> It's more efficient and cuts down on transaction costs. And surprisingly, it's safer. With in-kind assistance or vouchers, people are more susceptible to being exploited by gangs and criminals. They see refugees come out of a distribution point with in-kind goods and basically force the refugees to sell the goods to them, and then they sell it back on the market at inflated prices. Giving people cash is more discreet—when they use it at stores there's much less visibility and more privacy. . . . Also, whenever we [UNHCR] asked refugees, it was clear they were happy with cash. They said it was a real improvement in their lives even though it was never enough to meet all their needs. Just to be able to determine for themselves what they wanted to spend it on was very important.[2]

Cash programming takes two forms. "Sector-specific" cash supports sectors such as rent or food. For example, refugees are given vouchers or ATM cards they can use at participating grocery stores; an example is the WFP e-food card in Lebanon. "Cross-sector" cash programming allows households to decide how they want to spend the cash, without direction from humanitarian organizations. Households can spend the cash on such things as food, shelter, debt repayment, heat, or medical and educational expenses, as they see fit. Cross-sector cash programming can have conditions attached to the cash payment—for example, recipients might have to work (under programs known as "cash for work") or attend training sessions—or it can be unconditional, with no such constraints.

Cash assistance is useful only where there are functioning markets that provide the things refugees need and want to buy. In settings such as rural villages, cash is less useful because most locals are self-sufficient producers (farmers or pastoralists) and there is not much of a cash economy. Similarly, in camps and rural refugee settlements, the local street market might not be enough to provide for refugees' needs. In these situations, aid agencies continue to provide refugees with food or in-kind assistance or, depending on the context, some combination of cash and food assistance. For example, in Uganda's huge refugee settlements in the rural north, humanitarian assistance mainly takes the form of food, but cash is used as a supplement when long-term funding gaps mean that WFP can provide only part of the basic food ration.

The Cash Program in Lebanon

By 2015, the situation in Lebanon had worsened for everyone, refugees and hosts alike. More than a million registered refugees were living in 1,200 villages and all the main towns and cities across the country. Refugees and poor Lebanese struggled to find work and decent housing. Daily wages had fallen by 60 percent, and many Lebanese and refugees were resorting to loans and credit to meet expenses. Some had to sell their assets or send their children to work. Child marriages were increasing, especially among Syrian and Palestinian refugees.[3] More than a quarter of the Lebanese population had been poor long before the Syrian refugees came, but afterward things were much worse. As noted in Chapter 5, by 2015, a third of Lebanese were living below the poverty line—that is, they could not afford the minimum standards of living. Half of the heads of these households were unemployed.[4]

Poor Lebanese households were served by various assistance programs that made up the government's national poverty reduction strategy. Lebanon's National Poverty Targeting Programme provided eligible households with health and education subsidies and food assistance through e-vouchers.[5] Local NGOs also had relief programs, but they were not sufficient to cover all who needed help. Nor was the High Relief Commission, mandated to serve Lebanese communities in crisis, able to cover their humanitarian needs. Under these circumstances, giving aid only to refugees would be well beyond unfair—it also could antagonize locals who already blamed the refugees for their economic woes.

UNHCR was aware of these underlying dynamics, and from the onset of the Syrian influx, the agency sought to support Lebanese institutions and communities. By 2014, 15 percent of its annual budget and 24 percent of the interagency humanitarian appeal was dedicated to these efforts. Local support included the rehabilitation of schools, public health facilities, and municipal water and sanitation facilities, including provision of equipment; the building or renovation of community centers, roads, and playgrounds; and measures to improve livelihood opportunities through support to cooperatives, skills training, and income-generating activities. UNHCR also sought to increase social cohesion through youth development programs, community arbitration, and conflict management training. This community support increased from just US$24,000 in 2011 to over US$11 million in 2016.[6]

In countries like Lebanon that have a strong private sector and well-established, integrated markets, cash programming is a good option. Daily needs such as food and fuel are available in local markets, and ATM bank services are easily accessible. Early in the Syrian crisis, Ninette Kelley began negotiating with the government to get authorization to start a cash program for the most vulnerable Syrian refugees, in line with national programs that targeted similarly situated Lebanese. This was not an easy task: "At first, the government did not want us doing cash because they thought it would be resented by poor Lebanese who did not receive public assistance. It took many, many confidence-building meetings with the minister of social affairs and the Prime Minister's Office before we were able to get authorization for limited cash assistance." The government wanted to ensure that Lebanese citizens would also benefit from the humanitarian funds pouring into the country. At first, UNHCR turned to the World Bank to see whether UNHCR could work with them to support the government's poverty reduction strategy, which included cash disbursements to poor people, but this didn't turn out to be feasible. Finally, the government acquiesced to a cash program for refugees once UNHCR assured them that it would be in line with what the government was providing to poor Lebanese, "recognizing of course that the Lebanese also had access to certain benefits that refugees didn't have." UNHCR first inquired whether cash programs for refugees could be delivered through the National Poverty Targeting Programme, but the government did not approve of this, and the World Bank advised that even with political support, the task would be very difficult.[7]

Interagency cash programming in Lebanon began by using vouchers and eventually moving to cash loaded onto ATM cards. In November 2012, WFP joined UNHCR and nongovernmental organizations like the International Rescue Committee to deliver "multi-purpose cash" (that is, cross-sector payments) to Syrian refugees. The cash program was the largest humanitarian program in Lebanon, intended to stabilize or improve access to food and basic needs of refugee households deemed to be the "most vulnerable." But as the number of Syrian refugees increased through 2013–14, the agencies' humanitarian budgets were unable to keep pace. In host countries, there is seldom enough funding to provide cash assistance to all the refugees who need it, let alone the locals. Even in Lebanon, where the humanitarian budget was over a billion dollars in 2014, UNHCR did not have enough funds to support all the refugees. UNHCR therefore had to find a way to ration the cash assistance and give it only to the refugees who were most in need. This rationing is known in humanitarian parlance as "the targeting problem" (see Box 9.1).

Although the 2013 vulnerability assessment showed that 72 percent of refugee households were sufficiently vulnerable to warrant food and nonfood assistance, only 16 percent were targeted for assistance. Even among this number, funding was unable to meet the needs of all. In 2015 UNHCR reported that of the 29 percent of refugees in need of income support, it was able to provide cash assistance to only 5 percent.[8]

Cuts to budgets can lead to distressing consequences, as those who rely on cash assistance may be cut off relatively suddenly. Mahmoud's sister, Nada, heard the news that she was no longer eligible for cash support in the same way people on welfare in the United States learn about their access to government programs—by text. Nada had been receiving cash support for a year, and then one morning she awoke to a neutrally worded message from WFP informing her that she no longer qualified for cash assistance and her ATM card would not be reloaded every month.

As with all humanitarian programs, the funding for cash programs does not last indefinitely. UN funding in a country is often cut when a new emergency arises elsewhere in the world. In late 2023, a substantial uptick in the violence in Syria led to new displacement, but international attention had moved on to the Israel-Hamas war in Gaza, and there were continuing demands on humanitarian funding for Sudan and Ukraine. In 2022, UNHCR and WFP in Lebanon were disbursing cash supports to some 287,000 refugees, out of a total of over a million refugees (the number could be much higher, but only about 790,000 are officially registered because the Lebanese government

> **Box 9.1. Targeting Cash**
>
> Deciding which households make the "most vulnerable" list is a complicated—and controversial—procedure. In Lebanon, to ensure consistency across programs, UNHCR, WFP, and international NGOs, with advice from the American University of Beirut and the World Bank, developed a standardized methodology for assessing vulnerability. The assessment is based on a representative random sample of refugee households across geographic districts. Trained enumerators conduct regular household surveys that ask about household livelihoods, income, access to food and coping strategies, housing and sanitation conditions, access to healthcare and educational services, and safety and legal status. Refugee households' answers are scored, and each family is ranked according to their score. For instance, if UNHCR had funding to support 60,000 families, it would assign the funding to the 60,000 families with the highest vulnerability scores. When there were funding shortfalls, the target number was adjusted and those refugee households with lower scores had to be cut off. The results have been published annually since 2012.
>
> Source: Jad Chaaban et al., *Multi-purpose Cash Assistance in Lebanon: Impact Evaluation on the Well-Being of Syrian Refugees* (Beirut: CAMEALEON, 2020), https://www.nrc.no/globalassets/pdf/reports/camealeon-impact-assessment-of-multi-purpose-cash-assistance-for-syrian-refugees-in-lebanon/camealeon-mpc-impact-assessment.pdf.

ordered UNHCR to stop registering refugees in 2014). In November 2023, UNHCR announced "significant funding reductions," meaning that cash assistance, capped at a monthly maximum of $125 per household, would go to 88,000 fewer families in 2024 than in 2023. Only about 190,000 families would continue receiving the assistance.[9] UNHCR said that by November 2023 its Lebanon office had received funds to cover only 36 percent of its annual budget (at the same time in 2022, it had been 50 percent funded) and that the office had already cut staff and reduced programs and would likely make further cuts in 2024.

The Impact of Cash Programs on Cities

Cash programs have consequences for the host cities where refugees live. Refugees use the cash to pay their rent, and often sell their food vouchers—at a discounted price—to poor Lebanese. For refugees, paying rent is a much bigger concern than buying food, which they can get cheaply. Selling food rations is part of a long-standing global pattern of "trade-in-aid" in which refugees or other humanitarian recipients sell their aid in local markets. Although it is not official policy, humanitarian agencies like WFP factor the practice into their budgets and distribution plans. It is an important way in which humanitarian assistance also benefits the local population.[10]

The impact of cash programming on refugees in developing countries has been well studied, especially by economists and especially in camp settings.[11] But there has been very little research on how cash programming for refugees affects urban communities in host countries.[12] Much of the research looks at the overall (aggregate) impact at the national level, but as this book has argued, it is important to disaggregate impacts at the subnational level—that is, the urban or even the neighborhood level.

There are at least three possible kinds of urban impact from cash transfer programs. The economic impact is likely to be positive overall, but with some mixed elements. The injection of cash benefits local economies as local consumption rises, boosting local production and sales of goods and services, but there is also the risk that a cash program could lead to price inflation. This is more of a problem in camps, where there are fewer retailers and they have more market power. It's less of a problem when cash assistance programs occur in competitive markets like large cities. However, as with all injections of resources, cash transfers have distributional effects, meaning that in urban neighborhoods, some will benefit more than others.

These distributional effects in turn point to the second type of impact, reflected in the Canadian refugee scenario with which this chapter began. Cash programs potentially affect social cohesion in the neighborhoods where refugees live, especially when only refugees and not their equally needful neighbors get cash support. The resentment and resulting tension in host neighborhoods is potentially a significant problem for the entire city. There has been research on how donor programs affect social cohesion, and we return to the topic in Chapter 18.[13]

A third type of impact results from cash for work (CfW) programs, in which participants work on community projects in exchange for cash. These programs are designed to utilize low-skilled physical labor (to make the program widely accessible), and they focus on building community assets and infrastructure. There is a strong critique of CfW programs, based on their unsustainability—they are designed to provide short-term access to income—and on the claim that they are a hindrance to participants building a long-term livelihood strategy.[14] Jordan has been particularly successful in attracting such projects: 90 percent of its donor-financed social transfer programs for Syrians take the form of CfW projects run by WFP, UNHCR, UNICEF, and some NGOs. Between 2016 and 2019, the budget for these programs reached about €300 million, most of it financed by Germany through its Partnership for Prospects program.[15] As noted in Chapter 8 (see Box 8.1), Jordan has been successful in ensuring that donor projects include Jordanians.

Jordan's social transfer programs were focused mainly on the northern border towns of Irbid and al-Mafraq, where most Syrian refugees had settled. In these towns, the CfW projects resulted in improved infrastructure and services, including the collection and recycling of waste, tree plantings and the rehabilitation of nature reserves, renovations of schools and health clinics, and rural road construction. These upgrades improved residents' quality of life, but there were other CfW projects that also had a substantial economic payoff, although "the size of this effect is difficult to estimate."[16] These included agricultural intensification projects such as rehabilitating dams and irrigation systems and introducing protective measures against soil erosion. In sum, the CfW projects in Jordan had a significant positive impact, even if it was difficult to measure using standard econometrics.

An area-based approach in which cash assistance is given to the most vulnerable households in the urban neighborhood, not just refugees, is something city governments could push for. Faced with the problem of donors earmarking funds for refugees, they could follow the example of national governments like Jordan and learn to pressure donors. In this, they would potentially have a range of allies, including the international NGOs like the Mayors Migration Council mentioned earlier, as well as refugee agencies and UNHCR.

10

Trash Mountain

Through the city of Tripoli runs the Abou Ali, once a beautiful river lined with palm trees, now a thin stream of sewage contained in a wide concrete canal pocked with sewage outlets poking through ten-foot-high walls. The river trickles slowly toward the port, meeting the sea at the site where the city's garbage accumulates: a giant, brown, sand-covered landfill, ten stories high, stuffed with partially buried, mangled bags of garbage. It squats precariously on the edge of the bay, threatening to topple into the sea (and actually doing so periodically). The site is known as Trash Mountain (see Box 10.1). Without an alternative solution to manage solid waste in Tripoli, and because of the dangerous situation of the existing landfill, the Lebanese government decided to create a temporary landfill by reclaiming 60,000 square meters of sea. This new landfill—really a "seafill"—is the third waste site decided by the government, after the Bourj Hammoud (North Beirut) and Costa Brava (South Beirut) sites.

The inability of city governments to cope with their solid waste (garbage) is one of the most serious problems facing Lebanon's cities, as it is for many growing cities—and indeed, for our planet. In Tripoli and Beirut, the arrival of thousands of refugees aggravated the garbage problem, but the claim that they caused it lacks credibility. Lebanon's ongoing national garbage crisis was largely caused by the breakdown of the political system and the Syrian war's spillover effect on both the Lebanese economy and sectarian relations in the

Box 10.1. A Visit to Trash Mountain

On a bright autumn day in 2018, one of Tripoli's sanitation engineers drove Claire and me up Trash Mountain in his battered pickup truck. Part of his job was to monitor the mountain and the adjoining seafill construction site. Ahead of us, two overflowing garbage trucks toiled their way up the narrow track to dump their contents at the top. Below the drop-off to our right, the Abou Ali River completed its last hundred yards before reaching the sea; having drained through Tripoli picking up everything the city dumped into it, by now it was a toxic mix of sewage and industrial waste. On its banks, dump dogs resembling dystopic sci-fi creatures with stained and patchy fur scavenged around two old men who were fishing. (They sold their fish in the street market.) A shallow weir marked where the river met the sea, spilling its poison and filth into a channel that widened out into the bay. To our left, a concrete containment wall bulged under thousands of tons of garbage looming above. Huge empty garbage trucks careened down the mountain, swerving around our truck and making our driver edge closer to the murky river a few meters below.

We stopped at the top of the mountain, and the engineer suggested we tighten the filtration masks he had given us. We did not get out of the car, wary of the toxic air. Sanitation engineers worried that the landfill could explode from accumulating methane gas, or collapse under its own weight. The mountain has twice partially toppled into the sea, first in 2008, then again earlier in 2018. The dump truck ahead of us tipped its contents into a shallow ravine full of garbage bags. A bulldozer pushed sand over the new tip, then compacted it. (Finding sand to cover the garbage is an ongoing problem. Some sand came from the harbor dredge, or it is looted from construction sites or excavated from mountainsides.) Two spectral dump dogs worked the uncovered trash, expertly dodging the moving vehicles. "They are so contaminated, no one will touch them," said our driver. "We fear they might be radioactive."

> The port area spread out below, the sky and sea different shades of Mediterranean blue. White seagulls drifted above the poisoned river as it streamed quietly into the sea. To the south were the cranes of al-Mina's docks, and out at sea, container ships waited to unload their cargo. Closer in were the squat buildings of the waste management plant and the Sanitation Department. Directly below, jutting into the sea, was a broad expanse of smooth sand—the construction site for Tripoli's giant port development project, known as the Tripoli Special Economic Zone, funded by the World Bank and other donors. This was where the seafill was being built. About a quarter mile out to sea, a barge dredged a foundation for its seawall. The dredger wallowed in the choppy water, its cranes sticking out like insect legs. Hundreds of huge H-shaped blocks filled with concrete were lined up in orderly rows on the nearby sand. Each was ten feet tall and ten feet wide and weighed many tons. A tugboat helped the barge drag these giant blocks into the sea to form a barrier to protect the seawall from the waves. The seawall would enclose an area of several acres, rising six feet above the sea. Then it would be ready for more dumping and, Tripoli's municipality hoped, would solve the city's sanitation problems.

country. The national government's failure to find a solution to the garbage crisis had set the scene for Tripoli's problems long before the refugee influx. As one Lebanese author said, "Neither popular demonstrations nor the environmental catastrophe and health hazards created by mountains of garbage bags enticed them to place the country's wellbeing and that of its citizens above their narrow political and financial calculations."[1]

Refugees contributed only a relatively small proportion of Tripoli's overall solid waste, but in the neighborhoods where refugees were concentrated—the city "hot spots"—their impact was larger. What made a difference for Tripoli and other host cities is that the refugee crisis brought increased attention to the problem and then help from external donors. After 2012, Lebanon received much more international media coverage and became the poster child for countries being inundated with refugees. Some of the humanitarian and development funding that poured into Lebanon as part of the Lebanon Crisis Response Plan was aimed at offsetting the environmental impact of the refugees. Thus, the refugee crisis brought opportunity to Tripoli by way of the international support it attracted. A second important benefit of the refugees' presence was the usefulness of their waste management activities in the form of waste picking. This chapter first considers the infrastructure problems facing Tripoli, particularly the garbage problem, then explores how waste pickers, who are often refugees and other migrants, play a role in managing the waste of cities, particularly those in low- and middle-income countries.

Tripoli is typical of host cities that buckle as the influx of refugees creates more pressure on already rickety urban infrastructure and services. By 2015, the city had to provide electricity, water, and sanitation for at least 50,000 more households, and thousands more people used its poorly maintained roads and public spaces. Electricity availability throughout Lebanon had long been intermittent, with some areas cut off for days at a time, which meant only those who could afford generators had power.[2] For the thousands of people in the Palestinian camp or the informal settlements around the city, the only way to get electricity was to hook up illegally to the electricity grid, which put further pressure on the city's power supply.

Water management was also a problem: there was either too much water—when the city streets were periodically flooded—or too little. Like many coastal cities, Tripoli is frequently subject to flooding, and the people living in slum areas like Hay al-Tanak are the worst affected. In other ways, there was too little water. The water coming out of faucets was "nonpotable," meaning nobody drank it. As a result, Tripoli was awash with plastic PET water bottles. While PET is recyclable, in Tripoli there is neither a strong culture of recycling nor much recycling capacity, and plastic water bottles simply went into the landfill—as they do in most cities. Lebanon's water problems had been growing well before 2012. In 2010 Lebanon was the twenty-eighth most water-stressed country in the world; by 2019 it ranked third (after Qatar and Israel).[3] Was this change because of the refugee influx? Prior to the influx, population expansion after the civil war and inadequate water policies had transformed Lebanon from a water-secure country (around 2,500 square meters per capita in the 1960s) to a water-deficit country (less than 1,000 square meters per capita) just before 2012. The refugee crisis aggravated the problem by creating and sustaining extreme hot spots of water stress in urban areas, but other factors—especially agricultural water consumption, infrastructure deterioration, and poor water governance—contributed much more to Lebanon's increased water stress. Refugees' water use was only a small percentage of the total water use in Lebanon.[4]

Likewise, the arrival of the refugees added to Tripoli's garbage problems but did not cause them. Tripoli's crisis of waste management (as well as other public services) was part of a national crisis that had begun well before 2012. During Lebanon's civil war (1975–90), security and budget problems had devastated government and municipal services. Solid waste had been collected and dumped by communities or warring factions without treatment. After the Taif peace accord in the early 1990s, the government privatized public sector services and assigned one company, Sukleen, the contract for managing half of Lebanon's municipal solid waste. Between 1991 and 1999, solid waste management was transformed. Haphazard community efforts were superseded by the work of private companies with trucks and regular collection routes. Garbage was collected from street bins daily and transported to dumps outside the cities. In 1998, the Bourj Hammoud dump north of Beirut became too high, and the city built a new landfill at Naameh, eighteen kilometers south of Beirut, as a short-term alternative. The Naameh landfill remained open well beyond its intended lifetime and was closed only in 2015. By then there was widespread street dumping (some 20,000 tons of rubbish flooded the streets of Beirut) and burning of waste, along with massive street protests known as the "You Stink" campaign. In September 2015, the government responded by devolving waste management duties to municipalities—a central demand of the protesters—and authorizing the opening of two new landfills. But Lebanon had run out of space to put the trash, and dozens of illegal dumpsites sprang up across the country. More seriously, Lebanon was (and still is) dumping its rubbish directly into the sea, with serious implications for the Mediterranean coastal ecosystem and for public health.

Cities were affected by the decentralization of Lebanon's waste management system. Each municipality got a budget from the government to subcontract private companies, which were paid by the ton of garbage removed. This meant there was no profit for the companies in recycling (there is little sorting capability in cities anyway); the profit lay in maximizing waste tonnage. One expert we spoke to, who was also a former member of Tripoli's municipal council, was opposed to the new landfill and incinerators. This person's view was that the waste management problem in Tripoli was about corruption and deal making between LavaJet, the waste removal company, and the city government: "The municipality is not equipped to manage the waste, so they contract private companies like LavaJet to collect the trash. But LavaJet is not interested in an integrated waste management system that reduces the amount of garbage going into the landfill. The more daily tonnage, the more money they make."[5]

Even without these perverse incentives, the private trash collection companies could not handle the problem. Tripoli's landfill opened in 1998, and uncontrolled dumping meant the site was soon at capacity. The city planned to close it in 2006, but with no alternative site, the closure was delayed to 2012, which came and went without any solution to the problem of where to put the ever-accumulating piles of garbage. Some of Tripoli's garbage continued to get trucked up Trash Mountain, but there was plenty more on the streets and the beaches of the nearby islands. In addition, Tripoli's sewage system had also been unable to handle the volume even before the refugee influx began; only 15 percent of sewage water was being treated before it flowed directly into the Mediterranean near the port (see Box 10.2).

Tripoli's sea dumping and the runoff from Trash Mountain violated several international conventions, including the Barcelona

---

Box 10.2. A Visit to an Island

One day, the Captain, the owner of the seafood restaurant at which we and many expat aid workers ate dinner, invited Claire and me on an outing on his small boat to one of Tripoli's nearby small islands. We sat on the rocky beach and gazed toward the city, sipping from beer cans the Captain produced from his well-stocked cooler. To our left, a couple of sea miles away, Trash Mountain loomed against the clear sky. The island's coarse beach sand was laced with glass crumbs, and the rocks behind us were filled with plastic and other trash washed up by the sea. A young man and his father walked among the rocks, picking up the trash with long hooks and bagging it. They said they came every weekend to clean the beaches and get fresh air. After a while, the Captain said he wanted to hunt for octopus. We donned masks and fins and snorkeled around the rocks. The sunbeams in the water lit up shoals of small colorful fish that swam through a mist of half-dissolved litter. We didn't stay long in the water, and soon the Captain returned without an octopus, much to our relief. On the boat headed back, I trailed my hand through the water, but as we got close to the shore, the Captain told me to stop: the water quality was much worse here, he said.

Convention for the Protection of the Marine Environment and the Coastal Region of the Mediterranean, which Lebanon has signed.[6] Prior to the influx of Syrian refugees, but even more so afterward, international development agencies like the UN Development Programme offered to partner with the Tripoli municipality to upgrade the city's garbage treatment facility. It was agreed that a new landfill should be built, but the only place to put it was in the sea—a seafill.

"Seafills are extremely risky and even more expensive than landfills. But this is the only option we have," said one sanitation engineer we spoke to in Tripoli. There were few other places to put a new landfill and the waste treatment plant. The "not in my backyard" problem exists in Tripoli like everywhere else, and no neighborhood is willing to be the location for a new landfill and its associated slaughterhouse and other infrastructure. If a new landfill were built outside Tripoli, in the mountains, there would be the risk of groundwater—including Tripoli's drinking water—being contaminated. Sanitation experts also worry that building a new landfill outside the city, away from the public's view, would create more opportunities for environmental protections to be ignored or buried by bribes.

The other option was to incinerate the garbage, potentially using new, more efficient technologies.[7] But environmental activists in Lebanon tried to stop the construction of the incinerators because they feared the health and environmental consequences. Partial incineration is common in waste management in the United States and Europe. (Denmark and Germany, which have the most efficient waste manage processes, recycle 60 percent and incinerate 30 percent of their waste.)[8] The problem is that an incinerator needs to be managed well, and good management is lacking in Lebanon. It seems there are few good options for how Lebanon's cities could manage their garbage problem.

Tripoli's garbage problems and attempted solutions are mirrored in cities throughout Africa and the Middle East. Nairobi (Kenya) manifests the same patterns of overflowing landfills, nonenforcement of laws and regulations, and inadequate or poorly managed waste management infrastructure. Nairobi generates more solid waste than the city can handle, some 3,000 tons a day, of which only 400–600 tons reach the dumpsite.[9] Nairobi's single landfill, Dandora, on the bank of the Nairobi River, is at more than three times its capacity. There are many levels of corruption, from squabbles among unregistered waste collection groups for the millions controlled by Nairobi's city council to truck drivers having to pay a fee to touts at the dumpsites before they can offload. Nairobi's attempted solution—contracting a single private company to collect garbage, as Tripoli did—failed. Households in wealthier neighborhoods like Lavington pay private collectors to remove their trash. Most of the rest of the garbage goes into the streets of Nairobi's slums and informal settlements like Mathare and Kibera, where refugees and IDPs also live.

Many cities rely on one or two massively overburdened landfills, which become trash mountains like Tripoli's. These are sites of great danger for those who live near them or work at them, like the waste pickers (see Figure 10.1). There are many examples of landfills collapsing. In March 2017, a landslide occurred at the massive garbage dump on the outskirts of Addis Ababa (Ethiopia's capital), killing at least thirty-five people. A year later, a similar event occurred outside Maputo (Mozambique's capital), and in August 2024, Kampala's Kiteezi landfill collapsed, killing eighteen people.[10]

The Syrian Refugees' Impact on the Garbage Problem

The arrival of the Syrian refugees in 2012 was thought by experts to have worsened Tripoli's (and Lebanon's) solid waste and sanitation problems. The Tripoli engineer we spoke to said that an earlier study had projected the daily dumping rate to be 450 tons by 2030, "but we reached that in 2015. Before 2011, it was 220 tons per day." How-

Figure 10.1. Waste pickers at Kiteezi landfill, the solid waste disposal site near Kampala, May 2023. Source: Author's photo.

ever, although one would expect the Syrian refugee influx to have also worsened Tripoli's problems, trends in city-level data appear to indicate little impact. The data for Tripoli show that the amount of disposed waste for the period 2000–2017 had already begun increasing sharply in 2009, and there was no spike after 2011.[11] Although these data might be unreliable, the garbage crisis did not affect all parts of the city—or the country—in the same way. Like wealthier neighborhoods in most host cities, the upscale neighborhoods of Tripoli like Maarat did not experience an influx of refugees—and could afford to hire private garbage removal facilities. The poorest areas of the city where the refugees lived, like Beddawi or the informal slum areas and settlements like Hay al-Tanak, were the most affected by garbage problems, and their situation worsened considerably after 2012.

For host cities confronting infrastructure and services problems, there are two consequences of a refugee influx that could potentially make a positive difference. One is the technical support and funds from humanitarian and development actors that follow the refugees' arrival. Before 2012, international development agencies were already supporting Lebanon with multimillion-dollar projects to improve the country's infrastructure and services. The European Union had contributed almost €490 million toward the construction of the new seafill in Tripoli, and the United States had provided nearly $1 billion in economic support funding to Lebanon since 2010. After 2012, as the refugee numbers threatened to overwhelm Lebanon's services and infrastructure, there were additional development funds. These funds, targeted for both refugees and Lebanese, could also be used for access to clean water and sanitation.[12]

The issue was whether the funds would be made available to cities and then utilized to address the infrastructural problems rather than line the pockets of profiteers. Many activists and public scholars in Lebanon have raised the alarm about the negative consequences, including debt making, of public-private partnerships in waste management. Environmental activists in Tripoli believed that corruption and fraud had got in the way of new aid projects—and that the new seafill project was likely to make environmental problems worse. The development aid largesse created new problems or aggravated existing ones. The al-Fayhaa municipality lacked the technical and management capacity to absorb the funds. The best local staff—who had the necessary technical skills and knew how the city worked—were often snapped up by international agencies that paid much higher salaries, creating a brain drain within city bureaucracies. Many in Lebanon believed that corrupt officials and private companies had diverted international funds into their own pockets. It was not the refugees but rather the country's endemic corruption and profit seeking that were at the heart of the trash problem, fueling the waste crisis.[13]

A second consequence of a refugee influx that could make a difference for cities concerns the actions of civil society—the community organizations and individuals who step up to address issues, whether out of need for income or concern about their environment. Elizabeth Saleh, a Lebanese anthropologist in Beirut, writes about "the myriad of activities that revolve around collecting and sorting through Beirut's waste." These occur in a range of settings, from small scrapyards run by Syrian refugees often with underage waste pickers to community organizations and NGOs, to commercial operations.[14]

Waste pickers, or informal waste workers, play an important role in urban waste management. These people, often refugees or migrants, salvage scrap metals, recyclable plastic, and other goods that have some resaleable value, combing city streets, urban waterways, or landfills and dumps. They then sort the waste and sell it on to aggregators or commercial operations. Waste pickers are among the world's poorest and most invisible—and thus exploitable—workers. (Their plight was beautifully narrated in Katherine Boo's 2012 book *Behind the Beautiful Forevers: Life, Death, and Hope in a Mumbai Undercity.*) They have no access to rights because they are part of the informal sector, and most are very poor, carrying out hazardous and very low-paying work. Because most cities of developing countries have such poor waste management infrastructure, waste pickers are a significant force for waste collection and recycling. By 2050, worldwide municipal solid waste generation will likely increase by 70 percent to 3.8 billion metric tons (from 2.1 billion metric tons in 2023).[15] At present, this waste creates huge problems for cities in developing countries, especially in the poor areas of cities—those most subject to in-migration and environmental problems.

Environmental advocates, including global leaders like the head of the UN Environment Programme (UNEP), are envisioning a zero-waste society: "A lot of what we throw away is a valuable resource, so we must start rethinking the design and delivery of products and services to keep resources in the economy."[16] Simply managing waste (through recycling, incineration, dumping) will never be enough; we need to begin thinking of waste as a resource that can be "mined." A range of organizations, small and large, are now focused on going beyond waste management. For example, the Global Commitment, led by the Ellen MacArthur Foundation and UNEP, is a consortium of over 500 businesses and governments committed to changing how we produce, use, and reuse plastics.[17] One report outlines the steps needed to "break the plastic wave," which will require every nation to do its part. Low- and middle-income countries "should focus on expanding collection of plastic waste, maximizing reduction and substitution, investing in sorting and recycling infrastructure, and reducing leakage from waste sites."[18]

Waste pickers fit squarely into this vison. Waste pickers are people who make a living collecting, sorting, recycling, and selling materials that someone else has thrown away. They are present in all cities (including my own town of Brookline, Massachusetts, where an elderly Asian couple regularly pick through the recycling carts on trash collection days). Their number globally is estimated at twenty million people by the global network that supports them, Women in Informal Employment: Globalizing and Organizing (WIEGO).[19] There are efforts to organize them: the International Alliance of Waste Pickers is a union of fifty waste picker organizations that represents more than 460,000 workers across thirty-four countries, and there are a number of advocacy organizations, both for-profit and nonprofit, who support them.[20] It is difficult to find evidence of how much waste pickers collect, but back in 2010, UN-Habitat estimated that some eleven mil-

> **Box 10.3. Lunch at Abu Fadi**
>
> Claire and I left the waste engineer's office and headed for a late lunch at Abu Fadi, a famous fish sandwich place at the port end of Mina Corniche, a few blocks away. We took our food to a table on the sidewalk. Next to the table, a large trash barrel stood in a puddle of garbage. A middle-aged Syrian woman dragging a large shopping cart approached and began efficiently picking through the barrel, quickly putting plastic bottles, aluminum cans, and cardboard into her cart, then moving down the road to the next garbage pile. She was part of the army of waste pickers who are the only effective collectors of reusable and recyclable materials in Tripoli. On a per capita basis, their efforts were much more productive and cheaper than the sorting plant at the waste treatment center, which often broke down. We finished lunch and threw the sandwich wrappings into the trash barrel, gave our plastic water bottles to the waste picker, then headed home through Mina's street market. Vegetable detritus and cardboard packing boxes littered the alleyways. Waste pickers worked the trash, their shopping carts rattling over the cobblestones. Later that night, street sweepers would clear what remained, dumping everything into the receptacles headed for Trash Mountain.

lion waste pickers in developing countries collect about 60 percent of plastic waste. This number is likely to be much larger now.

In Lebanon, Syrian refugees have carved out a niche for themselves as waste pickers. Saleh writes about a group of young boys from a village in Syria, aged between eight and sixteen, some of them brothers or cousins, whose families sent them to Beirut when the Syrian war broke out: "They were under the care and supervision of the scrapyard muallim (master), a young man in his twenties, [from] the same community. Waste pickers would travel daily across the city pushing carts, with baskets attached, in search of scrap metal and plastic, clothes, shoes, games, books, and wooden furniture. Scrap metal and plastic were sold into supply chains for export and local recycling, respectively. Clothes and the like were sold by waste pickers' relatives at travelling flea markets around the Beqaa Valley."[21]

Saleh notes that in addition to providing waste disposal services, the waste pickers support Lebanon's scrap metal industry (scrap metal is one of Lebanon's main exports). In an urban salvage subeconomy, large scrapyards purchase scrap iron from small ones that rely on waste pickers to gather scrap and reduce it to manageable pieces. Saleh writes, "The smaller scrapyards are often located in abandoned or run-down buildings where, aside from hammers, pliers, and the occasional drill, . . . [it is] the hands and feet of mostly young boys who throw or stomp on old washing machines and fridges and tear wires apart." This waste picker subeconomy provides jobs and income for many poor people, including refugees and increasingly—as Lebanon's economy worsens—locals, too (see Box 10.3). As Saleh notes, war creates increased opportunities for salvaging scrap metal (from destroyed buildings). Given the current wars being fought in cities in Ukraine, Gaza, Sudan, and elsewhere, there will be plenty of opportunities for the urban scrap iron subeconomy to flourish.[22]

11

The Smuggling Economy

All cities hide illicit economies, and war and displacement provide opportunities for the growth of smuggling of both people and goods. This was certainly the case in Lebanon. During its own civil war and afterward, the smuggling of goods like building materials, medicine, and fuel became well established, as did the smuggling networks and routes between Lebanon and Syria.[1] Until 2014, there was relatively little smuggling of people. The border was essentially open, and people moved easily back and forth between the two countries, so people did not need to be smuggled. Mahmoud made his way to Tripoli using a taxi and buses. Most Syrians entered Lebanon via official border posts, mainly Masnaa and Ka'a (Qaa), but many used unofficial border crossings if they were closer and easier to access. As the war spilled into Lebanon, the Lebanese and Syrian governments made the border much more difficult to cross. Now Syrian refugees needed smugglers to help them find routes across the mountains into Lebanon, and then, for some, across the sea to other destinations. This demand gave the smuggling industry a significant boost. "The numbers of refugees coming into Lebanon kept going up, even in 2015 after the border was closed," said Ninette Kelley. "The smugglers were getting into gear."

Syrians crossed the border in both directions, for many reasons. Some traveled back to Syria to take advantage of the free health care in Syria, since in Lebanon they had to pay what they considered an exorbitant sum for health care. Others went to visit family still in Syria, or to check on their houses and farms. Mahmoud's mother, Umm Ahlam, frequently received jam and the dried apricots she loved, brought from her village by Syrian neighbors who now lived in Lebanon and frequently crossed the border. Syrians who were registered as refugees in Lebanon had to sneak back across the border because the Lebanese government did not allow refugees who went back to Syria to return to Lebanon. If Syrians didn't have the right papers or the right stamp in their passport, they needed a smuggler guide to cross back into Syria because the Syrian border guards would not allow them to return. Many of these "smugglers" were simply local young men who were either hired by smuggler bosses as guides or who acted on their own.

There were a range of options for smuggling people to or through Tripoli. The cheapest and simplest was passage across the closed Syrian border, guided by locals. For those who could afford a somewhat larger fee, some fishermen supplemented their incomes by hiring out their boats to migrants who wanted to attempt the journey of 233 kilometers across the sea to Cyprus. At the top end, for a much larger fee, Syrians or Lebanese could be moved from Tripoli to Europe. The main smuggling routes moved thousands of people through Türkiye to Greece, or via African cities to Libya and onto the boats crossing the Mediterranean. For example, after Türkiye changed its visa regime after 2014, Syrians who had the means and wanted to get to Europe made arrangements to travel to Sudan, which had become the only Arab country that did not require an entry visa. In Khartoum, smugglers used well-established networks to move Syrians, Sudanese, Eritreans, and Ethiopians through Cairo and on to Alexandria or elsewhere on Egypt's north coast.[2] These extremely long and dangerous journeys had high failure rates. Only wealthy migrants could ever pay the high sums charged for "door-to-door" service, which included fake documents and air transportation through transit countries to their destination.

Like all ports, Tripoli is a long-standing smuggling hub with many operations owned and run by Lebanese, providing a range of services and itineraries. One Lebanese smuggler, known by his nickname "Octoboot" (octopus in Arabic), had been smuggling goods between Lebanon and Syria for years. Before the war in Syria, his cargo had been goods like diesel fuel, cigarettes, and even gym protein powder, but now it was more difficult to smuggle goods across the border because of the Syrian checkpoints. So instead, he "helped" human beings cross the border (for a fee) using the long-established smuggling routes. Octoboot saw his smuggling operation as both lucrative and beneficial in that it provided a needed service for Syrians. He was one of many Lebanese smuggler bosses, each with their own routes and territories, and each known to the others.[3]

Tine Gade's scholarship has shown that during the Lebanon civil war and subsequent Syrian occupation, Tripoli's businessmen and militias and Syrian army officers were all heavily involved in the smuggling and trafficking of stolen and diverted goods. Syrian and Lebanese war profiteers enriched themselves through illegal construction, real-estate speculation, and the export of cannabis and opium produced in the Beqaa. The militias imposed illegal taxes on civilians and goods passing through the ports they controlled. Smuggling was rife in North Lebanon, and Tripoli's port has been used to smuggle hashish to Türkiye since the 1970s. As high taxes and other impositions made using the Tripoli port expensive, other ports to the north were opened, through which cigarettes, alcohol, and electrical appliances were smuggled into Syria.[4] Syrian commanders gave army officers and soldiers the opportunity to participate in this rent seeking to enrich or empower themselves. By the time the war began in Syria, much of Tripoli's economy had become, as Gade says, "a joint venture between the notable families of Tripoli and Syrian military officers. . . . Local politicians were interwoven into the Syrian orbit [so] that they constituted one social fabric. . . . The cooperation, shared economic benefits, and common interest in the perpetuation of Syrian influence in Lebanon helped modify norms and identities. . . . A common moral community and a common interest-based 'asabiyya were created."[5]

Smuggling networks—the 'asabiyya—were particularly strong between the cities of Tripoli and Homs. In 2011, the open border allowed trucks to smuggle fuel oil into Syria and return with food, household appliances and products, and much more. The weak Syrian currency made goods in Syria much cheaper, and Lebanese citizens frequently crossed to shop in Syrian towns. Weapons and fighters also came and went across the border. In the north, Syrian rebel factions came to support militias in Tripoli, and to the south, Assad's regime sent support to Hezbollah, which was supporting Assad in Syria.[6]

Human smuggling is a long-standing aspect of the migration industry, comprising different scales and types of activities. Some consider it a needed service for migrants, and indeed, there are thousands of straightforward transactions between smugglers and migrants in which both parties are satisfied with the outcome, even if the states involved are not.[7] But there are also hundreds of accounts of nefarious actions by smugglers, including ones where smugglers become traffickers. There is no clear line between smuggling (a business transaction between two parties) and trafficking, where the victim may be deceived, forcibly recruited, extorted, held ransom, or even enslaved.

The Impact of Smuggling on Cities

The issue of smuggling and trafficking is widely debated and researched, but there is still relatively little research on the impacts, positive and negative, that smuggling has on towns and cities. Yet, given the growth of the enterprise, the number of people involved, and its financial value, there must be urban consequences. In Tripoli, large-scale, organized operations like Octoboot's employed many people, linked multiple cities and regions, and made large profits. There were also small-scale smugglers who worked on a casual, opportunistic basis, such as the guides and fishermen. Migrants themselves sometimes worked for a large smuggling organization or simply took advantage of serendipitous opportunities to earn income and perhaps use the operation to have themselves or their families smuggled. As the demand for smuggling increased in North Lebanon, Tripoli's well-entrenched smuggling economy expanded, providing employment and entrepreneurial opportunities in a city where jobs were scarce.

Tripoli's rich smuggler bosses, already influential power brokers in poor neighborhoods like Beddawi, now became the arbiters of economic survival for refugees and Lebanese alike. In addition to providing transportation, the smugglers had a lucrative and long-standing side hustle in providing fake documents. Forged identity papers and work permits enabled refugees to find jobs and housing, and there was strong demand for fake passports, visas, and other documents needed for travel. This market for fraudulent papers is widespread globally and has been in place for decades.[8]

It's difficult to estimate how much of a city's local employment comes from smuggling and its associated illicit activities like providing counterfeited documents. Given the secretive nature of the industry, gathering empirical evidence is difficult, and there are no city records. But the presence of the smuggling industry has many indirect effects for towns and cities. For one, smuggling is a type of trade and migration that strengthens a city's business, employment, and communications links with other cities. Long-standing smuggling networks and routes link cities in the Middle East, North Africa, Europe, and the United States. One such smuggling route might start in a South Asian city (in Afghanistan or Myanmar or Nepal), and transfer clients to a city in South America before embarking them on a route through a Central American city (in Costa Rica or Mexico) to the United States. Still other networks extend throughout Africa (with smuggling city hubs in Ethiopia, Somalia, Sudan, Nigeria, or the Democratic Republic of the Congo). Migrants and refugees retain their connections with their families left behind, sending and receiving goods and money, and making return visits when they can. When the formal means to do these things are too difficult or expensive, people use informal means, as we explore in our discussion of financial transfers in Chapter 17.

A second consequence for smuggling hubs is the inflow of revenues. Smuggling operations often require migrants (including those who could qualify as refugees) to stay in transit cities for periods of time ranging from days to weeks or months until the smugglers are ready to move them out. The migrants must wait until the smuggler has gathered enough passengers to fill vessels to capacity (sometimes beyond safe capacity) or bribed the right officials, or for logistical or security reasons (to avoid inclement weather or the active presence of security forces or militias). Most smugglers' profits are based on a "pay-as-you-go" model: migrants pay different smugglers on different legs of their journey. Smugglers benefit from economies of scale, and most operations try to move large numbers of migrants simultaneously. Clients are therefore kept waiting in cities along the routes, where they must be fed and accommodated.[9] Although the smugglers try to keep these costs minimal, the presence of migrants concentrated in specific areas of the city means income for locals. The migrants' presence, though transient, can substantially increase demand for housing, goods, and services, especially if migrants have to stay for weeks at a time.

Small towns in particular benefit both from migrants in transit and from being used as a smuggler base, where a smuggling economy emerges. A well-known example is Izmir on Türkiye's western coast, a center of human smuggling from Türkiye to Greece. Smaller Turkish coastal towns also benefit. The migration researcher Luigi Achlli visited Elgar in late 2015 and described it as a sleepy tourist town whose economy normally slowed after the summer visitors left, but which seemed to be thriving because of the human smuggling industry. Town revenues came from fees for smuggling and counterfeit papers—"a black market in fake documents: forged passports, ID cards, work permits, and any other paper for the right price." The revenues flowing to the town were not from the illicit economy alone—the regular economy flourished, too: "Shops, boutiques, restaurants, grocery stores, bus and taxi companies, nightclubs, and pubs were crowded with migrants and smugglers. . . . Hotels offered half or full board accommodations at special rates for families of refugees; bus companies posted special offers and group packages for Syrians and other migrants on the windows of their shops. In the upmarket bazaar, boutique owners participated in the smuggling enterprise, for example, by selling lifejackets showcased on mannequins and helmets with night lights. Grocery stores sold various types of merchandise to migrants and refugees, while restaurants stayed open late to feed the masses awaiting the right moment to depart."[10]

Urban smuggling hubs host a range of actors, from professional criminal and militia groups to smuggler bosses and sketchy travel agencies, to petty criminals and ordinary citizens (hotel owners, taxi and truck drivers, travel agents, and money lenders), all of whom benefit from the profits from moving people.[11] In Africa, these towns can be port cities or inland smuggling hubs. Well-known African ports that are human smuggling hubs on the Mediterranean include eastern

Libyan towns like Tobruk and Benghazi, Sfax in Tunisia, and Tripoli in western Libya; from these towns migrants head to Italy. Less-known smuggling ports on the Horn of Africa's coast include Djibouti's Obock, 250 kilometers from the capital Djibouti City (itself a smuggling hub) and a departure point for Ethiopians going to the Gulf States; and Bossaso (Pundtland, Somalia), from which people are smuggled to Yemen and vice versa.[12] Many inland transit towns and cities are smuggling hubs too, as is the case with Agadez.

Agadez

The Saharan town of Agadez in northern Niger is about 900 kilometers northwest of the capital, Niamey, and 700 kilometers south of the Libyan border. Agadez was an important stop in the long history of the trans-Sahara trade that followed what was known as the Salt Route. After the fall of Libyan leader Muammar Gaddafi in 2011, it became a major transit town in the Niger–Libya–Algeria smuggling corridor for African migrants heading to Europe. In 2016 alone, at least 120,000 migrants passed through the town, whose regular population was around 110,000.[13] More than 6,000 newcomers were arriving every week and staying several days before moving on. Some were stuck for weeks or months if they lacked the fees needed to pay smugglers for the next leg of their journey. Smuggling in this region involves a mix of long-standing "senior" smugglers and more casual entrepreneurs. According to one senior smuggler from Agadez, "We mainly work on the basis of occasional agreements, including part-time. Anyone can be a smuggler for some time; you just bring your own car, and then leave with no fear of reprisals whatsoever."[14]

The smuggling industry in towns like Agadez provides employment and business opportunities to all kinds of people from across the region, including managers who oversee the entire operation; individual or group owners of transportation (Toyota Hiluxes, boats, camels, buses, trucks); cultural mediators and interpreters; drivers; lookouts; and security (bodyguards or other hired and armed muscle). Migrants are also employed in smuggling activities. "Each smuggler supports a hundred families," the president of the Agadez Regional Council told a reporter.[15]

State actors are also involved in Niger's smuggling industry, as they are in countries worldwide. In Niger, as Luca Raineri has shown, human smuggling is part of a highly resilient protection racket that is protected and enforced by state authorities. Material incentives in the form of substantial development aid offered to Niamey by the European Union have failed to curb irregular migration, especially after the 2023 coup.[16] The resilience of the smuggling industry, Raineri argues, is based on the social legitimacy of human smuggling, derived from a long history of smuggling rooted in the region's political economy. For poverty-stricken local people, migration and human smuggling are survival strategies, and for many, the smuggling industry is their only source of livelihood. Research across the Sahel shows widespread acceptance of smuggling practices, even including regular shakedowns at checkpoints where "people pay, sometimes 5,000 CFA, sometimes more, without much protesting. It is as if it was authorised. It is a practice, people find an agreement, and it works out well for everyone."[17]

In Agadez, as in Tripoli and elsewhere, state protection rackets rely on this social legitimacy and on networks of patronage politics. In many towns, locals have a positive view of the "big men," the powerful smuggler bosses. They wield a lot of influence, not least because they are often in league with city politicians or security forces. In Tripoli, Syrian refugees tend not to head up smuggling operations because they lack *wasta*—that is, relationships with the Lebanese authorities that ease the way for illicit activities. Smuggler bosses often locate the source of their power in their previous activities as rebel leaders or warlords. Raineri gives the example of Tuareg rebel leaders who, at the end of hostilities in Niger, were appointed to administrative and political offices in Niamey or Agadez and continue their smuggling activities, now as part of the state protection racket. The patronage networks protecting human smugglers also extend to commercial businesses: "The owners of major bus companies feature prominently among those who have benefitted from the protection of Niamey's authorities, despite their well-known involvement in all sorts of trafficking, including human smuggling. Two . . . major bus companies belonging to Nigerien businessmen . . . have grown suspiciously from a start in the early 2000s to now being among the most prominent and most profitable transporters in the whole of West Africa."[18]

The strength of the smuggling industry derives in part from its cultural acceptance by the local population, its contribution to the economy of cities like Agadez, and the financial interests of state actors. This organic strength has seriously weakened efforts by the European Union to stop migrant smuggling. Recent efforts such as the "operational partnership" launched in 2022 to tackle migrant smuggling between the European Union and Niger are likely to be similarly unsuccessful, beyond a few token efforts on the part of state governments.[19] As a result, cities that are smuggling hubs have prospered.

An additional boost for smuggling hub towns is the presence of international actors, including UN agencies and NGOs, which assist the migrants and refugees passing through—or stuck in—transit cities. Agadez hosts the offices of the International Organization for Migration (IOM) and UNHCR and several of their NGO partners. In 2014, IOM opened its fourth Niger transit and assistance center for migrants in Agadez. The new center accommodated up to 400 people regularly, but could host up to 1,000 "in periods of crisis." A few years later, there was a change in the composition of migrants in Agadez. In addition to the migrants heading north to Libya, now there were also returning people fleeing the violent conflict and abuse of migrants in Libya, as well as refugees who had been forced back (or "refouled") from Algeria. As UNHCR put it, "Niger is increasingly turning into an alternative space for protection, including for the asylum-seekers and refugees who fail to reach Europe." In response, in 2017 UNHCR Niger built another humanitarian center on the outskirts of Agadez and procured space in six guesthouses and in the Agadez suboffice for "the most vulnerable" (that is, children and mothers). UNHCR and IOM provided meals, health care, education, and other services for the refugees and asylum seekers. Notably for the town, the UN also built new infrastructure, including a permanent water pipeline to the humanitarian center. In all, the arrival of the UN agencies and international NGOs provided a significant injection of resources for Agadez. These resources included direct rent payments to local landlords for office space and for housing for staff brought in from outside, local employment of drivers, cleaners, security guards, and office staff, and new forms of expertise that could be passed onto locals.

Between the needs of the international agencies and the smugglers' requirements, the citizens of smuggling hubs can do quite well economically from the migrants and refugees passing through or staying for longer periods. However, the dark side of the smuggling industry also manifests in the host town. Migrants who are kept waiting by smugglers are often housed in miserable conditions, with minimal, if any, freedom; their presence is a dark shadow on towns. Many migrants and their families become deeply indebted to the smugglers. If they opt for "travel now, pay later" schemes, they go as far as their money will take them and then have to stop and work to earn enough money to pay off the smuggler or to pay for the next leg of their journey; this work often takes the form of indentured servitude. In smuggling hubs like Tripoli and Agadez (and Cairo, as we explore in Part III) there are often large numbers of migrants working without the legal status to do so. When migrants are indebted to their smuggler, they are vulnerable to exploitation, including being compelled to work in the smuggling industry.

PART THREE
Giant Cities: Cairo, Egypt

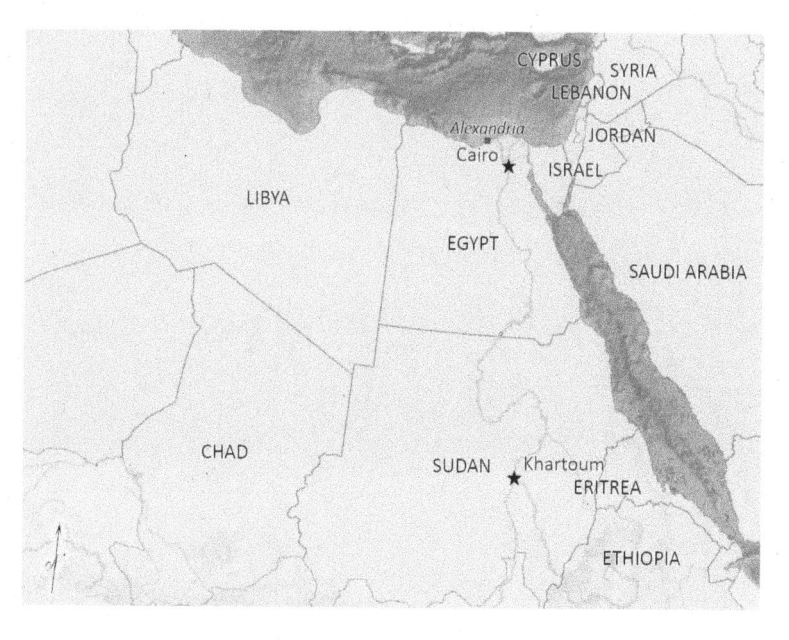

Figure III.1. Map of Eastern Mediterranean and Northwest Africa.
Source: ESRI, GEBCO, USGS, NaturalVue, and Natural Earth
(with thanks to Marcia Moreno-Baez).

12

Comparing the Experiences of Cairo and Tripoli

Whereas Tripoli represents the experience of smaller, secondary cities, especially those near the borders of refugee-sending countries, Cairo represents the experience of primary host cities (which include most of the capitals of poor countries), the giant megalopolises surrounded by ever-growing informal settlements. In such cities, even very large numbers of new arrivals get swallowed up. By late 2023, Egypt had over 500,000 registered refugees and asylum seekers, as well as many more nationals from the same refugee-sending countries. Most of these refugees lived in a few Egyptian cities, the majority in Greater Cairo.

Cairo's population of more than twenty million people means the refugees make little dent in the overall urban fabric. A visitor to Cairo would be hard-pressed to identify refugees among the crowds in Tahrir Square. Nor does the presence of humanitarian agencies make much difference to giant cities. Although UNHCR has been in Egypt since 1954, and there are many international and local refugee agencies working in Cairo, their presence is barely noticeable. Unlike in Tripoli's Mina area, where there are dozens of bars and restaurants frequented by expatriates, in Cairo there are no areas where humanitarian and development workers are visibly present or where they have changed the atmosphere of the area. In the high-end neighborhoods of Mohandiseen, Dokki, and Zamalek, where many INGOs have their offices, the coffee shops, restaurants, and hotels are filled with many more wealthy Egyptians than humanitarian agency expatriates. Yet, while the presence of refugees and the humanitarian industry is less apparent, this doesn't mean that refugees have no impact on large cities.

In all cities, even small ones like Tripoli, refugees tend to congregate in particular neighborhoods, where their impact is much more salient. These refugee neighborhoods have been transformed—in positive and negative ways—by the presence of refugees. Their impact is sometimes obvious, sometimes subtle. The obvious impacts—on housing and job markets, on services like health care and education, and on infrastructure like waste management—can be assessed or even measured in a relatively straightforward way, as we explored in the chapters on Tripoli. The more subtle impacts on city neighborhoods are more difficult to grasp and measure, but important to capture.[1] Some of these impacts include hidden subeconomies, the effects on neighborhoods' social cohesion, and the activism of community organizations. The Cairo chapters in this part focus on these more subtle impacts.

The refugee and migration experiences in Egypt and Lebanon are similar, with a few important differences. Historically, both Egypt and Lebanon were once part of Syria. (Briefly, from 1958 to 1961, Syria and Egypt declared themselves one country, called the United Arab Republic.[2] Syrians and Egyptians still refer to this historical relationship.) Both Lebanon and Egypt border on only one or two of the many refugee-sending countries: Lebanon borders on Syria, and Egypt borders on Sudan (at this writing, Egypt is also receiving Palestinian refugees from Gaza). Both countries, like all the countries of the Middle East and Africa, have long histories of receiving refugees and migrants from other African and Middle Eastern countries, and consequently they have large, long-standing diaspora populations. As in Lebanon, there was a large population of Syrians living in Egypt before 2011—some estimates are as high as 400,000—and there was also a large population of Sudanese who had been in Egypt for several decades. These long-standing diasporas play an important role in supporting newcomers. (For a geographical overview see Figure III.1.)

Both countries also have long histories of internal displacement and urban migration within the country, and their citizens have migrated (or been forcibly displaced) to neighboring countries and further abroad. As with Lebanon, we don't know the true refugee population in Egypt, or even the country's total population. In both countries, registered refugees are a subset of a much larger population of co-national migrants, many of whom would qualify as refugees if they were counted. In Egypt, IOM conducted a triangulation study of migrants in 2022 and concluded that their number had reached nine million, with Sudanese, Libyan, Syrian, and Yemeni migrants comprising the top four groups.[3]

In both Egypt and Lebanon, the arrival of Syrian refugees after 2011 was different from earlier refugee arrivals. This was because the 2011 displacement from Syria was much larger and occurred over a shorter period than previous displacements (this happened again in Egypt in 2023 with Sudanese arrivals fleeing the civil war in Sudan) but also because, for Egypt in particular, the Syrian refugees arrived at a time of great political turmoil in the country.

In terms of their national government's response to refugees, there are again differences and similarities between the two countries. Unlike Lebanon, Egypt is a signatory to the 1951 Refugee Convention and the 1967 Protocol. However, neither Egypt nor Lebanon has a legislative framework to manage asylum seekers and refugees. Both governments have a lax and variable response to refugees ("policy" is too strong a word). Both countries do not require refugees to live in camps—although Lebanon has a long history of Palestinian camps. As in Lebanon, UNHCR has played a strong role in managing the response to refugees in Egypt.

Part III begins with an explanation of Egypt's refugee context and policies (Chapter 13), then Chapter 14 explores how refugees are distributed across the landscape of Cairo. Chapter 15 takes us to one of Cairo's satellite cities, 6th of October City, where many Syrians—and UNHCR—have moved. This chapter explores what changes humanitarian funding has brought to Cairo. Chapter 16 explores how refugee entrepreneurs have boosted Cairo's economy, and Chapter 17 focuses on one subeconomy, the money transfer sector, and what the informal money transfer system known as the *hawala*, largely run by refugees, means for Cairo. The last chapter explores how social cohesion is affected by the presence of refugees, and the problems experienced by youth and women in two very poor neighborhoods, Ard al-Lewa and Hay al-Ashr (Chapter 18).

Hassan

The Cairo chapters that follow trace the experiences of Hassan, a Somali refugee who fled Mogadishu in 2007 when he was eighteen years old. At that time, life for young men in Mogadishu had become increasingly dangerous as opportunities for a decent life dwindled. Al-Shabaab, the jihadist organization (then and now) fighting Somalia's fragile government, was actively recruiting young men and threatening them when they refused. Schools and universities were no longer functioning, and the moribund economy provided few jobs. Hassan got permission from his father to leave, and he and two friends hired a smuggling service to take them across the border to Kenya. In Nairobi they joined the large and vibrant Somali community in the suburb of Eastleigh. Hassan lived in an apartment building owned by his aunt, a flourishing businesswoman, and worked for her, but his safety in Kenya was precarious. The Kenyan government's encampment policy required Somali refugees to reside in the long-standing Dadaab camps near the border. Refugees who left these camps—or bypassed them, as Hassan had done—were not permitted to live or work in Kenya's cities and were often the targets of police raids. Hassan spent a few months in Nairobi, keeping close to his aunt's house and avoiding the streets as much as possible. His goal was to reach Cairo, and with the support of his aunt, Hassan made the journey by bus and smuggler van to Cairo in 2008.

Hassan's journey from Somalia via Kenya to Egypt has been made by many thousands of Somalis since the 2000s. Even more refugees have come to Egypt from Sudan, Eritrea, Ethiopia, and other African countries since the 1980s, and in 2012 the Syrian refugees began coming. For many years, they were the largest refugee population in Egypt, but as of late 2023, their number has been surpassed by the arrival of Sudanese refugees that began in April 2023.

Field Research for the Cairo Chapters

In 2008, I began a series of research studies in Cairo in collaboration with the Center for Migration and Refugee Studies at the American University of Cairo. Until the pandemic brought travel to a stop in 2020, I visited Cairo regularly, staying for a few weeks at a time and experiencing the frustration and fascination of the great old city. I worked with Egyptian researchers and faculty and with Sudanese, Somali, and Syrian refugees, regularly visiting their neighborhoods, including the gated communities where wealthy Egyptians live and the very poor informal areas where most refugees live alongside poor Egyptians. Many of the following chapters draw on my visits to Cairo and on conversations and interviews by my research assistant,

Ryan Philip (he requested that his name be changed for anti-doxxing reasons). Ryan, a white American man, speaks fluent Egyptian Arabic and lived and worked in Cairo for four years before he came to the Fletcher School of Law and Diplomacy at Tufts University, where he was my student and research assistant. After graduating, he returned to Cairo and continued to help with this book, spending many evenings hanging out in neighborhood coffee shops and attending community events. Ryan was the same age as many of the young people whose views and experiences we were interested in, and he related to them easily. During the course of my research projects, my teams and I have talked to key informants from Somali, Sudanese and South Sudanese, Eritrean, and Syrian networks using different entry points, including community organizations, tribal associations, community schools, churches, refugee agencies, and activists in Nasr City, Maadi, Ard al-Lewa, Hay al-Ashr, 6th of October, and Barajil. We have had conversations with academics, interpreters, UN and NGO officials, and expats living in Cairo, including David Sims. In March 2019, as part of a study we conducted with Save the Children, we held a workshop on community violence with refugee service providers including international NGOs and UNHCR, as well as pastors from Sudanese and South Sudanese churches in Cairo.

To maintain our informants' confidentiality, we refer to them by their role and neighborhood or we made up names for them, unless they specifically requested that we use their own names.

13

Egypt: The Refugee Context

Humanitarian movements into a city do not always begin with an "emergency phase" or a mass influx. Sometimes the refugee flow resembles that of migrants: people arrive in smaller numbers over longer periods of time. The slow accumulation of refugee populations in cities occurs when the crisis in sending countries is drawn out. Usually, people are forewarned or intuit that things will get worse, and those who are able and willing begin to leave. Well-resourced people, including those with networks outside the country, leave first; they transfer their assets to safer places and relocate family members in a strategic way. As the conflict or crisis takes hold, increasing violence and loss of homes and family members push more people to seek safety, either elsewhere in their own country or in neighboring countries. This displacement pattern has characterized most conflicts since 2010, including Syria, Ukraine, and Ethiopia. But sometimes violent conflict descends very suddenly and unexpectedly on a country. That was the case with Sudan and Gaza in 2023.

Until 2012, the pattern of slow accretion characterized Egypt's refugee arrivals. UNHCR reported 70,000 Palestinians for many years, but this number was never validated. There were some 14,000 Sudanese refugees registered with UNHCR in 2005, but fewer than one thousand refugees of other nationalities. From 2010, refugee arrivals slowly crept up, then in 2012–13, Syrian arrivals doubled the number of registered refugees in Egypt. The number of refugees declined

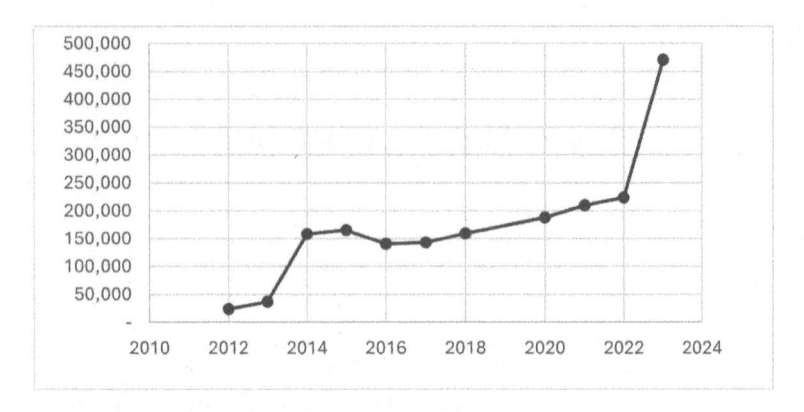

Figure 13.1. Registered refugees in Egypt, 2012–23. Source: "Refugee Context in Egypt," UNHCR, 2023, https://www.unhcr.org/eg/about-us/refugee-context-in-egypt.

slightly through 2016, then arrivals from all the main sending countries began to increase, and in mid-2023, the civil war in Sudan created a massive surge of displacement. By March 2024, Egypt hosted almost 550,000 registered refugees from Sudan, Syria, South Sudan, Eritrea, Ethiopia, Yemen, Somalia, and Iraq, as well as smaller numbers from other countries and a long-standing population of Palestinians (see Figure 13.1 and Table 13.1).[1] These numbers only include the refugees who had been registered by UNHCR. As we know, official refugee numbers are always uncertain, because of unrecorded departures and arrivals, and in all host countries, there are large populations of nationals from the refugee sending countries, who are not registered as refugees, for various reasons.

Egypt's History of Migration and Displacement

Egypt's displacement history is characterized by three themes. The first two are shared by Lebanon and most of the countries of the Middle East and Africa: a long history of external and internal movement, in-

Table 13.1. UNHCR Registered Refugees in Egypt, by Nationality, March 2024

Eritrea	34,406
Ethiopia	17,957
Iraq	5,650
Somalia	7,373
South Sudan	40,579
Sudan	279,293
Syria	155,896
Yemen	8,666
Total	470,577

Source: "Refugee Context in Egypt," UNHCR, 2023, https://www.unhcr.org/eg/about-us/refugee-context-in-egypt.

cluding refugee inflows, labor out-migration, internal displacement, and rural to urban migration; and (as a result) the long-standing presence of different refugee nationalities, including Palestinians, Sudanese (especially in Egypt), and Syrians—before the arrival of newcomers. A third theme, and one that differentiates Egypt from Lebanon, is the strength of Egypt's leaders—especially their views of themselves and of Egypt as a pan-Arab leader, welcoming others from countries like the Sudan (in the case of Nasser)—and their often heavy-handed attempts to re-engineer the city in the name of development and modernization. In Egypt, the aftermath of the January 25 Revolution in 2011 resulted in significant political changes that included a coup two years later and the installation of Abdel Fattah el-Sisi as president in 2014. As with Lebanon, these historical themes shaped the political and social context in Egypt for new refugee arrivals.

Egyptian migrants have historically been one of the biggest sources of labor in the Middle East, mainly after Nasser came to power in 1952—before that, there was little out-migration. Most Egyptians sought work in the Middle East and North Africa, but many went further afield and, like the Lebanese, contributed to a large diaspora worldwide, probably as large as ten million.[2] The number of Egyptian workers in Middle Eastern countries shrank in the early 2020s, in part because of the economic downturn, the COVID pandemic, and in Jordan, the influx of Syrian workers that reduced the demand for Egyptian workers. Thousands returned to Egypt, rejoining their families, often in the same poor neighborhoods where the refugees lived.

Egypt's internal migration—from rural to urban areas—began in the 1960s and continued through the 1970s, but today it has dropped off. From 1970 to 2018 there was little change in the proportion of Egypt's urban population. The urban share of the national population in 2018 was 43 percent compared to 41 percent in 1970, making Egypt the second-least urbanized country in North Africa and the Middle East, after Yemen.[3] Egyptians have also been subject to internal displacement over the past century. During the Suez War in 1956, the population of Port Said was displaced, and the construction of the Suez Canal in 1967 again displaced residents of the region's towns and villages. (The construction of the New Suez Canal, which began in 2014, is reported to have displaced 2,000 Egyptians in the Sinai Peninsula.) In 1964, the construction of the Aswan High Dam in Upper (southern) Egypt displaced much of the Nubian population living there. In 1974, the Israeli occupation of the Sinai after the 1967 Arab-Israeli War (the Six-Day War) displaced more than a million Egyptians, most of whom fled or were evacuated to Cairo.[4]

Refugees have been coming to and fleeing from Egypt since antiquity, but until the Palestinians began coming after 1947, most of the refugees arriving in Egypt were Christian, fleeing persecution by the Ottomans. Among the groups were the Syro-Lebanese or Levantine Christians, who fled the conflict between the Christian and Druze religious sects in Lebanon and Syria. (Lebanon was at the time still part of Ottoman Syria, or Bilad al-Sham in Arabic, hence the appellation "Shawam" or "Shami.") The Ottoman ruler of Egypt, Muhammad Ali Pasha, permitted Greeks, Armenians and Assyrians, and Jews, as well as Christians, to migrate to Egypt. Prior to 1952, Christian and Jewish populations thrived and were well integrated into Egypt's cosmopolitan society. In 1952, after the Free Officers revolution led by Gamal Abdel Nasser, nationalism swept Egypt. Nasser nationalized foreign enterprises and pursued import-substitution industrialization policies. As the political climate became more anti-western and less cosmopolitan, many Christians and Jews left Egypt, and immigration into Egypt declined. Since 1945, it is largely refugees from African countries and the Middle East who have been coming to Egypt.

Egypt also has a long history of expelling people or causing them to flee. The most well-known refugee story is the flight of the Jews, including Joseph and Mary, a few months before the birth of Jesus. Just short of 2,000 years later, during the Suez Crisis in 1956, it was the Egyptian government under Nasser rather than the pharaoh who again expelled stateless Jews.[5] Since then, Egypt's governments have repressed journalists, political groups, and human rights activists, and today there are almost 70,000 refugees and asylum seekers who have fled Egypt. As a side note, it is quite common for host countries also to be sending countries, and vice versa. For example, at the end of 2023, Sudan, with 1.5 million refugees in other countries and more than nine million internally displaced, was itself host to almost a million refugees from six countries.[6]

As in many host countries, in Egypt the different refugee nationalities are subject to shifting political exigencies. The Palestinians are a good example. Prior to his death in 1970, Nasser had welcomed and supported the thousands of Palestinians who came to Egypt after the first Arab-Israeli War (the *Nakba*) in 1948, and then again after the 1956 and 1967 Arab-Israeli Wars.[7] The Palestinian presence in Egypt accorded with Nasser's anti-Zionist, pro–Arab solidarity rhetoric and his desire for Arab leadership, and Nasser allowed Palestinians to work and use Egypt's health and educational facilities. Perhaps for this reason, UNRWA is not present in Egypt to support Palestinians, as it is in Lebanon and other Middle Eastern countries. By the mid-1970s, however, with Anwar al-Sadat in power, the situation for Palestinians had changed, especially after the 1971 Black September event in Jordan, and then in February 1978, the assassination of Egypt's Minister of Culture, Yusif al-Sibai (who was also a beloved Egyptian author), in Cyprus by the renegade Abu Nidal (Sabri al-Banna) Organization. The latter, an offshoot of the PLO, was opposed to Sadat's pursuit of bilateral rapprochement with Israel and the 1977 Camp David Accords, which had been negotiated without input from Palestinians. In Egypt, Palestinians lost their rights to legal residency, employment, and property ownership. Those Palestinians who had not acquired Egyptian citizenship (usually through marriage to an Egyptian national) continued to be refugees in Egypt.[8]

How many Palestinians are in Egypt? As in Lebanon, this figure is unknown. Since at least 2005, UNHCR has listed the number of Palestinians in Egypt as 50,000–70,000, but this number has never been verified. The oldest Palestinians have now lived dispersed in Cairo and other Egyptian cities for seventy years. As noted by Oroub al-Abed, Palestinians do not live in their own communities but instead are mixed into Egyptian society "socially, professionally and culturally," and "over time and due to intermarriage, it has become difficult to differentiate Palestinians from Egyptians."[9] Despite their small number and weak political power, Palestinians have consistently been viewed by Egypt's governments as a threat to the country's stability. State policies, surveillance, and intimidation by the media have forced Palestinians to hide or suppress their identity. Thousands of young Palestinians are "illegal"—essentially, stateless—despite having been born in Egypt.

Sudanese and South Sudanese refugees also have a long history in Egypt and likewise have been subject to changing political winds. The Sudanese began to arrive during the first war in Sudan in 1955, when South Sudan was still part of Sudan, and then again after 1983 when the Sudanese government established Islamic law (sharia) in southern Sudan followed by the outbreak of the Second Sudanese Civil War.[10] Until 1995, Sudanese citizens could enter Egypt without a visa and had unrestricted access to employment, education, health coverage, and property ownership. Then in 1995 there was an assassination attempt on President Mubarak, allegedly by Sudanese Islamists, and Egypt repealed the agreement, making it harder but still possible for Sudanese to enter Egypt. Ongoing conflicts in Sudan—in Darfur, the Nuba Mountains and Blue Nile, and East Sudan—continued to drive refugees into Egypt. After South Sudan became independent in July 2011, some but not all of the 10,000 Sudanese refugees in Cairo returned to South Sudan, and since then refugees from Sudan and South Sudan have continued to come to Egypt. Today there are South Sudanese who have been in Cairo for forty years but still consider themselves refugees, and at the end of 2023 there were well over 40,000 South Sudanese registered with UNHCR, some of them long-standing residents, others new.[11] The size of the unregistered South Sudanese population in Cairo is unknown, with estimates ranging from 750,000 to four million.

From the early 1990s, wars, conflict, and persecution in the Horn of Africa also drove Ethiopian, Eritrean, and Somali refugees to Egypt. When Hassan arrived in Cairo in 2008, he joined 5,000 other registered Somalis already living there. A substantial population of Iraqis, including political refugees from Saddam Hussein's Baathists, began to arrive following the escalation of violence in Iraq in 2006. Iraqi nationals were initially allowed to enter Egypt on tourist visas, which Egyptian authorities routinely renewed until November 2006. Then the Egyptian Ministry of Interior began to restrict these renewals, telling Iraqis that if they wished to remain in Egypt, they had to register with UNHCR. From January 2007, the Egyptian authorities began imposing highly restrictive new procedures for Iraqis seeking entry. Tourist visas now required face-to-face interviews by at least one family member at an Egyptian consulate, and since there was no Egyptian diplomatic post in Baghdad and Iraqis could not get to consulates in Syria or Jordan, it became virtually impossible for Iraqis to obtain a visa for Egypt. As a result, there was a significant drop in new Iraqi arrivals, as well as an increase in split families, where one or more family member made it to Egypt but other family members could not leave Iraq.[12] By 2008, some 10,000 Iraqis had registered with UNHCR, but it's likely that many Iraqis had not registered. Like the Palestinians, the Iraqis lived quietly, dispersed in more upscale neighborhoods, so as not to draw attention to themselves. All told, at the beginning of 2012, on the eve of the Syrian refugees' arrival, Cairo's non-Palestinian UNHCR-registered refugee population was about 56,000.

None of Egypt's previous inflows of refugees was as dramatic—or as consequential—as the refugees fleeing the Syrian civil war, who began coming to Egypt in earnest in late 2012. Egypt does not border on Syria, but there were several reasons why Syrians made their way there, mostly by airplane. For one, there was already a large Syrian population in Egypt who could provide a network of support for new arrivals, and many Syrian new arrivals already had business or family connections in Egypt. A second reason was timing: the Syrians' arrival came at a critical juncture in Egyptian history. The Egyptian revolution began on January 25, 2011, and by the end of 2011, the office of the president was vacant (Hosni Mubarak had been forced to resign in February). A military junta suspended the constitution, dissolved both houses of parliament, and proclaimed that it would rule for six months until presidential elections were held. In June 2012, Egyptians elected Mohamed Morsi, the Muslim Brotherhood candidate, to the presidency. The Sunni Muslim Brotherhood was an ardent foe of the Shia-backed Assad regime, and President Morsi welcomed the Syrians, most of whom were opposed to the Assad regime. Like the Iraqi refugees, the Syrians were allowed to enter on three-month tourist visas and to register with UNHCR. By the end of 2013, more than 121,000 Syrians had come to Egypt, vastly outnumbering all other refugee nationalities.

All governments' responses to refugees shift as the political winds change. In mid-2013, after months of street protests, the Egyptian military overthrew President Morsi in a coup and assumed power. Xenophobia and hostility toward Syrians began to rise. The Egyptian media cast Syrians as troublemakers who had supported the ousted Morsi and taken part in protests calling for Morsi's reinstatement. Human rights groups said hundreds of Syrians in Egypt faced prolonged detention or deportation. In a repeat of what had happened with the Iraqis, the new government toughened its requirements for Syrians. From 2013 on, they had to obtain a visa prior to arrival and register with the government once their visa expired.[13] Syrian arrivals declined dramatically in 2014 (the current president, Abdel Fattah el-Sisi, was elected in June 2014), but even so, more than 14,000 arrived and registered with UNHCR. In 2015 arrivals decreased further, to just under 6,000, but in 2016 Syrian arrivals more than doubled from the previous year, to 14,607, and the next year, arrivals increased again. By the end of 2022 there were well over 136,000 registered Syrian refugees in Egypt, and the number of refugees from other countries continued to grow.

After the Sudan civil war took hold in 2023, Sudanese fled the country and their arrivals in Egypt increased dramatically. By March 2024, Egypt hosted almost 550,000 registered Sudanese refugees. Syrians were no longer the biggest refugee group in Egypt. But as the next chapters show, they continue to make a significant impact on Cairo and other cities in Egypt.

Egypt's Policy toward Refugees

Unlike Lebanon and other Arab states, Egypt is a signatory to both the 1951 Refugee Convention and the regional OAU 1969 Refugee Convention. However, the implementation of its Convention-related obligations has been ad hoc, even haphazard. Egypt has no national asylum legislation or administrative bureaucracy related to refugees. Instead, the responsibility for refugees, including registration, documentation, and status determination, is delegated to UNHCR under a 1954 Memorandum of Understanding (MoU) signed with the government of Egypt. The MoU has meant that the government has left services for refugees to international and local NGOs working as implementing partners for UNHCR. Kelsey Norman calls Egypt's policy toward refugees one of "strategic indifference," but, she argues, this changed after the 2013 military coup, when the Egyptian government began to take a more "proactive, securitized, and repressive approach" to migrants and refugees.[14]

Since the 1970s, although refugees have been allowed to enter Egypt, the government has made little effort to help or accommodate them. Although refugees, including Palestinians, were never and are not now required to live in camps, most of them, especially non-Syrians, struggle mightily to make a living, find adequate housing, and find schools where their children are not abused and harassed. The government's indifference to the plight of refugees plays out in many ways. First, although it signed the 1951 Refugee Convention, Egypt submitted reservations on several clauses, including those related to public relief, education, and employment.[15] This means refugees are not legally permitted to work in Egypt except under certain circumstances (discussed in Chapter 16). Registered asylum seekers are entitled to public health services and their children have access to primary education, although many refugees avoid public schools if they have other options, because of the poor quality of schools and the harassment their children experience in them. (This kind of experience by refugee children in schools is by no means unusual in host neighborhoods around the world.)

One difficulty for refugees is that they must hold a residence permit to access public services or obtain a work permit. The first step is to register with UNHCR. Those who can show valid identification, such as a passport, obtain the Asylum-seeker Registration Card, known as the "yellow card," which is valid for eighteen months. Those who cannot show a valid passport or other identification get an Asylum-seeker Certificate (or "white paper"), which does not enable them to obtain a residency permit. Yellow card holders will eventually be interviewed by UNHCR for formal refugee status (the refugee status determination process). If their interview is successful, they are granted the coveted Refugee Registration Card ("blue card"), which means they are legally recognized as refugees by UNHCR, and the holder can obtain a legal residence permit for Egypt, valid for three years.[16]

Until 2019, refugees struggled to obtain or renew their residence permits because they had to navigate Egypt's excruciatingly slow and cumbersome bureaucracy. The permits were valid for only six months, and renewals required people to travel to the notorious Mogamma al-Tahrir, the huge administrative building in Tahrir Square where all residency and other visa documents were processed. Ryan, who worked with refugees for many years in Cairo, wrote this about the Mogamma in 2018:

> Refugees start lining up at 4 A.M. to make sure that they can get inside the building. Some come the night before and sleep in front of the Mogamma. Once inside, police treat refugees horribly: officers will scream, insult, and, from my own observation, once ripped up an application of a refugee who was nearly done acquiring the various stamps and stickers required from different windows. At any point in this process, a refugee can be told that they cannot renew their residency permit and be arbitrarily denied. When that happens, a refugee can alert UNHCR (or an INGO who alerts UNHCR), who then faxes a letter to the Egyptian Ministry of Foreign Affairs reminding them that this person is a refugee and entitled to a permit. If the refugee keeps trying, they may eventually receive their permit; however, a small number are never granted residency permits due to "security reasons." Refugees and their descendants need to go through this process for years on end.[17]

Making the trip to the Mogamma was expensive in terms of travel costs and lost work time, as it required refugees (and Egyptians) to wait in long queues all day. These bureaucratic requirements led to low rates of acquisition and retention of permits. UNHCR tried to work with the government to ease the process for getting birth certificates and residence permits, but the situation got worse. Then, in October 2019, Egypt's Passport and Immigration Administration upgraded the yellow and blue cards with new digitalized residence permit cards.[18] Whether the new system has improved the process of obtaining and renewing residency permits remains to be seen.

The process explained above is for non-Syrian refugees, who are usually from African countries. Many host countries have different policies for refugees, depending on their nationality. For example, Kenya requires Somali and Sudanese refugees to be in camps but allows Congolese refugees to live outside camps; Middle Eastern countries have different rules for Palestinians than for other refugee groups. Likewise, in Egypt Syrians are treated differently from other refugee nationalities. All Syrians registered with UNHCR automatically receive yellow cards, making them asylum seekers—but they cannot apply for blue cards that enable Convention refugee status.

If an applicant "fails" the asylum interview—that is, they are deemed by UNHCR not to have shown adequate evidence of being a refugee—they receive neither a yellow or blue card and are designated as "closed file" (that is, a rejected asylum seeker). As in most countries, when the government denies asylum to an asylum seeker, they are designated an "irregular migrant" and expected to return to their home country. For example, in the United States, when an applicant requests asylum at the border, a Department of Homeland Security asylum officer makes a decision—a "credible fear" determination—about whether the applicant is telling the truth and whether she will be able to demonstrate eligibility for asylum in immigration court. If the asylum seeker passes this screening, she is admitted into the United States and is given a court date when an immigration judge will determine whether she qualifies for asylum. If the applicant fails this screening, she can be placed in expedited removal proceedings and possibly deported.[19] Once the asylum seeker has gone before an immigration judge, if asylum is denied, the asylum seeker returns to whatever legal status she had at the time of application. She can appeal, but if her legal status has expired by the time of the asylum interview, she is placed in removal proceedings.

In Egypt, most rejected asylum seekers come from countries like Eritrea, Sudan, and Ethiopia, where it is a crime for citizens to seek asylum elsewhere. Those who return face the risk of detention and even torture. This means many people with "closed file" cases do not return home; they continue to live in Egypt without legal status. Historically, except for occasional raids, Egypt has not conducted mass deportations. But since 2010, there have been reports of increasing expulsions, particularly of Eritrean asylum seekers. UNHCR claims that the white paper provides some protection from deportation because it "serves as proof of an asylum application in Egypt." But Egypt has regularly been accused of deporting people with formal refugee status and also collectively deporting particular nationalities, such as Eritreans, without allowing them the opportunity to apply for refugee status.[20] This suggests that documentation does not necessarily prevent deportation.

Like undocumented migrants everywhere, rejected asylum seekers in Egypt are unable to apply for a residence permit and are not eligible for humanitarian assistance or government services. They live at risk of arrest, detention, and deportation, and they endure discrimination by employers and landlords who take advantage of their lack of legal status and consequent unwillingness to contact authorities. How many return home or migrate to other countries is unknown, but it is likely that a large proportion remain in Egypt. A 2017 estimate was that there might be 25,000–35,000 closed-file residents in Egypt.[21] The number is probably much higher today. In 2022, UNHCR Egypt had more than 63,000 pending asylum applications from ten countries. Of these, UNHCR made decisions on 28,852 cases—less than half (45 percent). Of those, 6,618 asylum seekers were granted refugee status (23 percent) and 22,234 (77 percent) were rejected or had their cases closed.[22] These closed cases added to the existing population of closed cases, or the undocumented immigrants who are still in Egypt from previous years. Some might have moved on to other countries or returned (or have been deported) to their home countries. We have no way of knowing their number, as neither the government nor UNHCR tracks closed cases.

The presence of a large population of closed cases has several implications for cities like Cairo. One consequence is that neither the government nor humanitarian agencies know the real size of the refugee population, and as noted in Chapter 2, the undocumented population is growing as they have children. Refugees' and migrants' children who were born and grew up in Cairo are not eligible for Egyptian citizenship, which is granted on the basis of descent (jus sanguinis), and they are at risk of becoming stateless. This means the refugee population continues to grow even if no more refugees enter the city. While UNHCR registers the children of already registered parents, there are uncounted numbers of closed-file and unregistered refugees and migrants whose children add to their numbers in the city. The presence of unregistered and therefore uncounted refugees and migrants in Cairo (and most cities) means we don't know the total number of non-Egyptians in Cairo.

A second consequence is that because closed cases and all undocumented immigrants must live and work in the informal sector, they can be more easily manipulated and discriminated against by employers looking for cheap labor and landlords seeking high rents, and may even become victims of traffickers and criminals. The presence of a growing, highly marginalized population in a city can never be healthy or beneficial for a city and its residents. Many cities today confront the issue of refugees and other migrants who fail to get asylum or other legal status but remain in the city where they have been living, at risk of deportation and at the mercy of those who bear them animus. They survive on charity, including the charity of officials who turn a blind eye, and on the support of their communities already living in the city. As we shall see in the following chapters, Cairo's housing and employment, its remittance networks, and its economic resilience are all caught up in the tension between the formal and informal spheres, between those who live in the shadows and those who take advantage of them.

14

Drops in the Bucket: Cairo's Refugee Neighborhoods

Zamalek is an old, affluent district of Cairo. It takes up the northern half of Gezira Island in the Nile River, but most Cairenes simply refer to the whole island as Zamalek. The district is full of charm, even though it is bisected by the heavily trafficked 26th of July Corridor. The tree-lined streets contain a mix of run-down belle époque and even some art deco buildings, grand but heavily secured embassies, and modern apartment buildings. Restaurants, bars, and cafés line the sidewalks along the highway. On the quieter streets there are boutiques, silversmiths, bakeries, tinsmiths, minimarts, and other small shops, interspersed with schools and the occasional upscale supermarket. It is not only the wealthy who live here. Cairo's byzantine rent control laws enable low- and middle-income Egyptians to live in Zamalek, but landlords rarely make improvements in low-rent apartments, and building maintenance is sporadic.

When in Cairo I stay in Zamalek, at the Flamenco Hotel, on the northwestern side of the island. The rooms with river views look out across the narrow western channel of the Nile as it divides around the island, over the historical (and now removed) houseboats moored along the shore of Kit Kat on the west bank, and southwest toward Giza governorate, where the pyramids and the Sphinx lie about sixteen kilometers away.[1] To the north is the low-income district of

Imbaba and to the south is the affluent neighborhood of Mohandiseen. This juxtaposition of wealthy and poor neighborhoods is typical of Cairo; even within wealthy neighborhoods like Zamalek, there are pockets of poverty.

Cairo's landscape reflects its history of rapid urbanization. The movement of people from rural areas began in the 1950s and lasted for a few decades, leading to the growth of informal housing and settlements both within the old city and in the peri-urban areas. This increase in informal housing occurred largely because of the Egyptian government's failure to provide affordable housing, but also because of rapid development and speculation on the part of land investors. As a result, in 2009, one estimate was that 70 percent of Cairo's population rent or have built housing semi-legally or illegally on privately owned or public lands.[2] As we know, informal housing and settlements are where most refugees and migrants live, too.

Greater Cairo is spread over 171,000 square kilometers, spanning both sides of the Nile, about 210 kilometers southeast of the port city of Alexandria, where the Nile delta reaches the Mediterranean (Lower Egypt). The city consists of three governorates, each with its own administrative structure led by a *muhafiz* appointed by the president.[3] (The management of these governorates is severely constrained by the fact that 80 percent of their budgets comes from central government allocations, of which 55–75 percent goes to salaries. This leaves very little for urban services and investment; the governors are unable to do much more than administer day-to-day affairs.) The three governorates are subdivided into dozens of "cities," districts, and neighborhoods, over half of them informal areas. Together they comprise the largest metropolitan area in the Middle East and Africa, home to about one-fifth of Egypt's estimated 105 million people. The three governorates consist of Cairo governorate (population in 2017: 9.57 million), Giza governorate (8.66 million), and Qalioubia governorate

(5.65 million), for a total of about twenty-four million people.[4] These numbers are likely to be undercounts, largely because the 2006 census left out many informal areas on the periphery of the city, and it's not clear that the 2017 census did any better at capturing these areas. Nor did the 2006 national census count refugees or migrants. During the planning for the 2017 census there were discussions about doing so, but the current data make no mention of refugees, migrants, or foreigners.

To understand the impact of refugees and migrants on an old and enormous city like Cairo, it's useful to know how the city landscape has evolved and where the different refugee groups live. Perhaps the best explanation of Cairo's urban landscape is put forward by one of its long-standing expatriate residents, the urban planner and historian David Sims. Sims divides Greater Cairo into three "urban forms": the formal city; the informal city; and the new desert cities. Each of these urban forms, Sims says, contains its own causes, rules, and norms, and with some overlapping at their edges, each is legally and physically separated.[5] For our purposes, using a migration lens reveals how each form contains neighborhoods that have been transformed by both the rural-to-urban migration of Egypt's own citizens and the arrival of refugees and migrants from other countries. Below, we briefly consider each of Sims's three urban forms.

Greater Cairo Proper: The Formal City

"Greater Cairo Proper" refers to the continuing growth of the formal city, which comprised most of Cairo until the 1950s. (By "formal," Sims means modes of city growth that are mainly legal—that is, real estate and land subdivisions that conform to laws and government controls.) This was the old city about which the Nobel Prize winner Naguib Mahfouz wrote. It included the inner city and "historic" Cairo, with its "narrow and winding streets and jumbled mix of decrepit and monumental buildings," where Egypt's poor and working classes lived in crowded tenement buildings. In districts of Cairo such as al-Gamaliyah, Bulaq, and Bab al-Shariyah, urban densities averaged 2.5 people per room in 1947. Through the 1950s and 1960s, more and more rural peasant farmers (known as *fellahin*) left their farms and moved into these densely populated districts, further exacerbating the "generally deplorable" residential conditions.[6]

This period of rapid urbanization began with the 1952 Egyptian revolution, or Free Officers movement, spearheaded by Gamal Abdel Nasser, which overthrew the Egyptian monarchy and installed a socialist government; it ended with the 1967 war with Israel and Nasser's death in 1970. Under Nasser, the government began partnering with private housing companies and developers to expand Cairo into the agricultural and desert areas around the city, especially along what is known as the Northeast Corridor. Two huge subdivision projects were Madinat Nasr (Nasr City) and Ain Shams, both of which today host large numbers of refugees in various districts. In the 1960s President Nasser established Nasr City, one of the formal city extension projects that made up his modernization plan, and he chose the name (*nasr* is Arabic for "victory"). It began as a 7,000-hectare (70-square-kilometer) concession on state desert land, and today it is the largest district in Cairo, occupying more than 250 square kilometers, with eight shopping malls, a conference center, the prestigious Al-Azhar University, the Cairo Stadium, and many multistory apartment buildings with commercial ground floors—as well as nightmarish traffic congestion. Nasr City is divided into East and West districts (*hayy*): East Madīnat Naṣr (Qism Awwal) and West Madīnat Naṣr (Qism Than), and twenty-five subdistricts. The wealthier subdistricts have upscale malls with international chain stores like H&M

and a suburban culture that reflects the Dubai architecture and upscale lifestyles of the Gulf States. These neighborhoods are populated by middle-class professionals and the nouveau riche, including migrants who have returned from working in the Persian Gulf or have received remittances that enable their families to purchase property in the neighborhood.. These wealthier subdistricts also house better-off refugees, including many Iraqis.

Nasser's government also initiated what Sims calls Egypt's "long and continuing love affair with state-subsidized public housing." This public housing was initially modest and intended to house factory workers, but by the 1960s, larger, more luxurious units were being built for government officials and army officers. Everyone paid nominal rents, however, and most significantly, the tenants and their heirs had rental contracts that gave them perpetual rights against eviction as long as the rent was paid.[7]

From 1967 through the mid-1970s, Egypt's economy was on a wartime footing (the war with Israel ended in 1979 with the Camp David Accord and the Egypt-Israel peace treaty). Army conscription "vacuumed up the labor force," as Sims puts it, and formal urban expansion ended. But by the mid-1970s, President Sadat's Open Door policy—part of his liberalization of the economy known as *al-Infitah*—began to transform Cairo. The economy surged, and Egyptians could travel abroad freely. Neighboring oil-rich countries (the Gulf States and Libya), awash with cash after the oil price hikes in 1973 and 1979, brought in migrant labor, and hundreds of thousands of Egyptian workers began to send remittances back to their families in Egypt. Local entrepreneurs, oil companies, banks, and import-export companies were established across Cairo. A real estate boom was accompanied by new infrastructure: bridges, highways, and the first metro line. Also rising was the largely uncontrolled building of tower block housing and floors added onto existing buildings.[8] This expansion of formal Cairo was mainly toward the northeast, and it continues in the present day.

From the 1980s through the 2000s, formal Cairo, especially the historic downtown area around Tahrir Square, underwent significant depopulation as the government cleared the tenement slums for prestige projects. The downtown area became commercialized as housing was converted into small factories, warehouses, and wholesale operations, and old and decrepit housing stock was not refurbished. People moved—or were relocated by the government—to the new urban development sites such as Nasr City. Many Somali and Sudanese refugees and migrants moved with the relocating Egyptian families. One such refugee was Hassan, who had moved into Ard al-Lewa, one of the many poor slum neighborhoods where migrants are concentrated, when he first arrived in Cairo. He left Ard al-Lewa in 2008 to move to Hay al-Ashr, one of the ten subdistricts of Nasr City. (Nasr City's first five subdistricts have names, but subdistricts 6–10 are referred to by their respective numbers; Hayr al-Ashr means "tenth neighborhood.")

When he first moved to "Ashr," as it is known, Hassan liked the area. Rents and living costs were more affordable, and at that time, the area was less congested and crowded compared to Cairo's old inner-city neighborhoods like Ard al-Lewa. As Hassan described it, Ashr had an open feel, and its wide main streets and buildings were laid out in a somewhat organized plan. Today, things are different. Nasr City is now just as congested as downtown Cairo, and getting downtown—or worse, across town—can be a one- to two-hour trip, depending on traffic and the combination of public transportation used. Public transportation might include *tuk-tuks* (three-wheeled motorized rickshas, of which there are an estimated four million in Cairo), microbuses or larger public buses, and possibly the Cairo metro, depending on the route one prefers.

In the poorer subdistricts of Nasr City like Hay al-Ashr, poor and working-class Egyptians live alongside refugees and migrants. There are South Sudanese and Sudanese from the states of Nuba Mountains, Blue Nile, and Darfur. There are Congolese, Nigerians, and other West Africans. The Somalis cluster in a part of Ashr called Saqr Quresh, where Hassan lived. Living conditions and the architecture are basic. The buildings are mostly old and decrepit apartment blocks that crowd together on either side of narrow dirt alleyways. Open spaces are filled with construction rubble and garbage, the territory of Cairo's street dogs. There are no parks, green spaces, or even trees other than the occasional dusty palm.

In March 2019, when Ryan and I visited Hassan, he was sharing a flat with two other Somali men. Their fifth-floor apartment was at the top of a crumbling stairwell with unglazed windows that let in the hot city air. The dimly lit flat had a spacious living room lined with floor cushions, a large TV, a small kitchen, and two bedrooms. At that time, the rent was E£2,000 per month (then about $400), and utilities cost another E£100 per month ($20). Hassan and his roommates were lucky to have a gas line for their stove, which meant they didn't have to lug a heavy gas canister (known as an *annboba*) up the stairs every few weeks. Their landlord, an Egyptian professor living in Spain, sent his wife or adult children—who lived nearby in a more expensive area—to collect the rent each month. This arrangement suited Hassan, as some landlords required their tenants to send their rent in the form of a money order, which cost additional fees. But Hassan worried about being able to pay the rent. When Egyptians couldn't pay on time, landlords would usually allow a grace period of three months, but they rarely did this for refugees. Instead, refugees got a warning, then had to pay or be evicted. At the time of our visit, Hassan's lease was for one year, and he knew the rent would go up when the lease ended. Recently, he told us, landlords had begun asking refugees to pay more rent even before the end of the lease—and refugees could do nothing about it. If they argued, the landlords told them they could leave; there were many other refugees who would take their place. Hassan knew families who had missed a single rent payment and been evicted.

In Cairo, as in many host cities, refugees usually pay higher rent than local citizens. Until the 1990s, Egypt's long-standing tenant laws protected poor Egyptians from rent increases, and many Egyptians had rent-controlled contracts that kept rents low and protected renters against eviction. A law introduced in 1996 allowed contracts to be renewed annually, removed rent-control limitations, and eased eviction procedures. Foreigners continue to pay higher rents because they are usually only able to rent (not to buy) under the new law and are less able to negotiate the rent.

The Informal City

The second type of urban form identified by David Sims is the informal city. Until the 1960s, there were no informal settlements in Cairo; today, some 70 percent of the city's population lives in such areas. Sims defines informal areas in Cairo by their "small building footprints, 100 percent plot coverage and little or no allocation for public open spaces or social facilities," and surmises that the first such settlements began in the early 1960s while the government was looking the other way, focused on "creating new socialist zones and prestige heavy industry."[9] These informal settlements grew during the war years, from 1967 to 1975, when formal expansion in Egypt had stopped. During this period, urban migration to the cities increased with (among other movements) the evacuation of nearly a million people from the Suez Canal Zone to Cairo, but the supply of formal housing stayed the same. Nasr City and other newly developed parts of formal Cairo absorbed many Egyptians and migrants, but starting in the 1970s, many more moved to Cairo's desert and agricultural fringes, where new housing was rapidly being built—without state authorization.

The informal settlements were built mostly by private entrepreneurs or developers who purchased the land from farmers. As state-owned land or privately owned agricultural land became subdivided, small traditional villages and farmland disappeared under the rush of construction. The rate of growth—both of population and of land development—was almost three times that of Cairo's formal city. Most growth was in the peri-urban areas north and south of the city. The expansion was "polycentric"—that is, existing villages and hamlets expanded into the surrounding agricultural plain where land and housing were cheaper and developers and individual buyers had less trouble with the government prohibition of development on agricultural land. This urbanization of agricultural land occurred because even though the agricultural land was highly productive, farmers could make more money from selling their land for building than from farming.

Once the buildings were constructed, the inhabitants or their landlords might have legal ownership rights to the land, but the structures and buildings themselves were illegal because the land was zoned for agriculture. This did not really create problems, however, because urban authorities took a laissez-faire approach, and their tolerance was supported by a "well-consolidated system of clientelism and corruption" that made residents dependent on the "benevolence" of public authorities.[10] Since the 1970s, these unplanned, informal areas, known as *'ashwā'iyyat* in Egypt, have vastly outgrown formal housing.[11] Cairo's informal areas are unlike the typical shantytowns with shacks made of scrap wood, metal sheets, and tarps found in cities in poor countries. Rather, Cairo's informal city consists of vast areas of multistory apartment blocks made of brick and concrete that look much like the buildings found in formal areas of Cairo. The difference is that the planning and construction of these apartment blocks are generally illegal, or semi-legal at best.

Until the 1990s, the government did little to incorporate informal settlements into formal Cairo. The settlements lacked services and public infrastructure like community water taps, sewage systems, and electricity. Residents made do by linking their apartments to available infrastructure, pirating electricity lines and septic tanks. During the 1990s the government began to worry about the growing popularity in the 'ashwa'iyyat of Islamist groups like the Muslim Brotherhood, especially after the 1992 earthquake, when the Brotherhood actively supported the recovery of the affected areas around Dahshur, about eighteen kilometers south of Cairo.[12] The government began to provide electricity, water, and sanitation in some informal areas, even though the buildings were technically illegal. Residents were then able to request connections from the water and electricity companies, which gave them an official government document with their name and address. These documents created a paper trail connecting the owner to the property and eventually provided residents with more stability and a degree of formality—a step toward tenure security.

By the end of the 1990s, many of Cairo's informal areas had access to infrastructure, and the building process shifted from an owner-built incremental approach, in which individuals added one floor or room at a time, to developers building high-rise buildings. Over time, as informal settlements grew and stabilized, the real estate market got in on the act. Developers brought in capital and flipped properties and land for profit. Unlike the older, incrementally built buildings, the new high-rises were usually completed before going on the market. Although such apartment buildings are capital intensive, and the insecurity of land titles would normally discourage investment, developers saw the market potential. Today these high-rise buildings—some as high as twenty stories—are a dominant feature of Cairo's landscape and occupy a large share of the housing market.[13] Demand is driven by people who can afford to buy or rent a fully built unit in a prime location with access to services and infrastructure, at a much lower price than a comparable unit in the formal market. The high-density informal settlements mean millions of people can live closer to work opportunities, with relatively decent living standards. However, because the ten- to twenty-floor buildings are often on streets designed for two-story buildings, they tend to have limited privacy, ventilation, and sunlight.

Cairo's informal areas are not restricted to the high-rise settlements on the periphery of the city. Within the formal city, there are pockets of 'ashwa'iyyat. As Deen Sharp notes, "Urban Egypt is not dominated by urban informality on one side and urban formality on another, but by haphazard urbanisation in which anything can be made to appear formal or informal if there is the will and power to do so." Since coming to power in 2014, the military regime of President Abdel Fattah el-Sisi has announced its intention to eliminate 'ashwa'iyyat as part of Egypt Vision 2030. The regime sees these areas as a threat to the nation.[14]

The third urban form identified by Sims is the "New Cities" in Cairo's western and eastern deserts. In Chapter 15 we discuss one, 6th of October City.

Where the Refugees Live in Egypt and Cairo

Refugees have settled in towns throughout Egypt, usually clustering by nationality in neighborhoods in both formal and informal cities. Most live in Greater Cairo and its satellite desert cities, but Alexandria, Egypt's second-largest city, hosts just under a quarter of

Table 14.1. Refugees in Greater Cairo and Egypt's Other Towns (2010-21)

	2021		2020	
	Syrian	Other	Syrian	Other
Greater Cairo	81,409	71,621	78,030	69,914
Cairo	23,561	44,479	22,866	44,018
Giza	38,185	26,918	36,940	25,679
Kalobeyei	19,663	224	18,224	217
Alexandria	21,459	1,293	20,809	1,243
Next-biggest cities				
al-Sharkia	10,824	165	10,170	161
Damietta	9,277	28	8,735	34
Dakahliya	3,586	75	3,170	103
Monofiya	2,468	17	2,313	18
Gharbeya	1,090	34	954	45

Source: UNHCR, Demographics with Locations.

the Syrian population (21 percent), and the delta town of Damietta hosts about 9 percent. Smaller numbers of Syrians live in al-Sharkia governorate, particularly 10th of Ramadan City, an industrial area where refugees find employment (see Table 14.1).

In Greater Cairo, refugees and migrants live in twenty-two districts and neighborhoods (see Table 14.2). Syrians—by far the largest population of refugees in Cairo—have tended to move away from central Cairo; over half the registered Syrian refugees resides in 6th of October City. They also live in another satellite city, al-Obour (about fifty kilometers northeast of downtown Cairo), and East Nasr City, 10th of Ramadan City, al-Rehab City, Jissr al-Swiss, Madinaty, Sadat

Table 14.2. Geographic Distribution of Cairo's Refugees by Nationality

Neighborhood	Syrian	Sudanese	South Sudanese	Eritrean	Ethiopian	Iraqi	Somali	Yemeni
Central-north Cairo (east side of the Nile)								
Ain Shams		X	X					
Matareya			X					
Abbassia		X	X					
Hadayek al-Zaytoun		X						
Helmiyat al-Zaytoun		X			X			
Heliopolis	X	X				X		
East Cairo								
Araba wa Nus		X	X					
Hay al-Ashr		X	X				X	
Hay al-Tasa'							X	
Hay al-Sabia							X	
Nasr City (esp. 10th district)	X					X	X	

(continued)

Table 14.2. (continued)

Neighborhood	Syrian	Sudanese	South Sudanese	Eritrean	Ethiopian	Iraqi	Somali	Yemeni
South Cairo (east side of the Nile)								
Arab Maadi		X	X		X			
Hadayek al-Maadi		X	X		X		X	
Helwan	X	X						
Maadi	X	X	X		X		X	
West Cairo								
Ard al-Lewa		X		X	X		X	
Baragel		X						
Bulaq al-Daqrur		X						
Dokki		X						X
al-Marg		X						
Faisal	X	X		X	X	X		X
Mohandiseen		X		X	X	X		

Satellite cities			
6th of October City	X	X	X
10th of Ramadan City	X		
al-Obour City	X		
al-Rehab City	X		X
Jissr al-Swiss	X		X
Madinaty	X		
Sadat City	X		
Tagmouh 1 and 5	X	X	

Source: Ryan Philip, "Getting By on the Margins," Cairo, Egypt Case Report (Refugees in Towns Project, Tufts University, 2018), https://refugeesintowns.net/all-reports/cairo-2018.

City (Menofia governorate), and Tagmouh 1 and 5. There are large concentrations of South Sudanese in Ain Shams, Matareya, Abbassia, and Maadi, and pockets of Sudanese in the other three central-north Cairo neighborhoods. In 6th of October they cluster in the subdistrict of Masaken Osman. Eritreans and Ethiopians also live in these areas, and in Ard al-Lewa, Mohandiseen, and Faisal, as well as 6th of October, Maadi, and Ain Shams. Eritrean refugees tend to separate into Christian and Muslim communities, and Ethiopian Oromos live separately from Amharas. Somalis live in the subdistricts of Nasr City like Hay al-Ashr, and in Maadi and 6th of October.[15]

Refugees of the same nationality tend to live near each other in specific neighborhoods because doing so provides the protection and resources that come from community networks. It is these neighborhoods, rather than the whole city, that are transformed by the presence of refugees.

15

The Bus to 6th of October:
The Desert Cities and UNHCR

It is 6 A.M., and Ramses Station, Cairo's main rail and subway station, is thronged with thousands of workers, heading to the subway stop called al-Shohoda (the martyrs) or to a microbus taxi to take them to work. The train station—officially "Mubarak" until the 2011 revolution, but everyone calls it Ramses—links other Egyptian cities to Cairo. Outside, there is a swarm of buses, microbuses, tuk-tuks, and cars, most of them honking. Even late at night, the noise is deafening. Microbus drivers shout out their routes, and street vendors hawking small goods and clothes have a megaphone playing a loop of what they are selling. To a newcomer, the place seems chaotic, but to Cairenes like Hassan, it is normal.

As he does every workday, Hassan caught a microbus taxi from Ashr to arrive at Ramses by 6 A.M., and now he threads his way through the crowd to the area where the microbuses and taxis are headed for 6th of October City. The drivers are standing around shouting out their route and encouraging passengers—they won't leave until their vehicle is filled. On weekday early mornings, some drivers head directly to UNHCR. As Hassan approaches, a driver grabs his arm and asks, "Mofwadiyeh?" as UNHCR is known.[1] Hassan knows that since he is a black man and at Ramses that early, the driver assumes he is a refugee going to UNHCR. The microbus is almost full, with eight passengers, and Hassan jumps into the last seat next to the driver. Everyone in the bus passes their fare (usually around one to three Egyptian pounds, or 30 cents) up to the front and the driver counts it to make sure everyone is covered. Then he pulls out into the traffic and Hassan assumes the duty of the person riding shotgun in a microbus—he organizes the money and distributes change to people who paid with a five- or ten-pound note. Already the passengers are preparing to sleep, making their jackets into pillows against the windows or leaning forward on their arms; they catch up on sleep during the commute that sometimes takes two hours in Cairo's snarled traffic. Hassan tips his cap over his eyes and dozes off as the driver wends his way across the crowded Nile bridge to the highway on-ramp. The highway west to 6th of October City is raised above the desert, and the taxi is at eye level with the upper floors of the high-rise, low-income apartment buildings of Giza. There is a short stretch where green fields of vegetables and palm trees relieve the bleak desert sand. But this greenness is shrinking as the cities of Giza and 6th of October expand toward each other, and soon the desert resumes until the sand-colored concrete buildings of 6th of October City emerge like a mirage.

As Cairo has grown, the government has created satellite cities on desert land, one of which is 6th of October, thirty-two kilometers west of Cairo. Named after the start date of the 1973 Arab-Israeli War, 6th of October is one of Egypt's first new desert cities, and part of President Anwar Sadat's legacy. Cairo is typical of old urban metropoles that government leaders see as having become overpopulated, traffic-clogged, and decrepit, and instead of tackling these problems, decide to build new cities. These may be satellite cities on the fringes of the metropole, or sometimes entire new capitals at a distance from the old cities. Nigeria, for example, in the 1980s planned and built the city of Abuja more than 700 kilometers away from Lagos, the country's capital and most populous city, and then made Abuja the new capital in December 1991. Likewise, Egypt has been building its New Administrative Capital (it does not yet have a name) since 2015 in a largely undeveloped area halfway between the Nile River and the Suez Canal, about forty-five kilometers east of Cairo.[2]

The idea of expanding Cairo into the desert has been around since the 1950s, but it was not until 1974 that President Sadat initiated an official policy of constructing desert cities throughout Egypt. The "new towns" policy was created by city planners who considered Cairo too difficult to rehabilitate and believed it would be easier to build new satellite cities in the desert. Urban development was thereafter directed away from Cairo and Alexandria and toward the new desert towns. By 2019 there were twenty-two completed or partly built new cities, and the New Urban Communities Authority had plans to build nineteen more. According to some estimates, about seven million people live in them, a much smaller number than the planners envisioned. Some new towns have seen population increases, including in the wealthy gated neighborhoods on Cairo's outskirts, such as those in Sheikh Zayed City. But most Cairenes cannot afford to move to the new cities, or they feel they are too far from "home," or they simply choose to avoid the "sprawling but largely lifeless suburbs" promoted by developers and the state. Instead, as noted in Chapter 14, most urban expansion has occurred "informally" in Giza and Cairo's peripheral areas, whose (largely uncounted) residents add housing as they find funds.

One of the most successful satellite cities is 6th of October. Construction began in the 1980s, with large areas allocated as industrial zones to draw investors. Over the years, public and private businesses moved there, and today there are eight shopping malls, including the giant Saudi-developed Mall of Arabia, the third-largest mall in Africa.[3] As with the other desert cities, the government aimed to have

6th of October attract public and private investment and draw people from Cairo, Alexandria, and the crowded Nile valley. At first, there was mixed success. Egyptians were slow to move in the numbers the government wanted. By the time Hassan arrived in Egypt in 2008, 6th of October had about 160,000 inhabitants, but relative to Cairo's population increase, its population had not grown by much.[4]

One group, however, immediately saw the benefits of moving. After Syrian refugees continued to arrive in 2012, some moved to 6th of October, and gradually others joined them.[5] If new arrivals had family or other connections there, that is where they headed. Today 6th of October is a good example of a city where refugees of the same nationality span the spectrum from poverty to affluence. Many Syrians live in districts like District 7 (where UNHCR is located), or the area around Al-Hosary Mosque, where they have rejuvenated the city with shops and restaurants. Other refugees live in low-income districts like Masaken Osman and Beyt al-'Ayla, where rents are lower but crime is higher. As we shall see in Chapter 16, the Syrians have had a dramatic effect on 6th of October.

One organization that chose to move to 6th of October City was UNHCR, which relocated from its Cairo location in 2006. This was a controversial decision. The move happened after events in 2005 when a refugee protest in one of Cairo's parks ended very badly. In September 2005, Sudanese refugees began occupying a protest camp in a park in front of Mustafa Mahmoud Mosque in Mohandiseen, an upscale suburb of Cairo, where UNHCR had an office. The camp had been organized by a Sudanese refugee group called Refugee Voices, and the refugees were protesting UNHCR's lack of services and low resettlement rates. Negotiations with UNHCR were unsuccessful, and UNHCR closed its office in mid-November, saying it was forced to suspend operations by the sit-in. Despite UNHCR's attempts to negotiate with the government, the occupation ended violently in December 2005, with the Egyptian police storming the park and shooting refugees. An estimated twenty-eight (or as many as 100) Sudanese were killed, and many more wounded. The Egyptian police forcibly dismantled the camp and detained more than 2,000 protesters. Refugees and their advocates blamed UNHCR for the outcome, and the organization was widely excoriated.[6] Its move to 6th of October City a few months later was widely seen as an effort to distance itself from the refugees in Cairo (see Box 15.1).

UNHCR's new location made it difficult for refugees who did not live in 6th of October to reach the organization's office. Besides the distance and time required to get there from Cairo, the office is barricaded behind security reinforcement. Like most UN compounds around the world, the office compound has a wall topped with razor wire surrounding it, and much of the street is blocked off with cement barricades known as Jersey barriers, intended to prevent truck and car bombs. These security measures were put in place after the attacks on UN agencies that began in the early 2000s. The most notorious occurred in August 2003, when a suicide bomber drove a truck full of explosives into the UN headquarters in Baghdad (Iraq), killing twenty-two UN staff and injuring 150 local and international aid workers. Since then, there have been other car bomb attacks on UN quarters, including the attacks on the UN offices in Algiers in December 2007, which killed seventeen UN staff members, and on the United Nations House in Abuja in August 2011, which killed twenty-three people including eleven UN staff and wounded more than eighty people.[7] There have been multiple attacks on individual UN and other humanitarian workers over the past two decades. Security measures are now required for all UN staff, including that they travel in vehicles that have been hardened against mines and gunfire.

In conflict-affected countries such as Sudan and Somalia, UN staff are heavily restricted in their movements. In Mogadishu, for

Box 15.1. Protests outside UNHCR

These kinds of protests outside UNHCR offices by refugees, especially Sudanese, have occurred in other countries too, with less deadly but equally unsuccessful results. In Jordan in late 2015, hundreds of Sudanese staged a sit-in outside UNHCR's Amman office, hoping to improve recognition of their rights as refugees and asylum seekers and to receive better treatment from the agency. A previous protest in 2014 had ended after Jordanian police made the Sudanese leave the site. This time, the Sudanese camped out for a month in the upscale neighborhood of Khalda before the police dismantled the camp. The police took some 800 protesters—men, women, and children—to a holding facility near the airport, and over the next few days the Jordanian authorities deported over one hundred protesters to Sudan. It was reported that they were detained and questioned on arrival in Khartoum and that some were harassed and intimidated by Sudanese authorities.

Protests by African refugees in African countries have similarly resulted in failure or deportations. In Cape Town (South Africa) in October 2019, there was a sit-in protest outside the UNHCR offices by refugees and asylum seekers from African countries. They wanted to be resettled outside South Africa because they did not feel safe from the ongoing xenophobic attacks in South Africa's townships. The protest campaign lasted five months, with hundreds of people taking part, including members of the Central Methodist Church in Greenmarket Square, which gave the protesters refuge. At the end, the police tried to forcibly evict them using stun grenades. The South African authorities then deported twenty refugees and asylum seekers.

What explains these responses by city authorities? It is possible that they reflect discrimination based on refugees' race or national origin or perceived cultural dissimilarities. There is plenty of scholarship exploring these factors in the differential treatment of refugees. But it is also the case that most cities are safe places of refuge only as long as the refugees refrain from political protest and behave like "good" or "deserving" refugees. As many have noted, this pressure to behave silences refugees and asylum seekers and undermines their sense of belonging.

> *Sources:* Rochelle Davis et al., "Sudanese and Somali Refugees in Jordan: Hierarchies of Aid in Protracted Displacement Crises," *Middle East Report* 46, no. 2 (2016): 2–10; "Refugees in South Africa: 'Give us a place where we can be safe,'" BBC News, February 2, 2020, https://www.bbc.com/news/world-africa-51284576; "South Africa Deports African Migrants after Protests," BBC News, November 6, 2020, https://www.bbc.com/news/world-africa-54845418; and Kelsey P. Norman, *Reluctant Reception: Refugees, Migration and Governance in the Middle East and North Africa* (Cambridge: Cambridge University Press, 2021), esp. chap. 6, "Differential Treatment by Nationality." Most of the substantial literature on the good refugee is focused on Europe and Australia. See, for example, Heidi Hetz, "The Concept of the 'Good Refugee' in Cambodian and Hazara Refugee Narratives and Self-Representation," *Journal of Refugee Studies* 35, no. 2 (2022): 874–892, https://doi.org/10.1093/jrs/feab075; and Rohan Miller Davis, "The 'Bad' and Exceptionally 'Good': Constructing the African Refugee," *Media International Australia* 179, no. 1 (2020), https://doi.org/10.1177/1329878X20926540. For a rare study of the phenomenon in Africa, see Clayton Boeyink, "The 'Worthy' Refugee: Cash as a Diagnostic of 'Xeno-racism' and 'Bio-Legitimacy,'" *Refuge* (Toronto English edition) 35, no. 1 (2019): 61–71, https://doi.org/10.7202/1060675ar.

example, all UN staff live and work in the UN compound near the airport and seldom venture into the city itself. If they do, it is always with a heavily secured armed escort, and there is very little interaction between the people on the ground and the UN staff in their large white Land Cruisers.[8] While such precautions are understandable, they have the effect of segregating UN staff from the local people with whom they work and whom they are there to protect. For the city, it means that the UN compound becomes an enclave cut off from the daily business of the city.

By 8 A.M., Hassan's microbus had made it to the UNHCR stop in 6th of October City. Hassan disembarked with the other passengers, a mix of refugees and UNHCR national staff who didn't own cars or who preferred taking the microbus to driving. (Most UNHCR international staff took the UNHCR bus from upscale neighborhoods like Zamalek where many expats lived, or they had their own cars with drivers.) Hassan walked down the street, winding past the Jersey barriers, until he reached the UNHCR building. Across the road, in a small vacant lot, refugees waited for their appointments with UNHCR intake staff, and Hassan stopped to greet a Somali woman he knew. The lot was often crowded, and the refugees' presence was not welcomed by the Egyptian neighbors—who sometimes called the police to remove them. Occasionally the refugees held protests outside the UNHCR office. In 2016, an Ethiopian refugee doused himself with gas and lit a match. Another refugee tried to put out the flames, but her clothes caught fire too, and they both died.[9] (In late 2021 the 6th of October municipality offered this vacant lot to UNHCR, which according to UNHCR "has improved the queueing and screening system, and streamlined security mechanisms, reducing the risk of unrest, violence and criminality in the outside waiting area.")[10] Today the area is quiet. Two women wearing Sudanese *thobes* (the traditional garments of Sudanese women, consisting of a long colorful fabric wrap worn over a dress) sat on the dusty grass under a palm tree with their children. Hassan showed his UN ID at the security office, put his backpack through the X-ray machine, and reported for work three hours after he left home at 5 A.M.

Hassan began working at UNHCR a year or so after he came to Cairo; he is one of the many staff, both Egyptian nationals and refugees, who are hired locally. These so-called national hires are different from international UN staff and contractors who are brought in from other countries, and they are paid on a different scale. Although Hassan's pay was reasonable, and working for a UN agency was and is widely regarded as a highly desirable job, Hassan didn't like working for UNHCR because of its unpopularity with the refugees. One reason was the lingering resentment dating back to the protest debacle in

2005, but a bigger reason was the unequal treatment of Syrian and non-Syrian refugees—which occurs throughout the Middle East.

These "hierarchies of aid" in the Middle East are well documented.[11] In Egypt, as elsewhere, international aid organizations such as WFP and UNHCR divide the refugee population into Syrians and non-Syrians (that is, Africans, Iraqis, Yemenis, and other groups) and mete out separate and unequal treatment. This is not entirely the aid organizations' fault: donor countries like the European Union and United States earmark relief for Syrians, which means Syrian refugees receive the most international assistance. For example, in 2016 WFP gave food vouchers to 30 percent of registered Syrian refugees in Egypt and no food assistance to non-Syrian refugees. This inequity was corrected in 2019, when WFP began providing food assistance to all refugees who qualified based on their needs, not just Syrians.[12] However, by the time this change happened, the view that Syrians received preferential treatment was well established and had created animosity toward both UNHCR and Syrians on the part of many refugees throughout the Middle East. UNHCR is also unpopular because refugees blame the organization for the lack of financial assistance and medical care and lack of support for education. Some refugees perceive UNHCR as a corrupt institution because they believe the organization receives a lot of funding and yet they see little help in their day-to-day lives.[13] What kind of funding does UNHCR Egypt receive, how is this funding disbursed, and do Egyptians and Egyptian cities benefit from it?

Humanitarian Funding in Cairo

As the refugees in Egypt know, there are indeed two different international responses to refugees, depending on their national origin. One is specifically for Syrian refugees, as set out in the Regional Refugee and Resilience Plan 2020–21 (3RP), which supports Syrian refugees and host populations in neighboring countries. The 3RP sought a budget of US$159 million from donors in 2020 and US$172 million in 2021. The other plan, for non-Syrian refugees, is the Egypt Response Plan (ERP) for Refugees and Asylum-seekers from Sub-Saharan Africa, Iraq, and Yemen, which was launched in 2019. This plan—which also includes funds for the host populations—sought US$89.6 million in 2020 and US$99.6 million in 2021.[14] In 2020–21 Syrians comprised 51 percent of the total number of refugees and asylum seekers in Egypt, but they were targeted for almost twice as much funding as non-Syrians.

Egypt's humanitarian funding profile fits the global pattern. In 2022, humanitarian funding in Egypt amounted to over US$165 million, of which 96 percent came from governments (mainly two: Germany and the United States together accounted for 87 percent of the total). As in most host countries, this funding was mainly channeled through UN agencies and it focused on food assistance for refugees. The WFP received 68 percent ($112.8 million), by far the largest proportion, and UNHCR received 15 percent ($25 million). Together, these two agencies received more than 84 percent of the funds. Almost all of the non-UN agencies that received humanitarian funding were international NGOs, often partnering with local community-based organizations that include Egyptians. The only listed local organization that received direct funding was St. Andrew's Refugee Services (a Christian church–based organization established and run mostly by expats), which received US$398,361, well under 1 percent of total funding.[15] In Egypt, as elsewhere, despite much rhetoric at the global level about channeling more humanitarian funding to local and national actors, this has not come to pass. In 2022 there was significant growth worldwide in humanitarian funding from donors, but no shift in how it was disbursed. The proportion of humanitarian assistance directly provided to local and national actors remained at just 1.2 percent (US$485 million).[16]

In terms of development assistance, unlike Tripoli, Cairo did not receive support for new infrastructure. Neither the Egyptian government nor Cairo city authorities leveraged the international community to obtain concessionary funding related to hosting refugees, as Jordan did.

Refugee Resettlement from Egypt

Many urban refugees hope for resettlement to western countries, but they sometimes have misconceptions about what UNHCR can and cannot do when it comes to resettlement. Some believe that UNHCR prevents them from being resettled, when in fact, UNHCR pushes hard in face of the fact that very few countries are willing to resettle refugees, as noted in Chapter 2. The global shortage of slots means UNHCR uses resettlement strategically, as a protection tool to help refugees who are at high risk. Risk factors include being a survivor of violence and/or torture or human trafficking or other forms of mistreatment and abuse. Other risk factors that make refugees eligible for resettlement are "compelling legal and physical protection needs arising from a lack of legal status in Egypt, women and girls and unaccompanied children at risk of exploitation, harassment and abuse, and individuals with serious medical condition or disability."[17] The need for this narrow focus means UNHCR estimates that only 10 percent of the refugee population are eligible for resettlement. Even then, there will never be enough slots. In Egypt, by the end of 2024, out of some 877,000 refugees and asylum seekers registered with UNHCR, only 3,000 refugees were resettled and another 2,060 refugees and asylum seekers departed the country after accessing what UNHCR calls "complementary pathways" (such as family reunification, labor mobility, education, and private sponsorship programs).[18] Together, less than 1 percent of the refugees in Egypt were given a way out of the country.

Although relatively few refugees ever get resettled from Egypt, the fact that UNHCR Egypt has a resettlement program at all is likely a draw for refugees from host countries that do not have such a program. Knowing that any resettlement occurs at all gives refugees the hope that they might be lucky and qualify, and the existence of a resettlement program is likely another draw for refugees to come to a city like Cairo—along with the hope of finding work, or because they have family or other community there, or because they are seeking to migrate on to another city or country.[19]

Misconceptions about resettlement persist because UNHCR is not good at communicating with refugees in cities about its programs and constraints. For one thing, UNHCR staff rarely come into direct contact with the refugees. Few refugees ever meet an officer after their initial interview to determine whether they warrant asylum status. This is in part because of the UN's strict security requirements. But even in countries with lower security thresholds, like Egypt, UNHCR staff do not spend much time in the neighborhoods where refugees live; they tend to keep to their fortified offices. During Hassan's time in Egypt, the UNHCR community officer, whose job it is to help refugees with their daily problems, was not permitted to travel to Cairo's poor refugee neighborhoods.[20] In my own experience, when I have asked refugees and their community leaders who live in cities like Kampala, Cairo, and Tripoli, most said they rarely encountered UNHCR staff outside their offices. This lack of contact means there is social distance between the organization and the refugees living in cities, and consequent suspicion and lack of faith on both sides. The disconnect between UNHCR and urban refugees is not helped by UNHCR's policy of rotating staff out of field offices every few years. No sooner does an officer start to understand the local politics—which can take years—then he or she is transferred to another work situation.

The kind of assistance UNHCR and other humanitarian agencies make available to refugees in Cairo is like that of other host countries without encampment policies. Most assistance takes the form of cash assistance to buy food. As in Lebanon, UNHCR in Egypt determines a refugee's eligibility to receive WFP assistance using a targeting process. At registration, UNHCR gathers information about the refugee's "vulnerability criteria"—that is, their financial situation, number of family members, access to other assistance, special needs, protection risks, medical conditions, and so forth. This information is scored and entered onto a spreadsheet, and then UNHCR's algorithms determine the cutoffs. Refugees who fall below the vulnerability score cutoff are eligible for food assistance. UNHCR then sends the list of eligible refugees (that is, those deemed to be in most need) to WFP, which then provides food assistance in the form of a cash transfer. A "personal beneficiary card" is issued to the refugee (or head of household) who can use it to get food at WFP partner retail stores or cash from over 140,000 points of sale nationwide.[21]

Other refugee assistance comes in the form of education and health care. The Egyptian government allows refugees and asylum seekers to access both public schools and public primary health care facilities, on par with Egyptian citizens—in theory. At these facilities, refugees receive care for free or at an affordable cost. However, refugees struggle to get good health care, and they are discriminated against in public schools and health facilities. UNHCR therefore supports its NGO "implementing partners" such as Caritas Egypt and Save the Children to provide health services to refugees who can't get the help they need at the public clinics or can't afford medicines, or for special cases like refugees suffering from HIV and/or tuberculosis infections. But whereas refugees don't need to show their refugee card at public facilities, at Caritas clinics, or for services by other UNHCR implementing partners, only registered refugees in good standing can get services.

In Cairo, the extent to which Egyptians benefit from UNHCR's presence or programs is minimal. UNHCR's NGO partners provide what's called "protection" services, mostly in the form of hotlines or safe spaces to deal with issues such as gender-based violence or legal problems. For example, Care Egypt runs two "women-friendly spaces" that hold "sexual and reproductive health awareness sessions, legal awareness sessions, basic psychosocial support sessions, self-defense workshops, gender training for children, and workshops to prevent child marriage."[22] These kinds of awareness-raising sessions and "women's empowerment" programs are made available to Egyptians and to (registered) refugees, so it is fair to say that UNHCR's funding supports Egyptians, too. But the overall reach and impact of such programs is minimal, given the great needs of both Egyptians and refugees.

In general, except for the "most vulnerable" refugees who get cash transfers, most refugees in urban areas receive little help from UNHCR, unless they are facing serious health or legal problems. There is little real support for livelihoods, which would go a long way toward enabling refugees to support themselves. However, UNHCR keeps a low profile when it comes to promoting the employment of refugees, because like many host governments, the Egyptian government does not permit refugees to work. Instead of directly assisting refugees to find work, therefore, UNHCR Egypt's Livelihood Unit supports "local social enterprises" that work with and train refugee artisans to develop a line of products. These are small-scale at best, and they benefit relatively few refugees. But UNHCR is constrained by its mandate as a member-state organization and must abide by host government preferences.

The overall lack of refugee assistance is mainly due to funding shortfalls and government opposition to certain activities, but it means that the refugees tend to have a low opinion of UNHCR, while at the same time, many believe they are owed more by the organization. On the other hand, this invisibility of UNHCR has led to independence on the part of refugees, who must rely on their own people and networks if they are to find work and housing and educate their children. In 6th of October, as in many other cities, refugees have organized themselves to address these problems, as we discuss in Chapters 16 and 17.

16

Refugee Entrepreneurs

When refugees arrive in a city, they need to start earning money—both to support themselves and to begin repaying the substantial debts they and their families back home have incurred to fund their journey. The need for income and a livelihood is paramount, but in most host countries either refugees are not legally permitted to work or it is very difficult and expensive to obtain the documentation needed to work or start a business. Some refugees do have the resources to start their own enterprises—especially the funds and networks, but also the necessary human capital such as mental and physical health and vigor. When they start businesses, it often means significant investment and revenues for the city. Many refugees, those both with and without such resources, work without documentation, which puts them at risk for discrimination or even loss of payment. Unscrupulous employers sometimes refuse to pay their refugee workers, or business partners abscond with funds; they know they won't be reported to the authorities.

These difficulties mean that many refugees seek work with or for their own people. In cities, this is easier because there are usually networks of co-nationals who support newcomers. Semiformal migration industries spring up to provide services to migrants of all kinds: home country foods, music, weddings, and, of course, cross-border activities, as we explored in Chapter 11. Because a city's migrant population—both newcomers and long stayers—often make up large proportions of the population, these migration industries have a significant impact on the cities, particularly for the urban poor (or the "unbanked," as the financial industry refers to them). A refugee influx, by virtue of its concentration of numbers, amplifies this migrant dividend.

One of the most important impacts of migrant and refugee entrepreneurs is how they link cities to the rest of the world, strengthening trade, financial, and communications circuits regionally and globally. Migrants and refugees are more likely than locals to have strong networks—friends, co-religionists, workmates, and family—both in their home countries and in their transit or destination countries. They sustain these connections over time and often derive livelihoods from them. These linkages take many forms; cross-border trade in goods and services is a common livelihood for refugees, who are well positioned to use their local knowledge and networks in both home and host countries. Cross-border trade in goods and services are part of regional subeconomies, which are well established in the cities of Africa and the Middle East (and, of course, elsewhere in the world). They range in size from small cross-border operations to global trading networks.

In Cairo, one example of an urban cross-border operation is health tourism. Hassan introduced Ryan and me to Ahmad, a thirty-year-old Sudanese man from Darfur who was making a good living acting as a *simsar*—a broker or agent who performs various services. In Ahmad's case, these services entailed helping people in Sudan who needed health services that weren't available in Sudan by bringing them to Cairo. Ahmad helped his clients make arrangements to travel to Cairo from Sudan, then met them at the bus station or airport when they arrived, helped them with the immigration authorities, and escorted them to the place he'd found for them to stay. During their stay, he would accompany them to and from the Cairo hospital, ensure that their needs were taken care of during their treatment, and organize their return journey. His services were much in demand, and combined with other part-time gigs around the city, he made a reasonable living.[1]

There were many such informal brokerage services provided by refugees for others from their country. Hassan himself occasionally picked up extra income by tutoring the children of Somali families returning from the United States, Europe, and Canada. (A small but substantial population of Somalis in Cairo and other Muslim countries have returned from western countries because they feel their children are not becoming good Muslims and are being corrupted by western ways.) The brokers draw on their knowledge of both Cairo and their home country. They understand the fears, needs, and desires of their visiting countrymen, and they help them navigate the city, not least because they speak the languages or dialects of both home and the city. These kinds of brokerage services represent the multifaceted livelihoods and gigs based in the informal economy that enable refugees to survive and even thrive in their host cities. New arrivals might join the existing businesses of co-nationals who came in earlier years, or they start entirely new industries or activities. Refugee entrepreneurs are of all nationalities, ages, and types, ranging from older women making a living selling traditional food from street stalls to high-powered businessmen in the tech industry.

Sixth of October is one area of Cairo that has been transformed in this way. It houses a large share of the Syrian businesspeople and investors who moved their businesses from Syria to Cairo after 2011, as well as young people who started new enterprises, sometimes with investment funds transferred from Syria. Many transferred their businesses to Egypt after the war broke out and then continued to invest in Egypt, often traveling back and forth between the two countries. The Syrians who arrived in Egypt early on consisted mainly of those with family connections, business ties, or personal networks, and they included industrial manufacturers. More recently, Egypt has attracted additional Syrian businesses and investors, both in manufacturing, especially the production of textiles and clothing, and in commercial and service sectors such as catering and retailing.[2]

The food sector in particular has flourished. Syrian cuisine is highly appreciated in the Middle East, and Lebanon and Jordan benefited from the arrival of thousands of Syrian food purveyors, large and small, who fled Syria. Egyptians love Syrian falafel (made with chickpeas rather than the fava beans from which Egyptian *taamiya* is made) and *muhammara* (a "salad" or dip containing roasted peppers, walnuts, and pomegranate molasses). Hundreds of Syrians established restaurants, fast-food chains, and street stalls in Greater Cairo, Alexandria, Damietta, and other towns.[3] In 6th of October, the streets of District 2 are filled with Syrian bakeries, restaurants, and other small shops, many with names that include *al-Sham* (the regional word for Syria). Even Egyptian shop owners use this name, both to attract Syrian shoppers and to acknowledge Syrian entrepreneurial prowess. Food shops sell Syrian cheese, flatbread and pastries, and specialty foods imported from Syria (see Figure 16.1).

After work one day, Hassan took Ryan and me to eat in Hossary Square, a bustling open-air food mall with restaurants, coffee shops, and bakeries, almost entirely run by Syrians. Most of the customers were Egyptian. This area used to be a rather run-down part of 6th of October, but now it is thriving. One of the most successful businesses is a Syrian fast-food chain called Rosto. Its founder, Hossam Mardini, had owned five stores back in Damascus, then sold his business and left Syria in 2012 and came to Egypt, where he lived off his savings, hoping he could eventually return home. As the Syrian war intensified, Mardini realized he could not go back, so he and seven friends combined their savings and started Rosto. We found a table in

Figure 16.1. Syrian shawarma shop, Cairo. Source: YouTube, April 9, 2021, from Reem Hanoud, "Syrians in Egypt: Social Acceptance and Successful Business," *Enab Baladi,* October 2, 2023, https://english.enabbaladi.net/archives/2023/10/syrians-in-egypt-social-acceptance-and-successful-business/.

Hossary Square's crowded outdoor courtyard seating area, near huge rotating spits of *mashwi* (roast chicken glistening with fat) and the deli section, which offers a dozen different Syrian "salads." A Sudanese waiter came over and took our order, then brought Ryan and Hassan a *shisha tufa,* the apple-flavored tobacco smoked through a hookah that is ubiquitous in Egypt. Rosto employs both Egyptians and Sudanese and other African refugees. The pay is not good, but it is steady employment. The seating area was crowded with men and women eating and drinking tea, coffee, and nonalcoholic drinks.[4] Next to our table, a group of young women lounged on rattan sofas, smoking shisha and peering at their phones. Smoking shisha used to be for men only, but increasingly, young women are partaking.

Most Syrian businesses in Egypt are small and medium-sized enterprises (employing fewer than fifty individuals). As businesses continue to leave Syria, the Syrian government, concerned about the drain, has sent government representatives to Egypt to encourage Syrian entrepreneurs to return and invest in their homeland, but few have done so. On the contrary, since 2021, more Syrians have moved to Egypt, attracted by investment opportunities there and concerned about the deepening economic crisis and lack of legal and security guarantees in Syria. There is wide speculation about how much Syrian private investment has occurred in Egypt since 2011. One widely cited estimate is that by 2017, Syrian private industry had invested nearly $800 million in Egypt.[5] The Syrian Businessmen Association (SBA) thinks that amount is low, and it has estimated Syrian investments in Egypt at $23 billion, but this cannot be verified. Khaldoun al-Mouakeh, the chairman of the SBA, claimed there were 30,000 Syrian investors in Egypt, of whom more than half are manufacturers employing tens of thousands of people, mostly in Egypt's towns and cities.[6]

Syrians have injected resources and skills into the urban economies of Egyptian towns such as New Damietta, a Nile delta port city that has close historical ties with the southern Syrian town of Saqba. The two towns were their countries' capitals of furniture making, and before the Syrian war, businessmen and artisans moved back and forth between them. When the Syrian war began, many Saqba residents moved to Damietta because of their existing relationships with Egyptians there, and Egyptians welcomed the refugees (at least, prior to the coup in mid-2013). The cost of living and doing business in Damietta was low, and Syrian craftsmen and artisans found jobs in furniture factories or workshops there. By mid-2013, over 8,700 Syrian refugees were living in Damietta. A local economy took root, with Syrian shops and restaurants, and Syrians settled there permanently, some marrying Egyptians. Then the mid-2013 coup occurred, along with a sharp rise in anti-Syrian xenophobia that changed the political climate across Egypt. Damietta, like other cities, saw a surge of anti-Syrian violence and harassment, and many Syrians left the city. Once things calmed down, the Syrians slowly returned. As of September 2021, there were 9,133 refugees in Damietta governorate, almost all Syrian—about 22 percent of the total population of 41,731. Most of them (around 8,500) lived in New Damietta, constituting about 12 percent of New Damietta's 71,342 residents in 2022.[7] They worked in Damietta's leather, furniture, clothing, and engineering industries.

As in many host cities, the potential impact of refugees and migrants on the business sector and the wider economy is constrained by Egyptian bureaucracy, the regulatory environment, and laws about foreign businesses. The regulatory environment for the food services sector alone includes more than fifteen different Egyptian governmental agencies. including the Ministry of Health, Ministry of Environment, local authorities, Ministry of Supplies, and many others that can potentially conduct inspections. Syrians who want to register their business must first register as a working foreigner and then find an Egyptian partner. Then there are six more steps to complete, each rife with the potential for corruption. The International Labour Organization (ILO) said there is "lack of law enforcement and coordination amongst the various entities, and the level of corruption has discouraged restaurant owners from formalizing their enterprises and a high percentage of them are in the informal sector."[8] In business partnerships with Egyptians, the refugee entrepreneur carries all the risk—if their partner absconds with funds or makes accusations, the refugee owner is seldom in a position to fight them in court. Syrian refugees sometimes circumvent these risks by registering their enterprises under Egyptian names or not registering them at all—but these actions also carry risks.

For refugee entrepreneurs, the legal obstacles involved in the bureaucratic process of registering and running a business lead many to forego the process and take their chances in the informal sector. The

ILO study estimated that in 2018, over 80 percent of Syrian food service businesses (including restaurants and all businesses along the food value chain) were in the informal sector.[9] Still, many enterprises persist with the formal route. Rosto's founder chose to find an Egyptian partner, and the Rosto chain started growing. In 2019, it had six branches and employed more than 150 Egyptian and Syrian workers. Other Syrians manage to transfer their savings to Egypt and then invest them in enterprises there. One thirty-five-year-old Syrian expert in IT management brought his family to Egypt ("I would have chosen to move to Dubai . . . but my family . . . wouldn't get a visa there," he said), then invested his savings in Networkers, a start-up that offers IT networking, training, and consultancy services. As his company grew, he settled with his wife and baby in al-Rehab, a city built by the private sector in Cairo's outskirts, where thousands of wealthier Syrian nationals live.[10]

The Egyptians are well aware of this economic transformation. Omar is a well-preserved Egyptian investment banker in his fifties who lives with his extended family in a large, elegantly furnished house with a well-tended rose garden, a lush green lawn, and a swimming pool in Sheikh Zayed City, a new city in Giza governorate between 6th of October and Cairo. Omar is a successful businessman and financier from a wealthy, high-status Egyptian family—"old money." He is well educated, with deep knowledge of Egypt's economy and financial sector. Omar is no liberal. On Egypt's election day in March 2018, he told Ryan and me over dinner that he had voted for General Sisi because Egypt needs a "strong ruling hand," and he liked that Sisi has improved infrastructure, including Egypt's road system, and has embarked on the Suez Canal enlargement. He made no mention of Sisi's dubious human rights record. His wife, who held more liberal views, was embarrassed that her husband had voted in the election at all—let alone for Sisi. (Many Egyptians refused to vote on election day in 2018.) Omar pronounced himself a fan of the Syrians but not of other refugee groups. He liked that the Syrians have transformed what was a moribund area of 6th of October City into a thriving economy, and he thinks Egypt has benefited greatly from their presence. "The Syrians are very much like us Egyptians," he said.[11]

Another Egyptian's view of the Syrian entrepreneurs was offered by Ahmed Alfi, a venture capital investor and the founder of the Greek Campus, Cairo's hub for start-ups and tech companies, located off Tahrir Square in downtown Cairo. Talking to a BBC journalist in October 2015, Alfi said, "Syrian people are by nature traders and merchants. They have always been on the crossroads, so they are very good at starting businesses." He thought that the Syrians who came to Egypt were different—wealthier, usually—than most Syrian refugees in other countries, who lack resources. "Egypt gets a different cross-section of the Syrian refugee population than Europe," Alfi says. "Distance becomes a filtration process, as those coming here are not those crossing the border on foot, and usually have some capital."[12]

The contributions of refugee entrepreneurs to their host cities across Africa and the Middle East, and no doubt, in other host countries, has become a well-researched area. Every city in Africa, large and small, has men and women either starting new businesses or reestablishing enterprises they had in their home countries. The neighborhoods where they locate themselves and their businesses flourish over time. In the Preface I described how Ethiopians and Eritreans have transformed part of the downtown area of Johannesburg, and there are dozens of similar examples. In some cities, business development associations formed by migrants and refugees have asserted their economic power to make claims against the city. In Eastleigh, Nairobi, the Somali business community has mobilized and become empowered over the years—and have begun to fight for their rights. They formed the Eastleigh Business District Association and have twice petitioned to bar tax collection by the Nairobi City County in Eastleigh because of the lack of service provision. Both petitions were dismissed by the High Court of Kenya, but many small-scale traders in Eastleigh said they did not pay taxes because of an "agreement with the government."[13]

As with all entrepreneurs, the kinds of enterprises refugees and migrants engage in include those that are legitimate and based in the formal sector, like Rosto, those that are clearly illicit (like the smugglers of Tripoli), and those that skirt the border between—what Anna Tsing calls the "unruly edge" of capitalism.[14] In Chapter 17, we explore one such enterprise, the informal money transfer business, specifically the Somali hawala in Cairo.

17

"Money Has Come": Remittances and Informal Money Transfers

Financial linkages with their home countries are particularly important for refugees and other migrants, both in terms of investment flows and private transfers. The latter, known as remittances, are the funds sent to refugees' families back home—an important source of revenue both for the families and for the economies of developing countries.[1] The World Bank estimates that officially recorded remittance flows to low- and middle-income countries reached $669 billion in 2023, more than foreign direct investment flows and overseas development assistance. Even during the COVID-19 crisis year 2020–21, remittance flows defied predictions of decline, and flows to low- and middle-income countries reached $540 billion, only 1.6 percent below the 2019 record, exceeding foreign direct investment by a wider margin. In 2023, Egypt continued to be the fifth-largest remittance recipient country in the world, receiving more than $24 billion. Remittances were 10 percent of its gross domestic product and the primary source of foreign income, making Egypt the top recipient of remittances in Africa. Lebanon, Somalia, and South Sudan were among the top five recipients in 2020 in terms of remittances as a share of GDP.[2] Experts surmise that unofficial transfers (that is, those that are not recorded by formal institutions like banks) could be equally as large as formal flows.

Remittances are an important source of support for both refugees in cities and their families back home. It is usually their families who finance the journeys of migrants and refugees, and most go into debt to do so. While some can sell or mortgage their homes or liquidate assets like gold jewelry, many take out loans (sometimes from smugglers) backed by land or livestock assets. Migration loans can be large, depending on the number of people traveling, the departure country, and the distance, and migration debt is sometimes compounded by the need for families to pay ransom money to secure the release of family members held captive by smugglers or traffickers during their journey.[3] On top of these travel-related debts, the families of migrants and refugees back home often have serious financial needs that are linked to the reasons their family members left in the first place. In Eritrea, for example, all Eritreans between eighteen and forty have to participate in unsalaried national service: six months of military training and twelve months of civic duty. Their service is often extended indefinitely, particularly due to the ongoing "no peace, no war" stalemate with neighboring Ethiopia, which in November 2020 erupted into full-scale armed conflict. Extended national service means workers struggle to provide for their families or fulfill their agricultural duties (Eritrea is still primarily an agrarian country). When young people flee the country to avoid national service, the state sometimes imprisons their families or forces them to pay steep fines "as a ransom for the seepage of human capital."[4] Eritrea is unusual only in that most sending countries don't have indefinite national service requirements that create serious financial problems for families. Across the world, refugees' families in their home countries are in similarly desperate straits from some combination of conflict, loss of livelihoods (often due to climate change), and national economic meltdown.

Refugees who reach transit or destination cities thus become vital sources of support for their families back home, who view them as having made it to a safe place and expect them to send financial support. There is unrelenting pressure on those who "make it" to send money home. Anna Lindley's aptly titled book *The Early Morning Phone Call* describes this pressure on Somalis living in London, who, though struggling financially themselves, are constantly pressed by their families in Somalia to send money home.[5] Refugees and migrants need to send money to their families, and they do. The main refugee-producing countries in Africa—Somalia, Eritrea, Ethiopia, Sudan, South Sudan, and the Democratic Republic of the Congo (all with thousands of refugees in Cairo)—are among the countries with the highest remittance rates in Africa. And it's not just Africa, of course. Conflict-affected countries like Iraq, Venezuela, Syria, Burma, Afghanistan, and the countries of Central America all have significant diasporas who send money home.

When refugees first arrive in cities, most of them are broke, having used up their funds or had them stolen or extorted along the way. Confronted with high urban costs of living, new arrivals are themselves in need of money and help. Hassan struggled mightily to make ends meet when he first arrived. He was better-off than many other new arrivals in that he did not have children to worry about, and he had a cousin in Norway who sent him fifty dollars a month. As Hassan put it, "In 2008, fifty dollars was enough to live off. Not enough to enjoy life, but enough to pay the rent and afford necessities."[6] Nonetheless, the pressure to start sending money home began soon after he arrived. It was not until Hassan landed his job with UNHCR that he could begin sending money back to his family in Somalia, and for years afterward he continued to support his family and pay his brothers' school fees.

The Money Transfer Industry

The need for refugees and migrants to send and receive money transfers has led to a huge remittance industry based in the cities of sending, transit, and host countries. This remittance industry spans the formal and informal sectors, including formal money transfer services provided by banks, agencies like Western Union, and digital services like PayPal, and informal money transfer services. One of the problems refugees and migrants face in host cities is the lack of access to formal financial institutions, like banks. Most banks do not want refugees as clients because they are too risky. For one thing, refugees often lack adequate documentation to meet "know your customer" (KYC) requirements.[7] Identifying information is difficult to verify, and refugees often come from highly risky countries. Banks require refugees and migrants to have state-issued documents that indicate the refugee is legally in the country, as well as proof of a recognized street address. In Cairo, to open a bank account a person must have a resident permit valid for more than six months, a passport, and a substantial minimum deposit. Opening a bank account is therefore not a common practice among refugees and migrants.[8]

In Egypt and in many other countries, bank staff might simply decide they don't trust refugees or migrants—perhaps because they don't like the look of them—and elect not to take the risk of allowing them access to bank facilities (see Box 17.1).

Without a bank account, it is not possible to send money to other countries through formal financial institutions. In recent years, new "fintech"—digital financial technologies–such as PayPal and M-PESA make sending remittances easier and cheaper. Older money transfer services like PayPal are expensive, have hidden fees, and offer less favorable exchange rates. Newer online services are constantly emerging.

Box 17.1. Problems with Banks

An example from Tijuana (Mexico) illustrates how some banks treat migrants and refugees. In Tijuana, interviews with bank employees in 2019 revealed that even if a migrant possessed all required documentation to open an account, they could still be denied one if a bank employee suspected the migrant might use their account for illicit purposes. The suspicion could be based entirely on the employee's perception and did not need to be backed up by evidence. Even after a foreign national had established an account, a bank could change its mind, as was the case with a Salvadoran who was denied access to his money by a Mexican bank because of his appearance. He told us that "[the bank employee] tried to humiliate me and claim I was a gang member. I had opened an account with them back when I worked at the manufacturing plant. I went to withdraw money one day and they requested my ID, so I gave them my residency card. Then they requested my passport, so I told them I didn't have one. They saw my tattoos and began to say I was a criminal and belonged to MS13.* . . . I pulled out my phone and called an attorney friend who works for the government. . . . Eventually they all had to take an antidiscrimination course and training on how to treat migrants. . . . They were in training for six months."

Source: Karen Jacobsen and K. Wilson, "Supporting the Financial Health of Refugees: The Finance in Displacement (FIND) Study in Uganda and Mexico" (working paper, Leir Institute, Fletcher School of Law and Diplomacy, Tufts University, 2021), 32.

* The Mara Salvatrucha, or MS13, is a notorious criminal gang that originated in the 1980s in Los Angeles. As the United States deported criminals who were gang members, the gang's power grew. Its reach now extends from Central America to Europe.

For example, WorldRemit, a mobile money transfer company started in September 2010 by a Somali refugee, Ismail Ahmed, has lower fees and is easy to use—with "just a few clicks" people can send money from anywhere, at any time.[9] Despite the growing market share of digital money transfer companies, brick-and-mortar banks and Western Union agencies are still important, especially in poor countries. This is changing as more people use cell phones to conduct their business digitally. But most digital bank and "mobile money" services are still part of formal financial institutions, and because customers must register their bank information with the digital transfer company, they must be existing bank customers. Even if refugees can surmount the KYC obstacles to opening a bank account, using banks or Western Union agencies to transfer to or receive money from other countries is prohibitively expensive and takes too long. (My own bank in Boston takes twelve dollars in wire transfer fees for incoming funds, regardless of the amount, and charges account holders more than forty dollars to send money to another country, which can take several business days.)

Some mobile banking systems, like Kenya's M-PESA, do not require users to have a bank account, but they do require a SIM card. Getting a SIM card requires registering with a phone company such as Safaricom by showing government ID such as the Kenyan national identification card or a passport. Ultimately, mobile banking is still a government-controlled money transfer, and government efforts to comply with international anti–fraud and money laundering regulations make it increasingly difficult for refugees to use mobile banking because of the ID requirements. These difficulties mean that refugees, like poor people in general, don't have bank accounts and can't use banks to send or receive money. Banks also lack branches in conflict-torn countries where a refugee's family might live.

Informal Money Transfer Systems: The Hawala

Given the difficulties and expense of sending and receiving money through formal institutions, there is fertile ground for alternative, informal methods for transferring money. Informal money transfer systems have a long history in many countries. Some people simply ask friends or people they trust to hand-carry money for them, or they make private arrangements to exchange money. The constant movement of people between cities and their home areas means there is usually someone who can be relied on and is willing to carry money. Even so, it is often more convenient for people—both refugees and locals—to use an established informal money transfer service. These services are known as *hawala* (in Arabic) or *hundi* (in Hindi and Urdu). *Hawala* means "transfer" or "wire" in Arabic banking jargon, and the "hawala system" refers to an informal channel for transferring funds through service providers known as hawaladars. The hawala system is well adapted to serve migrants, particularly in conflict-affected regions where formal bank and financial services are weak or nonexistent. Such money transfer systems originated in South Asia and are a long-standing part of urban financial systems. The money exchange market in Kabul (Afghanistan), for example, has existed for a hundred years along the Kabul River, near the gold and silver bazaars used by precious metal traders. Money exchange dealers provide traders with financial services that include currency conversions, international and domestic money transfers, deposit-taking services, and communication facilities. These are informal services, unregulated by the government and widely used by individuals and even international organizations.[10]

In Cairo, as in many African cities, there are several different hawala networks, usually based on migrant nationality. The best known is the *xawilaad* (the Somali rendering of the Arabic word *hawala*), which is run by the Somalis.[11] There are at least six Somali hawala organizations in Cairo and many more worldwide, headquartered in Dubai. In Cairo, each organization's representative, the hawaladar (broker or agent), has a team of fixers or runners. Hassan frequently used the hawala and had a friend who was a runner for one of the hawaladars. The scene described in Box 17.2 is quite typical in Cairo.

Hawala networks link the world's major trading and financial centers, operating through sophisticated financial networks that make their profits from trading on foreign currency markets in the Gulf rather than from customer fees. Much has been written about how unrecorded remittances have been used for money laundering, terrorist financing, and smuggling, but for ordinary citizens, the advantages of the hawala are its cheap fees, speed, and convenience.[12] Refugees come from conflict-affected regions, where formal bank services are minimal or nonfunctional and informal money transfer networks are the only options available. In countries subject to international sanctions (like Sudan or Syria) or where there is limited

---

Box 17.2. Coffee and Hawala

Friday is everyone's day off in Cairo, and after noontime prayers, Hassan was at the Souq al-Sayarat coffee shop in Hay al-Ashr's Swissry A street, smoking shisha and watching football on the large TV screen. The coffee shop was run by a Somali man, and all the customers were Somali men (in low-income areas in the Middle East, women do not frequent coffee shops). Sitting with Hassan was his friend, Sami, who acted as his hawala fixer when Hassan wanted to send money to his parents in Somalia or receive money from his relative in Norway. The other men in the coffee shop were all known to Hassan—some played football (soccer) with him on Saturdays, others were clan relatives. After chitchat, Hassan turned to the matter at hand. He told Sami the name and phone number of his father in Mogadishu and gave him E£2,000 in cash (about US$117 in 2018). Sami wrote the amount and information in a small notebook. After he left the coffee shop, he would head to the office of the hawaladar a few blocks away and give him the money. The hawaladar would then enter Hassan's father's information into an online spreadsheet and deduct a small fee. A few hours later, Hassan's father in Mogadishu would get a call, which would go something like this:

HAWALADAR: Are you Mohammed Dawar?
HASSAN'S FATHER: Yes.
HAWALADAR: Money has come for you. Come to Anyanle's coffee shop at 3 P.M.

At three o'clock, Hassan's father went round the corner to Anyanle's coffee shop, where he was approached by a man he recognized from the neighborhood who asked him to verify his phone number, then gave him the money. The entire transaction, from when Hassan gave Sami the money in Cairo to when Hassan's father received the money in Mogadishu, took six hours and cost about a dollar. Hassan says, "Even if you live in a faraway area, they can deliver your money to you, but you have to pay an extra fee for this. Otherwise, you have to go to them to get the money."

formal banking infrastructure (Afghanistan), even large international humanitarian organizations make use of the hawala system. In the early 2000s, the International Monetary Fund (IMF) wrote about Afghanistan that "the hawala system was praised by foreign and local aid agencies for its efficiency. . . . Nearly all nongovernmental organizations, aid donors, and development agencies used the hawala system to deliver humanitarian relief and developmental aid to Afghanistan and to move funds around the country. There was no limit to the volume of funds the hawaladars of Kabul could process, either individually or severally. Single transactions in excess of US$500,000, especially between Peshawar and Kabul, were not uncommon. Smaller organizations regularly remitted US$20,000–30,000 through the system to meet expenses."[13]

Hawala transfers are also fast. A transfer from Cairo to Somalia can happen within a few hours when it's going to Mogadishu, as was the case with Hassan's transfer to his father. Formal transfers through banks take longer because the funds need to be converted via foreign exchange depending on the destination country, and often there are a number of different banks involved in the transfer process.[14] Sending via hawala doesn't require bank-accredited documentation; the hawala system is based on trust and knowledge of the community, so the recipient needs to do nothing other than answering the phone call and showing up at a coffee shop to pick up the delivery.

Somali hawaladars are easily found throughout Cairo's poor and informal areas, especially where there is a large refugee presence, such as 6th of October, Ard al-Lewa, Hay al-Ashr, and Araba wa Nus. To make deliveries, hawala organizations hire young Somali men like Hassan's friend. He is paid a fixed salary and gets tips from recipients. Hassan prefers using his friend's hawala because their transaction fee (a few dollars) is the cheapest one. Hassan says of the competition among hawalas, "The newer ones are looking for customers, so they keep their prices low. But the hawalas are also built on the Somali clan system. Many tribes have their own hawalas, and people prefer to send through their own tribal hawala. The guys working there are almost always from the same tribe." Hassan's subclan doesn't have its own hawala, so he uses his friend's. The trust between them means there's a fair amount of credit in the system. Sometimes Hassan sends money to his family in Somalia and only pays his friend a month later. "Some hawalas let you do this," he says, "but they don't trust everyone and won't do it for just anyone. They check your background and make sure people know you. My hawala guy knows I have a full-time job and a steady income." It can be a serious matter if you don't pay the hawala loan back. "Then they won't let you use their service again. But more, they go to your relatives, who they know because of your name, and tell them to intervene. People are very embarrassed when this happens, and it can ruin their reputation. So not being paid back is not really a problem for the hawala."[15] High levels of collaboration across clan lines have enabled the Somali xawilaad to expand across Africa, with implications for the development of cities' financial infrastructure and other business sectors.[16]

Different nationalities have their own hawalas. The Eritrean hawala has been in place for decades, strengthened by the long war for independence from Ethiopia that began in 1961 and ended with independence in 1991. That war gave rise to a large Eritrean diaspora, which the Eritrean Liberation Front mobilized to provide money and services during the war. Still today, the Eritrean government levies a 2 percent diaspora tax on Eritreans living abroad, even though this has been found to be illegal under international law.[17] Those who try to avoid it are denied Eritrean consular services, and their relatives in Eritrea are punished. To renew one's passport, apply for a business permit in Eritrea, or even send goods or money to one's family, Eritreans living in other countries must visit the Eritrean embassy to obtain "clearance." This entails showing proof of earnings and then paying the 2 percent tax on them to the Eritrean authorities. In addition to directly taxing the diaspora, the Eritrean state tries to get its hands on the remittances sent to families in Eritrea. The volume of remittances sent to Eritrea is unclear, like all the financial data in Eritrea, given the lack of published government budgets and the incomplete knowledge of the size and profile of the Eritrean diaspora. However, scholars emphasize "the scale of remittances, their centrality to the Eritrean economy, and the level of government control over them."[18] The Eritrean state's attempts to control remittances is a clear reason why Eritreans prefer to use informal methods like their hawala.

In Cairo, people tend to use the Somali hawala system because, compared with other hawalas, it is perceived to be more reliable, quicker, and less corrupt. There is some associated risk because users cannot complain to the police or the bank if a problem arises. However, people have faith in the Somali system, and non-Somalis use it, too. As Hassan and his friend were leaving the coffee shop, an elderly South Sudanese woman approached them and said, "I have money coming to me, but where do I get it?" Hassan pointed to his friend and said, "Ask that guy, he will tell you."

Implications of Informal Money Transfer Systems for Cities

The presence and wide usage of informal money transfer services has several implications for host cities. First, as with entrepreneurs and trade networks, hawala systems strengthen a city's linkages with migrants' countries of origin and with countries where there are large diasporas. These linkages embed the city more deeply into regional and global financial, communications, and trading networks. When refugees conduct cross-border business, the efficiency and relative cheapness of the hawala system serve their financial needs, thereby supporting regional trade. It is not only refugees and migrants who benefit, local businesses do, too. Second, within the city, the hawala infrastructure gives rise to an urban subeconomy that provides jobs for refugees and locals alike as runners and fixers, and for hawaladars and their office staff. It is difficult to estimate how much employment is created, as data are hard to come by, but there are many examples across Africa of urban subeconomies. Perhaps the most famous is Nairobi's Eastleigh area, known as Mogadishu Ndogo (Swahili for "Little Mogadishu"), whose long-standing population of Somali refugees and migrants has, over the years, created an urban subeconomy based on the hawala.[19]

A third consequence is that in cities with uncertain business climates, a hawala system supports the business climate, especially by providing credit. A study in Afghanistan found that "despite their reputation for being the bankers of terrorists and criminals," most of the hawaladars' customers were Afghan merchants. They relied on "credit-hawala" to protect their supply chains from the interruptions of cash flow that are prevalent in the Afghan economy. This use of the hawala both for credit and for transfers is useful for local merchants, too.[20]

Hawala systems also support the formal money transfer system. People transfer money between host cities and cities in conflict zones, using both formal and informal services, depending on what works best. People, businesses, and organizations like aid agencies frequently use hawala to make transfers to countries under sanctions. Although formal services can be expensive—with high fees and weak exchange rates—informal money transfer service providers often make use of them when it's convenient.[21] Thus, because the hawala system is not fully delinked from the formal financial system, it provides a form of support for the city's formal economy.

Finally, remittances sent by refugees and migrants back to their families at home also support their hometowns and cities. In Harare, Zimbabwe, remittances from other countries, particularly South Africa, but other countries around the world too, have historically funded transportation networks (by enabling family members to purchase cars) and the education system (by contributing to school fees). Many migrants and refugees who return to Harare have established businesses that contribute to services offered in the city. In his study of Zimbabwe, Whitehead Zikhali notes how the informal sector and particularly informal remittances and "black market" currency trade have become as central to people's livelihoods as daily trade.[22]

Cairo's informal remittance economy is one example of an urban subeconomy run by refugees and migrants. Like the smuggling subeconomy, it operates underground, skirting the bounds of legality but providing a service to the poor and marginally legal, both refugees and locals. Likewise, the ways in which refugees transform host cities are not obvious to western or middle-class eyes. A tourist is unlikely to know about the hawala system unless she ventured into the poor areas of large cities and started asking locals in a coffee shop about how to send money to Somalia. After a few weeks, assuming that the tourist's Arabic was adequate, and that she had a trustworthy Somali friend to vouch for her, and that she did not resemble a government figure, she might be able to use the hawala. But it would be unlikely that she would ever get that far.

18

Ard al-Lewa: Drinking, Women's Work, and Social Cohesion

What makes a neighborhood neighborly? Perhaps neighborliness grows when it is challenged by problems and then comes together to try to address those problems. Large numbers of refugees can change the character of a city neighborhood by remixing its ethnic or religious balance and thereby creating or aggravating cultural or religious fault lines that stir up tension and conflict. In Tripoli, some Lebanese families moved away from neighborhoods that many Syrian refugees had moved into, in part because the Tripolitans found the Syrians too religiously conservative. In some of Cairo's refugee neighborhoods, tensions and conflicts arose over the behaviors of subgroups and the lack of systems in place to handle such problems. This happens in many host cities as the children of refugees grow up. Their difficult experiences as teenagers or young adults can bring new problems to a neighborhood, with consequences for social cohesion and for the women living there. In turn, refugee communities, including women, youth leaders, and elders, organize themselves into community groups to address these issues, and they are often joined by sympathetic members of the host population who act as their advocates. This chapter explores how the difficulties faced by women refugees and their children impact the social life of one neighborhood, Ard al-Lewa, and how refugees and their advocates come together to try to address these problems.

The concept of social cohesion refers to connectedness and solidarity among neighbors—both one's sense of belonging to the community and one's relationships with other members in it. It seems likely that the arrival and continuing stay of a new group like refugees would affect a neighborhood's social cohesion, but whether, how, and why this occurs in poor urban neighborhoods is not well understood. Most research on refugees and social cohesion in low-income host countries focuses on refugee camps and the surrounding population, rather than on cities. What research there is focuses on how humanitarian assistance such as livelihood programs promotes or undermines (or has no effect on) the relations between refugees and hosts.[1] But the refugees targeted by humanitarian programs are only a small proportion of the populations of most neighborhoods, especially in huge cities like Cairo, and there is no evidence that humanitarian programs have any real impact on social cohesion. The daily lives of refugees and their hosts and the relations between them play out with little influence by outside actors.

It's difficult to conceptualize social cohesion in terms of an entire city. Social cohesion or lack of it manifests at the neighborhood level, and changes occur there first, sometimes spreading outward. A city neighborhood is like a small town. When a new social group differs in visible ways—language, skin color, behaviors—their impact on the neighborhood is mixed. The new arrivals often bring entrepreneurial energy and skills, and sometimes an injection of financial resources like credit and cash (sometimes in the form of humanitarian resources). They might also bring behaviors that the locals don't approve of, or unwelcome changes to the old ways. This happens everywhere (see Box 18.1).

Ard al-Lewa is a very poor neighborhood in Cairo that has received many refugees since the 2010s. It is one of the older 'ashwa'iyyat of Greater Cairo, in the Agouza district of Giza on the west side of the

> **Box 18.1. A Changing Neighborhood**
>
> My own neighborhood, Brookline, is an urban suburb that borders the city of Boston and is thus part of Greater Boston. Brookline is surrounded by six neighborhoods, some very wealthy, like the city of Newton, and others more working class, such as Allston, a low- to middle-income neighborhood that is part of the city of Boston. For years, Allston has had a diverse population of students, city workers, and artists. One stretch of Harvard Avenue was known for its quirky mix of independent shops (including a magic shop called Ritual Arts and a secondhand bookstore, Bookistan, run by an old Iranian refugee), coffee hangouts, bars, and restaurants. In the last few years, a significant number of these establishments have been bought out and replaced by Korean barbecue places. The neighborhood has been not so much gentrified as replaced by an entirely different community. Street signs and shop advertisements are in Korean, and gradually the population around Harvard Avenue has changed. There is no real neighborhood tension around this shift, aside from some grumbling by locals. But what would happen if the Koreans were to start stirring up trouble on the street? Or if they were to flout local religious beliefs or social norms? What would happen in your own neighborhood, reader, if an outside group who did not speak your language moved in, took over the local watering holes, and began practicing animal sacrifice on the high school sports field? How quickly would neighbors start calling the police, and how soon would the group become pariahs?

Nile; part of is it under the highway that goes to 6th of October. Unlike similar areas of Cairo that were subject to the government's slum upgrading program, such as nearby Bulaq, Ard al-Lewa has not so far been targeted for demolition or relocation of its residents. It retains its old feel—it is a neighborhood of alleyways and narrow streets crowded by run-down apartment buildings and street life. Most of Ard al-Lewa's population are Egyptians, but there are also many Sudanese and South Sudanese and refugees from other African countries. A small number of Eritreans and Ethiopians were already living in Ard al-Lewa in 2015 when the situation in Eritrea worsened, the smuggling routes changed, and the number of Eritreans migrating to Cairo spiked. Unlike earlier Eritrean refugees who sought asylum through UNHCR, many of the newcomers intended to move on to Europe and were looking to hire smugglers and "take the boat" from Alexandria. Smuggling prospects deteriorated in Egypt, however, as the route became more dangerous and smugglers increased their prices. Many migrants held back, waiting in Cairo for the situation to stabilize. In 2018, some 8,000 Eritreans and Ethiopians were registered with UNHCR; by 2022, UNHCR had registered more than 16,500 Eritreans and almost 6,000 Ethiopians, and probably many more had not registered.[2]

In March 2018, Ryan and I visited Ard al-Lewa with Asmarina (not her real name), a young Eritrean woman who worked at a local refugee agency in Cairo. Asmarina gave us a tour of the neighborhood that she knew well, then took us to meet some Eritrean friends. As we walked through the narrow streets, it became clear that although they make up only a small part of Ard al-Lewa's population, the resident African refugees, like the Syrians in 6th of October, had rejuvenated the neighborhood. Ryan described what we saw:

> Refugee-run businesses are visible as soon as you descend the Silm Azela stairs that connect Ard al-Lewa to Dokki. There are dozens of Eritrean and Sudanese coffee shops, clothing stores, restaurants, call centers, and even a few bars. The shops sell Sudanese and Eritrean goods: coffee pots, coffee beans, and spices imported from Ethiopia, traditional clothing for weddings, and *injera* [the Ethiopian bread made from fermented grain]. The coffee shops and PlayStation cafes are popular hangouts for male youth, who also

use them to smoke hash and *bango* [marijuana]. . . . Egyptians have opened cafes decorated and geared toward Eritrean customers, with Eritrean wait staff. The shops cater to the Eritrean, Ethiopian, Somali, or Sudanese niche markets, but many shops are popular with Egyptians.[3]

Underneath all this shopping and socializing in coffee shops, tensions simmered. One source, Asmarina told us, was the bars in Ard al-Lewa and the behavior of male refugees. These bars are illegal (the owners produce their own alcohol) and they lead to public drunkenness in the neighborhood. Rowdy, drunken young men gather on street corners, disturbing the public and getting into fights. Unlike Somalis and Syrians, many Eritrean and South Sudanese refugees are Christian. While this does not bother the mostly Muslim Egyptian population, the fact that some male refugees publicly drink alcohol and get drunk is a problem. Alcohol consumption is frowned on by Muslims, especially the more religiously observant, and in accordance with Islamic traditions and sharia law, Egypt's constitution forbids drinking. Compared with countries like Saudi Arabia and Sudan where sharia law is strictly observed, Egypt is more tolerant; it is not a dry country (except during Ramadan), and the Egyptian police take a lenient approach as long as people don't drink openly.[4] In some upscale neighborhoods, there are even small liquor stores run by Coptic Christians. In Zamalek, for example, the tiny liquor store called Drinkies sells Egyptian beer and wine. But in poor neighborhoods like Ard al-Lewa, public drinking was deeply resented by conservative Egyptians, some of whom were already antagonistic toward the refugees. When drunken young men got into fights and caused other problems, neighborhood hostility came to a boil, and the police were called. A group of fifteen Egyptians in Ard al-Lewa wrote a letter to the local police in 2017, demanding that all refugees be expelled from the neighborhood. Later that year, an Egyptian news site published an article titled "Egyptian Complaining: An African Colony in Ard el Lewa."[5]

The presence of an out-group like migrants or refugees increases the social and cultural diversity of a neighborhood in ways that both please and displease the locals. In Ard al-Lewa, locals appreciated the increased economic activity brought by refugees, but the refugees also created more competition for jobs, retail space, and customers. Economic resentment added to tensions from the presence of drunken youth and the locals' perception that refugees were responsible for increased crime and spikes in housing prices and (especially) that they got more or all of the available humanitarian assistance. These tensions led to disputes between refugee and Egyptian shop owners, with the Egyptians complaining that the refugees should not have businesses in Egypt and the police and Egyptian youths hassling the refugee shop owners.

The ways in which increased diversity and tension affect neighborhood levels of trust and social cohesion has been widely theorized, mostly in Europe and North America. Two competing theories predict different outcomes. The "contact hypothesis" (that is, contact between locals and the "out-group" of newcomers) predicts that increased diversity provides more opportunities for positive intergroup contact. When increased contact is on equal terms, it can enhance positive experiences and lead to positive attitudes toward the out-group, thereby increasing social trust within the community. The competing "conflict hypothesis" argues the opposite—that diversity fosters distrust, mainly because of competition over limited resources but also because of the groups' different values. Following this hypothesis, Robert Putnam's "hunkering down" theory predicts that increased physical proximity with people of another race or ethnic background leads to reduced trust in the "other" and more "hunkering down" and solidarity among the in-group.[6] Both processes were in play in Ard al-Lewa: the African refugees brought more economic activity and opportunities for positive social contact, but they also brought increased economic competition and negatively perceived behaviors that led to tensions and diminished social cohesion.

In many host cities, neighborhood tensions are correlated with harassment of refugees and migrants from African countries, often stemming from a combination of economic resentment and racism. Across Cairo, the experience of prejudice and racism, linked to harassment and assault, is well documented in the lives of Africans, and racism is pervasive in the media and in law enforcement. One researcher in Ard al-Lewa noted that almost all her participants reported daily harassment in the form of racist slurs or physical assaults from Egyptians. Her refugee respondents said they had been hit, or had their phone snatched, or had garbage thrown at them. These kinds of refugee experiences are long-standing. In our 2012 survey of 788 Sudanese in Cairo, 82 percent of our respondents reported facing harassment from Egyptians, 40 percent had been robbed, 36 percent were physically assaulted, 24 percent were harassed by the authorities, and 18 percent were arrested or detained by police in the previous year. African refugee women in Cairo frequently experience sexual harassment on the street and are often called prostitutes.[7]

In Ard al-Lewa, as more Eritrean women migrants arrived, the host population's negative views extended to them, not because the women drank but because they were viewed as loose and immoral through their association with the drinkers. This perception undermined the already compromised safety of all women in the neighborhood, Egyptians and refugees alike. Street-based sexual harassment of women in Cairo is a long-standing problem, particularly in poorer areas like Ard al-Lewa.

Mariam, a young Eritrean woman, was one of the women living in the small dark flat we visited with Asmarina in Ard al-Lewa. Mariam was pregnant when she made the long and extremely arduous journey across Sudan to Cairo in 2016, and during our visit, her two-year-old daughter played with a flyswatter on the floor (very few people in Ard al-Lewa can afford toys for their children). Like her roommates and neighbors, Mariam worked as domestic help in Sheik Zayed City (the wealthy neighborhood near 6th of October), which meant a microbus commute of at least an hour each way, depending on traffic. Her employer had offered Mariam a room in her house, but the offer did not extend to her child, so Mariam had to turn it down. The commute meant Mariam had to make difficult decisions about childcare. Sometimes she could leave her daughter with her roommate or drop her off with a friend, but when neither of these options was available, Mariam had no choice but to leave the child alone in the flat until she got home from work. On those mornings, she would breastfeed her daughter, then lock her in the childproofed bedroom with the TV on to ensure she didn't wander around the apartment and turn on the stove, as a neighbor's child had done. The long commute meant Mariam often got home late. But she had no choice: without her job, she couldn't pay the rent. On the streets at night when Mariam came home from work, she walked as fast as she could, keeping her head down and her face covered with her scarf.

Many African refugee mothers, like Mariam, work long and physically draining hours as house cleaners, often in distant parts of the city, returning home late at night. Long work hours and exhaustion, stress about money and street safety, and lingering psychosocial distress (often linked to past exposure to violence) can mean they have little interaction with others in the community—or with their children.[8] They lack the social networks that Syrian and Egyptian women enjoy, which are particularly helpful for women with children. Egyptian and Syrian women often have relatives to help them. The smaller population of Eritrean refugees meant there was not a critical mass for a functional network, without which it was difficult to get help with childcare, or find employment, or have others around to ensure safety in the streets.

Mariam and her roommates face a worrisome spiral of isolation. Rather than deal with street harassment, Eritrean women in Ard al-Lewa keep to their homes, especially at night. They don't speak Arabic; among themselves they speak Tigrinya, the language of Eritrea, and with employers they use basic English. They might have learned some Arabic from watching TV, but homesick for a world they knew, they prefer to watch Ethiopian programs beamed in from Addis. Their only community activity is attending a small nearby Eritrean church. After work and on the weekends, they mostly stay inside, sometimes visiting other Eritrean women in the same building or nearby. On the street they slip through the crowds, trying to be invisible until they reach the safety of their apartment. Their self-isolation reinforces tensions with their Egyptian neighbors—the lack of communication means the neighbors view them with suspicion, especially if men ever visit the women.

As the number of refugees coming to transit cities grows, so does the number of women refugees (usually about half the refugee population), many of whom travel on their own or with their children. The experience of refugee women in Egypt is not well documented. They undoubtedly face the same problems as all women in Egypt: high levels of harassment on the street and in public transportation, discrimination at work, and—for those who live with husbands—violence at home. There is widespread evidence that across the world, violence against women tends to increase during and after emergencies, including pandemics. People's experiences of intense stress, the disruption of protective social networks, increased economic hardship, and decreased access to services all increase the risk of violence toward women. The World Health Organization says the Eastern Mediterranean region, which includes Egypt and Lebanon, has the second-highest prevalence of violence against women (37 percent) worldwide, which means that one in three women experience violence in these countries. This violence stems from high gender inequality in these societies, compounded by political and socioeconomic instability. Even before the COVID-19 pandemic, which compounded domestic violence problems because people were required to stay indoors, women and girls in the Eastern Mediterranean were at high risk of violence. Women and girls who are also migrants and undocumented workers, or who have disabilities, or who are caught up in armed conflict are even more vulnerable to multiple forms of violence.[9]

In Ard al-Lewa, as elsewhere in Cairo, refugee women are part of these extra-vulnerable groups. They are isolated, discriminated against, and incriminated along with their fellow refugee men for the problems of the neighborhood, all while doing their best to work and keep their children safe and fed. They seldom have time or energy to seek help from the few services in Cairo that support women. Nor are they likely to join the Egyptian women who protest Egypt's violence against women and discriminatory legislation. In Cairo there has been a massive grassroots response to violence against women, both on the part of local women and by international advocacy organizations. In 2011, during the Arab uprising protests, there was a major outbreak of sexual violence against women on the streets of Cairo. In response, women activists started organizations such as OpAntiSH (Operation Anti-Sexual Harassment), whose mission was to rescue women being attacked and escort them to safe houses. Attacks against women on the streets surged again two years later, this time during the protests against President Morsi. Many believed the attacks in 2011 and again in 2013 were coordinated by state security forces seeking to control and terrorize women (and all the protesters). The culture of impunity and the willingness to blame women for the attacks was clearly manifested in the response from Egypt's authorities and media. Egyptian members of parliament blamed women protesters, and a media mogul, Ahmad Mohamed Abdullah (known as Abu Islam), the owner of the al-Ummah television station, posted a video online in February 2013 in which he said that women protesters had gone to Tahrir Square because they wanted to be raped, and that such women were "devils." The public response to these comments and to the sexual attacks was intense, pitting those who supported the comments against those who resisted them, including not just advocacy organizations but members of the public, too.

In 2021, crowds of Egyptian women protested regressive (draft) revisions to Egypt's Personal Status Law (PSL), and in 2022 three Egyptian women's rights groups proposed alternative legislation—the "Just Family Law." The Just Family Law challenges both the proposed PSL revisions and Egypt's existing legislation that promotes a culture of impunity for domestic violence perpetrators. Grassroots efforts such as street protests and legal action by activist groups take a long time but can lead to change. The campaign to eliminate female genital mutilation (FGM) in Egypt lasted five years, then in June 2008 Egypt adopted comprehensive human rights legislation (Law 126) that raised the minimum age of marriage from sixteen to eighteen and criminalized FGM.[10]

These grassroots efforts by Egyptian women rarely trickle down to the poor neighborhoods where refugees live. It is likely that refugee women were caught up in the surges of street violence in 2011 and 2013, but away from the media gaze and the visible protests like those around Tahrir Square, what happened in the streets of poor neighborhoods like Ard al-Lewa went unnoticed. In these neighborhoods, as in many host cities, the culture of impunity that blamed women for being attacked was entrenched, and there were few organizations present to shine the light on these acts. The only people likely to help refugee women were other refugees.

Refugee Community Organizations

In all cities, refugees and their advocates form support groups and organizations to address problems such as isolation, mental health struggles, street violence, and difficulties navigating local bureaucracies and schools. They can be informal or formally constituted, aimed at particular groups such as women, or based on a nationality, such as Syrian organizations in 6th of October. Some focus on supporting arts and creativity. For example, Ettijahat was founded in 2011 to support independent Syrian artists in Lebanon and other countries. Some community organizations try to reduce community violence and problems with street gangs.[11]

The most widespread refugee community action is the creation of schools for their children. Cairo's situation is typical of the difficulties refugees face in finding decent schools for their children. Although UNHCR's agreement with Egypt allows refugees to register their children in local schools, Egypt's public schools are overcrowded and chaotic and have a poor reputation, even among Egyptians.[12] For refugee children and their parents, especially those from African countries, going to public school can be a fraught experience. (Syrian children seem to have fewer problems in public schools, and attendance is higher for Syrians than for other refugee nationalities.) To register their children at a public school, parents must show appropriate documentation, which they don't always have, and the costs for school fees and school uniforms are very burdensome. If they are registered, African refugee children face several difficulties in school: some (Somalis, Eritreans, Ethiopians) do not speak Arabic, but perhaps the worst problem is the bullying, discrimination, and harassment they often face. In Ryan's 2018 study, one informant recounted how a Sudanese family enrolled their children in a public school, then pulled them out after a week and enrolled them in a Sudanese school in Araba wa Nus: "The Egyptian students in the school touched the children's bodies, saying, 'Why are you so black? What did the sun do to you?'" While at the Egyptian school, the children had been unable to eat and went home and cried at night. . . . Some parents reported their children being beaten, hit with stones or glass bottles, and ignored by teachers. Some parents tried to talk to the teachers and the principal about these problems but reported that no one was interested."[13]

In response to these problems, refugee volunteers and refugee-led community organizations (RCOs) have established community-run schools in refugee neighborhoods. For example, Faysel Community Schools was founded in 2018 by refugee volunteers in Cairo. Sudanese schools use the Sudanese national curriculum and are supported by the international NGO Catholic Relief Services after an accreditation process. In 2016, one such Sudanese school in Araba wa Nus served 450 students ranging from kindergarten to grade 12, including Somali and Palestinian students. Both the Sudanese and Egyptian school curriculums are in Arabic, so the Somali community center in Hay al-Ashr offers Somali language classes for young children to prevent them from forgetting their native language.[14]

Refugee community organizations include informal women's groups that try to help women with finances or simply to provide companionship and support. For example, in Ard al-Lewa, Sudanese women form *sanadiq* (informal savings groups; sing., *sanduq*). One sanduq had thirteen members and met every Thursday, but nonmembers participated in social events, too. A UNICEF child protection officer went with a Sudanese friend and described the event: "Invitees brought along families and friends to exchange information, talk, and laugh, as exceptional hospitality is a custom that they have brought to Cairo and continue to practice." The women sold Sudanese products to each other and shared information about life in Cairo. "The host served Sudanese food and drinks, and women played the *dalouka* (Sudanese drums), sang, and danced in a room full of laughter" and *wanasa* (companionship). At the end of the meeting, the women passed around an envelope for each sanduq member to put money in, and a notebook "to write down how many memberships they had paid for—with each membership worth 50 EGP (US$3.19 in 2021)."[15]

Two important themes emerge from RCOs in host cities like Cairo and Tripoli. First, like all community organizations worldwide, RCOs provide partial solutions for the problems they address. Refugee-run schools help, but they don't have the resources and capacity to meet the needs of all the refugee children in a city, let alone the many requests from nonrefugees for spaces in the refugee schools. RCOs often extend their reach beyond refugees to address the problems faced by locals, too. There are many refugee schools in Cairo and Tripoli (Mahmoud's schools, for example) where locals try to place their children because they are much better than the public schools. These demand pressures on RCOs point to the wider problems, such as the poor public schools in Cairo and Tripoli, which are not being addressed by city or state governments. Nor are these problems being adequately addressed by the international organizations who are mandated to do so. A study of RCOs in Kampala (Uganda) points to their lack of institutional support by UNHCR, even while UNHCR's activities in Kampala were only minimally addressing the problems of the thousands of refugees living in Ugandan cities because their programs were largely focused on the refugee settlements in the north.[16]

The second theme concerns the role that RCOs might play within the formal humanitarian system, for which there is growing acknowledgment, as part of the much vaunted "localization agenda." RCOs provide an important alternative to the traditional model of refugee assistance, discussed in Chapter 8, in which international donor governments fund UNHCR or other international organizations, which then subcontract international NGO "implementing partners" to provide services to refugees. Yet, RCOs are generally locked out of formal funding mechanisms and lack any power. Two recent studies, one of Kampala and the other of Türkiye, make these points. The Kampala study authors argue that "refugee-led organisations that emerge to fill gaps in services find themselves in a delicate situation; able to legally register and run, but having to operate in ways that do not disturb the existing official or organisational balance of power."[17] The Turkish study notes that in Türkiye, "although RCOs have captured a space in the national migration governance for providing assistance to refugees, they are increasingly bound by the rulemaking and monitoring of the central state." Host countries like Türkiye, Egypt, and Uganda have "centralised, administrative structure and limited space for active citizenship and civil society . . . and [their governments are] suspicious of both foreigners and civil society organisations in general."[18]

Studies of refugee-led organizations raise the question of whether they can meaningfully carve out a sphere of influence through civic activism, given the architectures of migration governance in host countries.[19] The question could better be aimed at host cities. RCOs are most prevalent in cities, and the ability of RCOs to contribute to a city's migration governance is likely to vary from one city to another, depending on the response of the city government. It is possible that host cities that are some distance from the capital, where national governments are usually seated and more in control of city matters, could be more willing to allow RCOs some governance space when it comes to dealing with the issues facing refugees and migrants.

Epilogue: Strengthening Host Cities

Refugees are increasingly moving to or through cities. We know that humanitarian populations grow each year, but we don't know how many refugees and migrants of all kinds live in cities because the data are very unreliable. Still, the number of registered refugees is growing, and they are only a subset of the true number of displaced people. This book argues that the implications for cities are important because a humanitarian influx is different from other "regular" migration in several ways.

First, a humanitarian influx is different by virtue of its rapidity and scale, compared with the slow and steady pace of regular urbanization. Mass arrivals of refugees over a short period of time transform the physical and social landscape of cities. When a large population of refugees moves into a neighborhood, they change its social and cultural character, sometimes causing local residents to move away. With a humanitarian influx, demand for housing increases sharply, and as rents go up, locals often have to move elsewhere. Developers see opportunities for profit in new construction and enlarge the city's physical footprint—often destroying green space and local ecologies in the process. Refugee entrepreneurs and businesses might be welcomed in neighborhoods, but when refugees aren't seen as "good" or "deserving," when they compete for jobs and housing, create public disturbances, or engage in protests, their actions roil neighborhoods. When locals react with anger, the police (or vigilantes) are summoned and social cohesion disintegrates, and often it is the refugees who suffer the most serious consequences.

Second, the arrival of refugees (but not migrants) is followed by funding and other kinds of international assistance, along with the humanitarian industry. Although most of this funding is aimed at helping refugees, aid agencies and donors increasingly recognize that host cities must be helped too, and this means supporting both the host population in the neighborhoods where the refugees live and the city-wide infrastructure and services that cannot cope with additional demands. When humanitarian agencies bring cash assistance programs, they increasingly try to include host populations, too. Aid agencies improve city housing through landlord agreements and the rehabilitation of buildings, and they support cities' health and education facilities, among many other inputs, all of which strengthen cities and stimulate urban economies. The humanitarian industry also injects funds and other resources into cities by renting and rehabilitating office space and staff housing, by employing and training local staff, and by increasing demand for all kinds of goods and services. All these productive inputs can be taxed by city governments, thereby increasing their precious own-source revenues. In short, refugees transform cities because of the humanitarian industry that follows them. As with all economic changes, some city residents benefit and others lose out. There are sometimes negative market impacts, including potential inflation. More empirical research is needed to understand how urban housing, employment, and credit markets react when confronted with a large refugee influx and the ensuing humanitarian assistance.

A third difference between humanitarian influxes and other types of migration is that some host countries require refugees and IDPs to live in camps, which are often near or in cities. As the Palestinian camps in Tripoli demonstrate, camps have both positive and negative effects on cities. They can create security threats, as we saw in Lebanon. But camps are also sources of cheap labor, camp schools and health centers provide services for locals, and camps are often places where locals can find cheap housing. The funding and projects that humanitarian agencies provide for camps have spillover effects for nearby cities. One example is Zaatari camp, near the border town of al-Mafraq in Jordan, where UNHCR constructed a 12.9-megawatt solar photovoltaic plant in 2017. The plant provides 80,000 Syrian refugees in the camp with power, and it is connected to Jordan's national grid, so any unused power is fed back into the network to support Jordan's energy needs and help the country meet its renewable energy goals.[1]

For refugees and migrants, cities are sites of refuge and assistance, but also places of precarity and danger. In crowded cities refugees can choose to fade into anonymity, away from the state's gaze or humanitarian attention, and find comfort, support, and familiarity among culturally similar people in refugee neighborhoods. In these neighborhoods, people help them even when they don't qualify for formal humanitarian assistance. One of the main arguments of this book is that to understand both refugees' experience in cities and their impact on cities, especially very large ones, we need to focus on neighborhoods or areas of cities.

Given these positive and negative implications of a humanitarian influx, the outcomes for city neighborhoods—and the future of host cities—depend on the response of the actors involved: the citizens and the refugees themselves, the city leaders and government, and international aid agencies and donors. It behooves all these actors to work together to take full advantage of the benefits refugees bring and to find ways to minimize the problems. What can these actors do, and how can they be supported?

EPILOGUE

For one thing, city leaders—mayors, politicians, and business leaders—can learn to leverage the funds and development financing that flow to host countries in exchange for willingness to host refugees. Until now it has been national governments like Türkiye and Jordan who have extracted major concessional financing from the European Union (Chapter 9). City governments have not been good at capturing or leveraging these funds. But therein lies an opportunity for mayors and city municipalities to find ways to work directly with funders.

Over the past ten years, a global network of refugee activists, researchers, and advocacy groups have pushed humanitarian agencies and donors to recognize that the growing number of refugees in cities is a game changer for refugee assistance and protection—and for the cities themselves. Advocacy groups like the Mayors Migration Council have focused their attention on cities (Chapter 8). International agencies and the UN are (more slowly) coming to recognize the importance of host cities in humanitarian matters. This awareness is often sparked when wars and disasters occur in cities, as in Sudan, Ukraine, and Gaza. International support is usually aimed at national governments, but funders are beginning to recognize the importance of supporting city actors.

The set of actors comprising the refugees themselves and the host city population together influence outcomes in important ways. The response of the host population to refugees is usually more favorable and sympathetic than it is to regular migrants. As we saw in Lebanon and Egypt, this response is partly a consequence of the host city's own history and experience with displacement. We also saw how this response can change over time, and how politicians can manipulate and take advantage of it. If supported with funding and other resources, local sympathy and assistance for refugees (and migrants) can provide a significant boost both for the refugees and for the city. The host population includes three important groups: co-national migrants who have long lived in the city (the diaspora); sympathetic citizens and refugee advocates; and community organizations.

First, in regard to the long-standing migrant population, host cities' history of in-migration and displacement means that well before a new influx there is usually a population of co-nationals established in a city. Some have become citizens or permanent residents; others are de facto integrated into the city—that is, even if they don't have permanent legal status, they are socially accepted and economically integrated (with varying degrees of success) into the neighborhoods in which they live. There were thousands of Syrians, Sudanese, and Palestinians living in Cairo and Tripoli long before the most recent arrival of refugees from those countries. This long-standing migrant population is perhaps the most important source of support for new arrivals to a city. They provide housing and food, help them find health care and jobs, invest in their businesses, and help them navigate the red tape and bureaucratic requirements of both the city government and the humanitarian organizations. Supporting the diaspora is thus a low-cost way to assist both the migrants and city residents.

Second, there are many citizens who sympathize with and want to help refugees. (Of course, there are also many who are vehemently opposed to them.) There is a long history of locals who open their hearts, wallets, and even their homes to refugees and asylum seekers. Citizens welcome refugees for all kinds of reasons. Some see themselves and their cities as part of a shared global humanity. Others recognize that embracing and taking advantage of the benefits refugees bring serves their own interests more than resisting and trying to obstruct the newcomers. Often, host citizens—especially those in border cities and towns—have long histories of cross-border movement for trade, shopping, entertainment, visiting family, and so forth, and they are therefore more open to the migrants. Host citizens support refugees through their churches, temples, mosques, or secular neighborhood associations. While this generosity might be severely taxed when the numbers get too high, most host cities have a strong and resilient norm of hospitality that city and national governments could draw on and support.

A third source of local support is community organizations, led by either refugees or host city advocates. These organizations wax and wane, often struggling mightily to find consistent funding and staff. Successful community organizations are wondrous groups of committed individuals with seemingly endless abilities to withstand burnout, low pay, and lack of visibility and appreciation. They are an essential part of the support architecture for refugees and for host cities in general, as they have experience in how to manage city bureaucracies, legal requirements and laws, and the immediate needs of refugees who lack local sources of support. Without them, both the refugees and the neighborhoods they live in would be much worse off.[2] Refugee-supporting community organizations are ubiquitous in host cities and should be supported by city governments, international organizations, and private donors.

Finally, the refugees themselves. This book shows how a city's refugee population, both long stayers and new arrivals, is composed of diverse groups, nationalities, education levels, wealth levels, and identities. Not all refugees arrive poverty-stricken and in desperate need. Indeed, not all refugees have made long and perilous journeys; some have the resources to take a direct flight to their destination city. Their experience of persecution and violence occurred before they were able to leave. (A wonderful illustration is the Netflix show *Mo*, which is loosely based on the comedian Mo Amer's family of Palestinian asylum seekers in Houston, Texas.) A refugee population usually includes people who are able to transfer some of their assets to their destination city. These assets include human capital in the form of entrepreneurship, as well as the technical and professional skills brought by refugees trained as nurses, doctors, teachers, lawyers, engineers, technicians, farmers—the list is long. Most of all, refugees and migrants bring a strong work ethos based on the desire to rebuild their lives and the need to earn income. Many small and medium towns need such human capital, whether it be health care workers, dentists, electricians, elder care nurses, or restaurant busboys. Resettled or formally recognized refugees are usually allowed to work, but they are usually only a small proportion of the displaced population in a host city. Asylum seekers (who have not yet been legally granted formal refugee status) face national regulations that prevent them from working legally; cities lose out from these regulations. In most cities, refugees and migrants who lack work authorization either confront enforced idleness or work anyway, under the table. This means cities lose out on the benefits of their work, including in income taxes. In addition, workers' unauthorized status contributes to a city's lack of information about its working population and its overall population.

Finding ways to support asylum seekers who want to work legally would be a major boon to cities. The city of Denver, Colorado (United States) is an example of a host city that has created apprenticeship programs and public-private partnerships that take advantage of the influx of asylum seekers that occurred in 2023–24. WorkReady Denver is a job skills–building program that creates a pipeline for industries with labor shortages in the Denver area and connects job seekers with employers. The program provides job training and certification for asylum seekers waiting to receive work authorization.[3] The city of Denver and its recent mayors have shown remarkable leadership in harnessing the potential of refugees and asylum seekers, while working closely with the state of Colorado, the business community, and local institutions. There are many cities all over the world that actively

EPILOGUE

support refugees; the Mayors Migration Council frequently showcases these cities.[4]

Cities like Denver offer models for a future in which cities are certain to hold more refugees and migrants than they do today. Such support goes well beyond designating "sanctuary cities" that offer safety to asylum seekers. Citizens who try to mobilize support for refugees do so in the face of the current anti-immigrant political climate, where asserting pro-refugee, humanitarian values often conflicts with national immigration policies. Most governments of destination countries in Europe and North America prefer to keep refugees out in the first place by creating walls and border restrictions, or by "resettling" them in other countries (as the United Kingdom tried unsuccessfully to do in 2023, by sending asylum seekers to Rwanda).[5] Transit countries try to siphon migrants and refugees off their territory, often in collusion with smugglers, or by sending them back to their origin countries. But siphoning off or returning refugees and migrants is unlikely to work, given other countries' reluctance to take in both types of migrants.

These problems are unlikely to diminish any time soon, because migration is not going away. The millions of refugees registered by UNHCR or the host government in the cities of Africa, the Middle East, Latin America, and Asia are just a small subset of the unregistered population of migrants living in those host cities, especially in their informal settlements or low-income neighborhoods. Many of these migrants would probably qualify as refugees. Most want to move to other cities—and many will find ways to do so. As migrants make it to their destinations in Europe and the United States, they find ways to bring their families, and as these family and co-national networks grow larger and stronger, they enable more migrants to join them. These networks help overcome inhibiting factors that prevent would-be migrants from traveling (like not having enough money to pay a smuggler). Someone in the family network will simply send

EPILOGUE

money, often via the hawala. Hardened borders and restrictive policies won't stop all or even most migration; it simply sends the migrants underground, into the hands of smugglers whose prices rise accordingly.

Those who choose not to go the smuggling route wait it out in transit cities, their numbers growing every year. Whether it occurs in smaller (but rapidly growing) border cities of the world or the informal settlements and poor neighborhoods of giant capital cities, urban displacement will ramp up with climate change and environmental disasters. In the coming years, rising waters will threaten thousands of coastal cities. Loss of farmland and rangeland from lengthening droughts or catastrophic flooding will push millions to move from rural areas to cities. This process is already happening, aggravated by urban sprawl. Conflict over loss of land and resources will displace even more people. It is likely that most of those displaced will move to the cities of their own countries. But millions will also leave their countries to join those who have already moved and who make it easier for their kin to move, too.

Refugee arrivals are part of the wrenching social change wrought by urbanization that all cities experience. Their impact depends on the responses of government agencies at city and national levels, of humanitarian and development agencies (and their private sector partners), of civil society organizations including the media and politicians, and of the refugees themselves. These actors have different ideologies and agendas and varying abilities and willingness to work together. Their interactions have consequences for how refugees are received, what happens to them as their stay lengthens, and what overall impact they have on their host city. When city actors mobilize to address the problems and take advantage of the benefits refugees bring, they mitigate the negative impacts and maximize the positive effects of an influx for the entire city.

EPILOGUE

In 2018, when I began writing this book, Syrians constituted the largest population of displaced people in the world, and they still hold that position in mid-2024. The experience of refugees and their impact on cities like Tripoli and Cairo are still illustrative today. The host cities of Africa and the Middle East hold lessons for the future for all cities, in rich and poor countries alike. Since 2018 there has been a sharp resurgence of long-standing conflicts—Ukraine, Ethiopia, Sudan, Gaza. People displaced from these new and old wars will join the millions of refugees and IDPs living in protracted situations. Perhaps other wars will have begun by the time you read this. It is almost certain that in the future, no matter how harsh the refugee and immigration policies, no matter how secure the borders, and no matter how resentful and xenophobic host populations are, people displaced by conflict, persecution, and disasters will flee to cities and towns. Many citizens will help them, they will help themselves, and with foresight and leadership, the cities will flourish.

Postscript: Update on Mahmoud and Hassan

Hassan lived in Cairo for more than fifteen years. Like most refugees, he wanted to move to Europe or the United States, but he had been turned down for resettlement. Like other refugees, he and his friends debated their options—whether to take the boat to Europe, return to Somalia, or stay in Cairo. Ryan encouraged Hassan to look into graduate programs in the United States and helped him apply and find funds for a scholarship. Then came the pandemic, and international travel ceased for a while. While he waited and filled out paperwork, Hassan moved to a new apartment in 6th of October. The daily trek from Ashr had become too arduous, and 6th of October is a safer, more upbeat place to live. Then in 2022 he was granted a student visa by the United States, and he traveled there, got a master's degree, then found a job in Minneapolis (home to a large Somali community).

We lost track of Mahmoud after the COVID pandemic, but last we heard, he is still in Tripoli taking care of his family. His two schools attract more refugee and Lebanese students every year, but he struggles to make payroll. Syrian refugees in Lebanon were being pressured by the Lebanese government to return to Syria, well before the conflict there ended on December 8, 2024, when Assad's regime fell to the rebel forces.[1] In the two years preceding that, many more Syrians fled to neighboring countries. Lebanese politicians made antirefugee speeches and offered refugees incentives to return. But Mahmoud had

POSTSCRIPT

been in Tripoli for ten years, and the longer people live in a place, the harder it is for them to uproot themselves. Syria has been destroyed by years of war, and the economy was in ruins. More than this, Mahmoud's family and community have been dispersed across the globe; there is no "home" to go back to. Mahmoud and his family will either stay in Tripoli, where they have made a life for themselves, or go back to their home country. If they return, it will likely be to a city.

Notes

Chapter 1. Cities and Humanitarian Influxes

1. For example, Benjamin R. Barber, *If Mayors Ruled the World: Dysfunctional Nations, Rising Cities* (New Haven: Yale University Press, 2013); Benjamin R. Barber, *Cool Cities: Urban Sovereignty and the Fix for Global Warming* (New Haven: Yale University Press, 2017); Ella Jisun Kim, *Cities, Climate Change and Public Health: Building Human Resilience to Climate Change at the Local Level* (London: Anthem Press, 2020).

2. *Statistical Annex 2022* (Geneva, Switzerland: UNHCR, 2022), table 1. Continent totals taken from "UN Major Regions."

3. Since August 25, 2017, more than 700,000 Rohingya refugees from Myanmar have fled to the Cox's Bazar district of Bangladesh, joining the 200,000 Rohingya who had fled years before. The 2017 surge is among the largest, fastest movements of people in recent history. The Rohingya, a mostly Muslim minority ethnic group in predominantly Buddhist Myanmar, are escaping what the United Nations has described as genocidal violence that follows decades of persecution and human rights abuses. Sevil Omer, "Rohingya Refugee Crisis: Facts, FAQs, and How to Help," World Vision, last modified September 20, 2023, https://www.worldvision.org/refugees-news-stories/rohingya-refugees-bangladesh-facts.

4. Forced Displacement and Development Study Group, *Refugee Compacts: Addressing the Crisis of Protracted Displacement* (Washington, DC: Center for Global Development and International Rescue Committee, 2017), xi.

5. Karen Jacobsen et al., "Unstable Ground: Environmental and Health Problems in Informal Settlements Related to Plastics Waste and Flooding in Kampala, Uganda" (working paper, Climate Policy Lab, Fletcher School, Tufts University, Medford, MA, February 2024); and Erin Nolan and Hurubie Meko, "After Intense Floods, New York City Lurches Back to Life," *New York Times*, September 30, 2023, https://www.nytimes.com/2023/09/30/nyregion/nyc-flooding-storm.html.

6. "Uganda," OCHA Financial Tracking Services, accessed October 30, 2024, https://fts.unocha.org/countries/233/summary/2022; and "Uganda," UNHCR, accessed October 30, 2024, https://data.unhcr.org/en/country/uga.

7. For Fargo, see Jennifer L. Erickson, *Race-ing Fargo: Refugees, Citizenship, and the Transformation of Small Cities* (Ithaca, NY: Cornell University Press, 2020). For Vermont, see Pablo S. Bose, *Refugees in New Destinations and Small Cities: Resettlement in Vermont* (Cham, Switzerland: Palgrave Macmillan, 2020); Susan Hartman, *City of Refugees: The Story of Three Newcomers Who Breathed Life into a Dying American Town* (Boston: Beacon Press, 2022). For Lewiston, see Catherine L. Besteman, *Making Refuge: Somali Bantu Refugees and Lewiston, Maine* (Durham, NC: Duke University Press, 2016).

8. Susan Hartman, "How Refugees Transformed a Dying Rust Belt Town," *New York Times*, June 3, 2022, https://www.nytimes.com/interactive/2022/06/03/realestate/utica-burma-refugees.html.

9. Shamil Alimia, *Refugee Cities: How Afghans Changed Urban Pakistan* (Philadelphia: University of Pennsylvania Press, 2022); Daniel G. Kassa, *Refugee Spaces and Urban Citizenship in Nairobi: Africa's Sanctuary City* (Lanham, MD: Lexington Books, 2019); Marc Sommers, *Fear in Bongoland: Burundi Refugees in Urban Tanzania* (New York: Berghahn Books, 2001).

Chapter 2. The Actors and the Numbers

1. Karen Jacobsen and Nassim Majidi, eds., *Handbook on Forced Migration*, Elgar Handbooks in Migration (Cheltenham, UK: Edward Elgar, 2023), 4.

2. John Cerone, "Migrant Categorization under the Patchwork of International, Regional, and National Law," in Jacobsen and Majidi, *Handbook on Forced Migration*, 34–44.

3. For example, the regional definition of "refugee" in the Organisation of African Unity (now African Union) Convention Governing the Specific Aspects of Refugee Problems in Africa (1969) includes "every person who, owing to external aggression, occupation, foreign domination or events seriously disturbing public order in either part or the whole of his country of origin or nationality, is compelled to leave his place of habitual residence in order to seek refuge in another place outside his country of origin or nationality." In Latin America, the 1984 Cartagena Declaration on Refugees similarly defines refugees broadly. This definition has been adopted by several Latin American states.

4. "Libya's Expulsion of UN Refugee Agency Puts Thousands at Risk," Amnesty International, June 10, 2010, https://www.amnesty.org/en/latest/news/2010/06

/libyas-expulsion-un-refugee-agency-puts-thousands-risk/. In 2013, the Sudan government expelled twenty UNHCR international staff and thirteen international NGOs. Sara Pantuliano, "Where to Now? Agency Expulsions in Sudan: Consequences and Next Steps" (working paper, Overseas Development Institute, London, March 26, 2009), https://odi.org/en/publications/where-to-now-agency-expulsions-in-sudan-consequences-and-next-steps/. Usually, the country representative is expelled as a symbolic gesture, and most of the UN team stays in place to continue its work.

5. UNHCR's global budget for 2024 was US$10.622 billion. See "Budget and Expenditure," UNHCR Global Focus, accessed October 24, 2024, https://reporting.unhcr.org/dashboards/budget-and-expenditure.

6. Faith-based organizations include the Anglican Communion, Caritas Internationalis, Church World Service, HIAS (Hebrew Immigrant Aid Society), International Catholic Migration Commission, Islamic Relief Worldwide, Jesuit Refugee Service, Lutheran World Federation, the World Council of Churches, and World Vision International. See Volker Türk, José Riera, and Marie-Claude Poirier, *On Faith-Based Organizations, Local Faith Communities and Faith Leaders—a Partnership Note* (Geneva, Switzerland: UNHCR, 2014), https://www.unhcr.org/sites/default/files/legacy-pdf/539ef28b9.pdf.

7. *Cities of Refuge in the Middle East: Bringing an Urban Lens to the Forced Displacement Challenge* (Washington, DC: World Bank, 2017), https://hdl.handle.net/10986/28901.

8. "United States of America: 2022 Contributions," UNHCR Global Focus, accessed October 24, 2024, https://reporting.unhcr.org/donors/united-states-america. For the US Department of State, see Congressional Presentation Document, Fiscal Year 2023, Bureau of Population, Refugees, and Migration (FY 2023 Statement by Assistant Secretary Julieta Valls Noyes), accessed October 24, 2024, https://www.state.gov/wp-content/uploads/2022/07/PRM-FY-2023-CPD-FINAL.pdf.

9. "Governments," UNHCR, accessed October 24, 2024, https://www.unhcr.org/us/about-unhcr/our-partners/governments.

10. Since 2010, the IKEA Foundation has contributed to UNHCR activities in sixteen countries; its current geographic focus is on four countries in Africa—Ethiopia, Kenya, Rwanda, and Uganda. "IKEA Foundation," UNHCR, accessed October 24, 2024, https://www.unhcr.org/us/about-unhcr/our-partners/private-sector/ikea-foundation.

11. "Private Sector for Refugees," World Bank, accessed October 24, 2024, https://www.worldbank.org/en/programs/private-sector-for-refugees.

12. "Private Sector," UNHCR, accessed October 24, 2024, https://www.unhcr.org/about-unhcr/our-partners/private-sector; "Private Sector Pledges US$250 Million for Refugee Assistance," UNHCR, accessed October 24, 2024, https://www.unhcr.org/news/stories/private-sector-pledges-us250-million-refugee-assistance; *Ensuring Prosperity for Refugees and Host Communities: Priority Actions for the 2nd Global Refugee Forum* (New York: International Rescue Committee, December 12, 2023), https://www.rescue.org/eu/report/ensuring-prosperity-refugees-and-host-communities-priority-actions-2nd-global-refugee-forum.

13. "Global Refugee Forum 2023," Global Compact on Refugees, accessed October 24, 2024, https://globalcompactrefugees.org/about/global-refugee-forum/global-refugee-forum-2023.

14. "Global Trends at-a-Glance," UNHCR, accessed October 24, 2024, https://www.unrefugees.org/refugee-facts/statistics/.

15. According to Jordan's Department of Statistics, in 2015 Syrians made up 13 percent of the population of Jordan and 43 percent of non-Jordanians. Ibrahim Alhawarin et al., "Migration Shocks and Housing: Short-Run Impact of the Syrian Refugee Crisis in Jordan" (IZA Discussion Paper No. 13969, IZA Institute of Labor Economics, Bonn, 2020). The UNHCR numbers come from *Statistical Annex 2015* (Geneva, Switzerland: UNHCR, 2015), table 5.

16. IOM's Displacement Tracking Matrix (DTM) gathers and analyzes data through "a large and diverse network of Key Informants." "About DTM," Displacement Tracking Matrix, IOM, January 31, 2023, https://dtm.iom.int/about-dtm. IOM states that the purpose of DTM data is not to provide counts or estimates of the numbers of displaced, but rather to help humanitarian practitioners design programs. For more on IDMC, see "How We Monitor," Internal Displacement Monitoring Centre, accessed October 24, 2024, https://www.internal-displacement.org/monitoring-tools.

17. Caroline Krafft et al., "Syrian Refugees in Jordan: Demographics, Livelihoods, Education, and Health" (working paper 1184, Economic Research Forum, Cairo, 2018).

18. See, for example, Nyasha Bhobo, "Black Market SIM Cards Turned a Zimbabwean Border Town into a Remote Work Hub," *Rest of World*, April 6, 2022, https://restofworld.org/2022/black-market-sim-cards-zimbabwe-border-work-hub/.

19. Elizabeth Fussell et al., "Measuring the Environmental Dimensions of Human Migration: The Demographer's Toolkit," *Global Environmental Change* 28 (2014): 182–191.

20. See Hagir Osman Eljack and Awatif El Awad Musa, "Sudan Experience in Conducting Population Censuses" (working paper, University of Alneelain, Khartoum, Sudan), accessed October 24, 2024, https://iaos-isi.org/wp-content/uploads/2023/03/Awatif_Musa_paper.pdf. See also *Sudan Labour Force Survey 2011–2012* (Geneva, Switzerland: International Labour Organization, 2011), https://webapps.ilo.org/surveyLib/index.php/catalog/5350.

21. Jean-Dominique Bérard-Chagnon et al., *Recent Immigrants and Non-permanent Residents Missed in the 2011 Census* (Ottawa: Statistics Canada, May 22, 2019), 8.

Chapter 3. Informal Cities

1. In February 2024, Germany had the highest number of Ukrainians: more than 1.1 million Ukrainian refugees and another million asylum seekers. "Ukraine Refugee Situation," UNHCR, accessed February 26, 2024, https://data.unhcr.org/en/situations/ukraine.

2. Rebecca Rosman, "Polish Border Town of Przemyśl Is a Revolving Door for Ukrainian Migrants," *The World*, October 18, 2022, https://theworld.org/stories/2022-10-18/polish-border-town-przemy-l-revolving-door-ukrainian-migrants.

3. International Crisis Group, "Hard Times in a Safe Haven: Protecting Venezuelan Migrants in Colombia" (Latin America Report no. 94, August 9, 2022), https://www.crisisgroup.org/sites/default/files/094-protecting-venezuelans-in-colombia_0.pdf.

4. "Alexandria Population 1950–2023," Macrotrends, accessed October 25, 2024, https://www.macrotrends.net/cities/22804/alexandria/population; "Documents & Reports—UNHCR Egypt," UNHCR, accessed October 25, 2024, https://www.unhcr.org/eg/resources/unhcr-egypt-documents.

5. Dennis A. Rondinelli, "Dynamics of Growth of Secondary Cities in Developing Countries," *Geographical Review* 73, no. 1 (1983): 44, https://doi.org/10.2307/214394.

6. Griet Steel et al., "The Urban Land Debate in the Global South: New Avenues for Research," *Geoforum* 83 (July 2017): 1–4, https://doi.org/10.1016/j.geoforum.2017.03.006.

7. Karen Jacobsen, *Internal Displacement to Urban Areas: The Tufts-IDMC Profiling Study. Case 1: Khartoum, Sudan* (Medford, MA: Feinstein International Center, Tufts University, 2008), https://fic.tufts.edu/wp-content/uploads/Tufts-IDMC-Profiling-2008-Khartoum.pdf.

8. One estimate claims that during the 1980s, informal housing increased from 17 percent of settlement in Khartoum to more than 60 percent. Aziza Ahmed et al., "Prospects for Improved Upgrading Mechanisms in New Residential Areas: Al-Fath, Omdurman," in *Recent Urbanisation Trends in Khartoum State: Case Studies from the EARF Project "The Urban Land Nexus and Inclusive Urbanisation in Dar es Salaam, Mwanza and Khartoum,"* ed. Enrico Ille et al. (Khartoum: Faculty of Architecture, University of Khartoum, in collaboration with the Institute of Development Studies, University of Sussex, 2020), 71, https://www.researchgate.net/publication/350048354_Recent_Urbanisation_Trends_in_Khartoum_State.

9. "Khartoum Demolishes Camps for the Internally Displaced," South African Institute of International Affairs (SAIIA), April 25, 2008, https://saiia.org.za/research/khartoum-demolishes-camps-for-the-internally-displaced/.

10. *Sudan Humanitarian Update* (Geneva, Switzerland: OCHA, July 29, 2024), https://reliefweb.int/report/sudan/sudan-humanitarian-update-29-july-2024-enar.

11. Deen Sharp, "Haphazard Urbanisation: Urban Informality, Politics, and Power in Egypt," *Urban Studies* 59, no. 4 (2022): 737, https://doi.org/10.1177/00420980211040927.

12. The Darfur trip was from September to October 2009. Karen Jacobsen et al., "Developing a Conflict-Sensitive Microfinance Model for Darfur" (Feinstein International Center, Tufts University, December 2009), accessed October 25, 2024, https://fic.tufts.edu/research-item/developing-a-conflict-sensitive-microfinance-model-for-darfur/.

13. The "Jungle" migrant camp in Calais was cleared in 2016, but the migrants created new camps near Calais and Dunkirk. In 2021, "some 2,000 migrants—including hundreds of unaccompanied children—[were] living in wooded areas, . . . disused warehouses, and under bridges in and around Calais. Several hundred more are staying in a forest in Grande-Synthe, a commune adjacent to [Dunkirk]." French police raid the camps, conduct mass evictions, and obstruct distributions of food and water by humanitarian groups. Such efforts have not deterred the migrants. Bénédicte Jeannerod, *Enforced Misery: The Degrading Treatment of Migrant Children and Adults in Northern France* (Paris: Human Rights Watch, October 7, 2021), https://www.hrw.org/report/2021/10/07/enforced-misery/degrading-treatment-migrant-children-and-adults-northern-france.

14. Sherif Maher Hassan and Ron Mahabir, "Urban Slums and Fertility Rate Differentials," *Population Review* 57, no. 2 (2018): 47–74, https://doi.org/10.1353/prv.2018.0006. Their study of seventy-two developing countries from 1990 to 2014 found support for the "positive effect of slums on fertility rate"—that is, fertility

rates are more likely to be higher in slums. See also Khan et al., "All Slums Are Not Equal: Maternal Health Conditions among Two Urban Slum Dwellers," *Indian Journal of Community Medicine* 37, no. 1 (2012): 50–56. https://doi.org/10.4103/0970-0218.94027.

15. See D. B. Resnik, "Urban Sprawl, Smart Growth, and Deliberative Democracy," *American Journal of Public Health* 100, no. 10 (2010): 1852–1856, https://doi.org/10.2105/ajph.2009.182501; H. Zhang, "The Impact of Urban Sprawl on Environmental Pollution: Empirical Analysis from Large and Medium-Sized Cities of China," *International Journal of Environmental Research and Public Health* 18, no. 16 (2021): 8650, https://doi.org/10.3390/ijerph18168650.

16. R. Ben Penglase, *Living with Insecurity in a Brazilian Favela: Urban Violence and Daily Life* (New Brunswick, NJ: Rutgers University Press, 2014), http://www.jstor.org/stable/j.ctt9qh1fx.

17. Romola Sanyal, "A No-Camp Policy: Interrogating Informal Settlements in Lebanon," *Geoforum* 84 (August 2017): 117–125, https://doi.org/10.1016/j.geoforum.2017.06.011.

18. "Footage Shows Egypt Police Dragging Warraq Islanders Out of Homes as Development Plans Move Forward," *Middle East Monitor*, August 17, 2022, https://www.middleeastmonitor.com/20220817-footage-shows-egypt-police-dragging-warraq-islanders-out-of-homes-as-development-plans-move-forward/.

19. *The Guardian* reported that "four days after the State Ministry of Waterfront Infrastructure Development issued a 72-hour quit notice to residents, a band of machete-wielding men laid siege to Makoko's buildings. Five days later, . . . the assault escalated: the demolition workers set fire to targeted structures and deployed armed police who allegedly fired gunshots indiscriminately. One resident was killed, shaming the demolition workers into suspending their efforts. By then, 30,000 people had been rendered homeless." See Tolu Ogunlesi, "Inside Makoko: Danger and Ingenuity in the World's Biggest Floating Slum," *The Guardian*, February 23, 2016, https://www.theguardian.com/cities/2016/feb/23/makoko-lagos-danger-ingenuity-floating-slum.

20. Libby George, "Mass Evictions Prompt Protests as Nigerian Housing Crisis Mounts," Reuters, January 24, 2020, https://www.reuters.com/article/us-nigeria-housing/mass-evictions-prompt-protests-as-nigerian-housing-crisis-mounts-idUSKBN1ZN1B9. See also Ope Adetayo, "The Scramble for Lagos and the Urban Poor's Fight for Their Homes," African Arguments, January 26, 2022, https://africanarguments.org/2022/01/the-scramble-for-lagos-and-the-urban-poors-fight-for-their-homes/.

21. Monika Streule et al., "Popular Urbanization: Conceptualizing Urbanization Processes beyond Informality," *International Journal of Urban and Regional Research* 44, no. 4 (2020): 652, https://doi.org/10.1111/1468-2427.12872.

Chapter 4. How Refugees Get Stuck in Cities

1. *Statistical Annex 2023* (Geneva, Switzerland: UNHCR, 2023), table 9.

2. T. Albers et al., "The Role of Place Attachment in Promoting Refugees' Well-Being and Resettlement: A Literature Review," *International Journal of Environmental Research and Public Health* 18, no. 21 (2021): 11021, https://doi.org/10.3390/ijerph182111021.

Chapter 5. Lebanon

1. About half the Lebanese returnees were of mixed Syrian-Lebanese nationality. *Lebanon Crisis Response Plan, 2017–2020* (Geneva, Switzerland: UNHCR, 2018), https://reliefweb.int/report/lebanon/lebanon-crisis-response-plan-2018-annual-report. The UN agency responsible for Palestinians in the Middle East, the United Nations Relief and Works Agency for Palestine Refugees in the Near East (UNRWA), claims there are 475,000 Palestinian refugees registered in Lebanon, but UNRWA doesn't keep track of people leaving the country. A 2017 survey by the Lebanese government suggested there are 174,000 Palestinians in Lebanon. *Population and Housing Census in Palestinian Camps and Gatherings in Lebanon—2017: Detailed Analytical Report* (Beirut: Lebanese-Palestinian Dialogue Committee, Palestinian Central Bureau of Statistics, 2019), https://lpdc.gov.lb/publications/detailed-report-of-the-population-and-housing-census-in-the-palestinian-camps-and-gatherings-in-lebanon/.

2. *Housing, Land and Property Issues in Lebanon: Implications of the Syrian Refugee Crisis* (Nairobi: UN-Habitat, 2014), https://unhabitat.org/housing-land-and-property-issues-in-lebanon-implications-of-the-syrian-refugee-crisis. See also *An Evaluation of the NRC Shelter Occupancy Free-of-Charge Modality in Lebanon* (Oslo: Norwegian Refugee Council, October 2018), 13, https://www.nrc.no/globalassets/pdf/evaluations/ofc-impact-evaluation/ofc-impact-evaluation-report-october-2018.pdf.

3. John T. Chalcraft, *The Invisible Cage: Syrian Migrant Workers in Lebanon* (Stanford, CA: Stanford University Press, 2009); Élisabeth Longuenesse, "Travailleurs étrangers, réfugiés syriens et marché du travail," *Confluences Méditerranée* 92 (2015): 33–47, https://doi.org/10.3917/come.092.0033; Are Knudsen, "Syria's Refugees in Lebanon: Brothers, Burden, and Bone of Contention," in *Lebanon Facing*

the Arab Uprisings: Constraints and Adaptation, ed. Rosita di Peri and Daniel Meier (London: Palgrave Macmillan, 2017), 135–154. See also Estella Carpi, Jessica Anne Field, Sophie Isobel Decker, and Andrea Rigon, "From Livelihoods to Leisure and Back: Refugee 'Self-Reliance' as Collective Practices in Lebanon, India, and Greece," *Third World Quarterly* 42, no. 2 (2020): 421–440.

4. Ninette Kelley, UNHCR representative in Lebanon, personal conversation with author, 2015.

5. In 2011, Lebanon's Human Development Index (HDI) value was 0.77, positioning it at 66 out of 188 countries. Today its HDI value has fallen to 0.70 and its ranking has dropped to 112. "Human Development Index (HDI) of Lebanon," Country Economy, accessed October 25, 2024, https://countryeconomy.com/hdi/lebanon. See also *Lebanon Crisis Response Plan, 2017–2020*.

6. *Annual Report 2014: Operational Highlights* (Washington, DC: World Bank, 2015), https://www.worldbank.org/content/dam/Worldbank/AR14_OperationalHighlights.pdf.

7. Kathleen Murphy, *The Lebanese Crisis and Its Impact on Immigrants and Refugees* (Washington, DC: Migration Policy Institute, 2006). Lebanese are especially in the United States, Australia, Canada, and Brazil. See also Tomas C. Archer, "Lebanon: Civilians Pay the Price," *Forced Migration Review* 26 (August 2006), 4–5.

8. Hezbollah first participated in Lebanese elections in 1992 and entered the cabinet in 2005. It has since held one to three seats in each government. After the 2022 legislative elections it held 13 out of 128 parliamentary seats. *Lebanese Hezbollah* (Washington, DC: Congressional Research Service, May 10, 2024), https://crsreports.congress.gov/product/pdf/IF/IF10703.

9. Maja Janmyr and Lama Mourad, "Modes of Ordering: Labelling, Classification, and Categorization in Lebanon's Refugee Response," *Journal of Refugee Studies* 31, no. 4 (2018): 544–565.

10. The kafala system derives from Islamic jurisprudence on legal guardianship, and began in the early 1900s, then expanded after oil was discovered in the 1950s and the Gulf states needed foreign workers. The system was intended to protect local firms where migrants often comprised the majority of the work force (and of the population in Gulf countries), and also sought to offer protection to workers. However, over the years, the power imbalance between sponsors and workers and sponsors' legal impunity have led to numerous abuses of workers. See Kali Robinson, "What Is the Kafala System?," Council on Foreign Relations, November 18, 2022. https://www.cfr.org/backgrounder/what-kafala-system.

11. Carpi et al., "From Livelihoods to Leisure," 421–440.

12. Chaden El Daif, *Access to Legal Stay and Labor for Syrians in Lebanon: Status and Prospects* (Beirut: Refugees=Partners and Lebanese Economic Association, 2022), https://lb.boell.org/sites/default/files/2022-07/Access-to-legal-stay-and-residency-EN.pdf.

13. On August 4, 2020, ammonium nitrate stored at the Port of Beirut exploded, causing at least 218 deaths, 7,000 injuries, and US$15 billion in property damage, as well as leaving an estimated 300,000 people homeless.

14. "Forced Return of Syrians by Lebanon: Unsafe and Unlawful," Human Rights Watch, July 6, 2022, https://www.hrw.org/news/2022/07/06/forced-return-syrians-lebanon-unsafe-and-unlawful. In May 2023, there were reports that the Lebanese Armed Forces were raiding the houses of Syrian refugees and deporting them to Syria. "Joint Statement: Lebanon Must Halt Summary Deportations of Syrian Refugees," Human Rights Watch, May 11, 2023, https://www.hrw.org/news/2023/05/11/joint-statement-lebanon-halt-summary-deportations-syrian-refugees.

Chapter 6. Tripoli and the Changing City Landscape

1. Jennifer Alix-Garcia et al., "Displaced Populations, Humanitarian Assistance, and Hosts: A Framework for Analyzing Impacts on Semi-urban Households," *World Development* 40, no. 2 (2012): 373–386.

2. UNHCR staff, interview with author, Tripoli, October 2018.

3. Radoslaw Trojanek and Michal Gluszak, "Short-Run Impact of the Ukrainian Refugee Crisis on the Housing Market in Poland," *Finance Research Letters* 50 (2022): 103236.

4. *Housing, Land and Property Issues in Lebanon: Implications of the Syrian Refugee Crisis* (Nairobi: UN-Habitat, 2014), https://unhabitat.org/housing-land-and-property-issues-in-lebanon-implications-of-the-syrian-refugee-crisis.

5. The calculation is based on the Living Condition Survey of Refugees and Host Communities in Lebanon, which reports an estimate by the former mayor that 17,000 refugees resided in Halba in 2018. This is much higher than the number of UNHCR-registered Syrian refugees. The survey found that registration with UNHCR is almost universal (98 percent) among refugees in Halba. (Of course, it is possible that many refugees did not come forward to be registered, for the reasons discussed in Chapter 2.) Dima Mahdi and Mona Harb, *Halba City Report: Lebanese Municipalities and Syrian Refugees: Building Capacity and Promoting Agency* (Beirut: Lebanese Center for Policy Studies, 2023), https://api.lcps-lebanon.org/content/uploads/files//Halba-City-Report.pdf. See also Estella Carpi, Jessica Anne Field, Sophie Isobel Decker, and Andrea Rigon, "From Livelihoods to Leisure and Back:

Refugee 'Self-Reliance' as Collective Practices in Lebanon, India, and Greece," *Third World Quarterly* 42, no. 2 (2020): 421–440.

6. Mona Fawaz et al., "Unplanned Links, Unanticipated Outcomes: Urban Refugees in Halba (Lebanon)," *Environment and Planning D: Society and Space* 40, no. 3 (2022): 487–488.

7. Fawaz et al., "Unplanned Links, Unanticipated Outcomes," 488–489.

8. *Housing, Land and Property Issues in Lebanon*, 45; Fernando Murillo, "Migrants and Rapid Urbanization: A New Agenda for Humanitarian and Development Urban Planning?" (paper presented at United Nations Expert Group Meeting on Sustainable Cities, Human Mobility and International Migration, Population Division, UN Secretariat, New York, September 2017).

9. *Housing, Land and Property Issues in Lebanon*, 6–7.

10. *Housing, Land and Property Issues in Lebanon*, 54.

11. See "March 2018 Report on Informal Settlements in Lebanon" (factsheet, Inter-Agency Mapping Platform, UNHCR, March 2018), https://data.unhcr.org/en/documents/details/63631; *VASyR 2021: Vulnerability Assessment of Syrian Refugees in Lebanon* (Geneva, Switzerland: UNHCR, UNICEF, and WFP, 2022), 11, https://reliefweb.int/report/lebanon/vasyr-2021-vulnerability-assessment-syrian-refugees-lebanon.

12. UNHCR and UN-Habitat, *Housing, Land and Property Issues*, 48.

13. There are no official statistics regarding Palestinians living outside the official camps. UNRWA does not have a mandate to provide shelter or water and sanitation assistance in such areas. See *Needs Assessment in the Palestinian Gatherings of Lebanon—Housing, Water and Sanitation* (Beirut: Première Urgence and Norwegian Refugee Council, 2009); Nasser Yassin et al., "Organized Chaos: Informal Institution Building among Palestinian Refugees in the Maashouk Gathering in South Lebanon," *Journal of Refugee Studies* 29, no. 3 (2016): 341–362; Diana Martin, "From Spaces of Exception to 'Campscapes': Palestinian Refugee Camps and Informal Settlements in Beirut," *Political Geography* 44 (2015): 9–18.

14. "Steps on Birth Registration," UNHCR Lebanon, accessed October 25, 2024, https://help.unhcr.org/lebanon/en/steps-on-birth-registration/.

15. Marylin Chahine, "How Uneven Aid Distribution Creates Divisions in Hay al-Tanak," *Beirut Today*, May 3, 2021, https://beirut-today.com/2021/05/03/how-uneven-aid-distribution-creates-divisions-in-hay-al-tanak/.

16. *VASyR 2022: Vulnerability Assessment of Syrian Refugees* (Geneva, Switzerland: UNHCR, UNICEF, and WFP, 2022), https://reliefweb.int/attachments/be9ca6d1-7774-4be8-8e7c-6349abceacaf/WFP-0000149219%20%281%29.pdf.

17. "Shelter," UNHCR Lebanon, https://www.unhcr.org/lb/shelter; "UNHCR's Shelter Program—Lebanon Factsheet" (factsheet, UNHCR Lebanon, December 2021), https://www.unhcr.org/lb/wp-content/uploads/sites/16/2022/02/UNHCR-Lebanon-Shelter-Fact-Sheet_December-2021.pdf.

18. *Impact Evaluation of the NRC Shelter Occupancy Free-of-Charge Modality in Lebanon* (Oslo: Norwegian Refugee Council, 2018), 47, https://www.nrc.no/globalassets/pdf/evaluations/ofc-impact-evaluation/ofc-impact-evaluation-report-october-2018.pdf. The British agency Habitat for Humanity UK supported a period of free rent for refugees and increased housing stock by building new homes, upgrading unfinished ones, and converting nondomestic buildings like warehouses. It also renovated existing buildings and upgraded water and sanitation facilities. These efforts reach relatively few people (some 1,500 families). "How We Help Refugees: Lebanon's Housing Crisis, Part 2," Habitat for Humanity UK, October 2016, https://www.habitatforhumanity.org.uk/blog/2016/10/how-we-help-refugees-lebanon-housing-crisis-part-2/.

19. *Impact Evaluation of the NRC Shelter*, 47.

20. Fawaz et al., "Unplanned Links, Unanticipated Outcomes," 500.

21. *Impact Evaluation of the NRC Shelter*, 47.

22. Urban Settlements Working Group, *Area-Based Approaches in Urban Settings: Compendium of Case Studies* (Geneva, Switzerland: Urban Settlements Working Group, 2019), https://reliefweb.int/report/world/area-based-approaches-urban-settings-compendium-case-studies-may-2019-edition. As of 2019, the compendium had documented thirty-one cases worldwide, but there are likely many more. See also James Schell, Mohamed Hilmi, and Seki Hirano, "Area-Based Approaches: An Alternative in Contexts of Urban Displacement," *Forced Migration Review* 63 (2020): 16–19.

23. "Supporting Urban Rehabilitation for Syrian Refugees and Host Communities in Tripoli," in Urban Settlements Working Group, *Area-Based Approaches in Urban Settings*, sec. N4; see also sec. N6. The Lebanon Humanitarian Fund funded the El Hay project from November 2016 to January 2018.

Chapter 7. The Camp and the City

1. *Statistical Annex 2022* (Geneva, Switzerland: UNHCR, 2022), table 18, author's calculation. See also "Jordan" (factsheet, UNHCR, May 2019), https://reliefweb.int/sites/reliefweb.int/files/resources/69826.pdf.

2. Jennifer Alix-Garcia et al., "Do Refugee Camps Help or Hurt Hosts? The Case of Kakuma, Kenya," *Journal of Development Economics* 130 (2018): 66–83. Un-

like Alix-Garcia, most economists who write about the impact of refugee camps mainly cite other economists' work and approaches. See, for example, Edward Taylor et al., "Economic Impact of Refugees," *Proceedings of the National Academy of Sciences* 113, no. 27 (2016): 7449–7453.

3. Clayton Boeyink, "The 'Worthy' Refugee: Cash as a Diagnostic of 'Xeno-Racism' and 'Bio-Legitimacy,'" *Refuge* 35, no. 1 (2019): 61–71.

4. According to the UNHCR's *Emergency Handbook*, "Persons who pursue military activities in a country of asylum cannot be asylum-seekers or refugees, may not stay in or enter refugee camps, and may not benefit from humanitarian assistance provided by UNHCR under its international refugee mandate." *Emergency Handbook*, UNHCR, accessed October 25, 2024, https://emergency.unhcr.org/protection/legal-framework/civilian-and-humanitarian-character-asylum.

5. Lewis Turner, "Explaining the (Non-)Encampment of Syrian Refugees: Security, Class and the Labour Market in Lebanon and Jordan," *Mediterranean Politics* 20, no. 3 (2015): 386–404.

6. Ninette Kelley, personal conversation with author, August 2022. See also Ninette Kelley, "Responding to a Refugee Influx: Lessons from Lebanon," *Journal on Migration and Human Security* 5, no. 1 (2017): 84.

7. Diana Martin, "From Spaces of Exception to 'Campscapes': Palestinian Refugee Camps and Informal Settlements in Beirut," *Political Geography* 44 (2015): 9–18. See also Kelley, "Responding to a Refugee Influx," 82–104; Are Knudsen, "Syria's Refugees in Lebanon: Brothers, Burden, and Bone of Contention," in *Lebanon Facing the Arab Uprisings: Constraints and Adaptation*, ed. R. D. Peri and D. Meier (London: Palgrave Macmillan, 2017); and Romola Sanyal, "A No-Camp Policy: Interrogating Informal Settlements in Lebanon," *Geoforum* 84 (August 2017): 117–125. For a list of Palestinian camps, see "Palestinian Refugee Camps," Wikipedia, accessed October 25, 2024, https://en.wikipedia.org/wiki/Palestinian_refugee_camps; "Beddawi Camp," UNRWA, accessed October 25, 2024, https://www.unrwa.org/where-we-work/lebanon/beddawi-camp.

8. Fatah al-Islam first appeared in Nahr al-Bared in 2006. Its aim was "reform[ing] the Palestinian refugee community in Lebanon according to Islamic sharia law before confronting Israel." The Lebanese government links the group to Syrian intelligence and the former al-Qaeda affiliate Hayat Tahrir al-Sham. "Salafi Jihadis: Fatah al-Islam in Lebanon," European Council on Foreign Relations, accessed October 25, 2024, https://ecfr.eu/special/mapping_palestinian_politics/salafi_jihadis_fatah_al_islam_lebanon/.

9. The remaining residents continued to live in temporary accommodations near Nahr al-Bared camp and in Beddawi camp. Some 958 shops have been reconstructed, and traders have begun to rejuvenate the camp's economy and social fabric. Today, much of the camp has been rebuilt. "Nahr el-Bared Camp," UNRWA, accessed October 25, 2024, https://www.unrwa.org/where-we-work/lebanon/nahr-el-bared-camp.

10. Palestinian refugees displaced from other camps in Lebanon, such as Nabatieh and Tal al-Zaatar (destroyed in 1974 and 1976, respectively), had also moved to Beddawi camp.

11. Lars Erslev Andersen, *The Neglected Palestinian Refugees in Lebanon and the Syrian Refugee Crisis* (Copenhagen: Danish Institute for International Studies, 2016).

12. "Kakuma Refugee Camp," UNHCR Kenya, accessed October 25, 2024, https://www.unhcr.org/ke/kakuma-refugee-camp; Utz Johann Pape et al., *Understanding the Socioeconomic Conditions of Refugees in Kenya*, vol. B, *Kakuma Camp: Results from the 2019 Kakuma Socioeconomic Survey* (Washington, DC: World Bank Group, 2019), 18–23.

13. Karen Jacobsen, *The Economic Life of Refugees* (Boulder, CO: Lynne Rienner, 2005). See also Eric Werker, "Refugee Camp Economies," *Journal of Refugee Studies* 20, no. 3 (2007): 461–480; Naohiko Omata, *The Myth of Self-Reliance: Economic Lives inside a Liberian Refugee Camp* (New York: Berghahn Books, 2017).

14. See Allan Mukuki, "What Does Kenya's New Refugee Act Mean for Economic Inclusion?," interview by Izza Leghtas and David Kitenge, *Refugees International*, May 4, 2022, https://www.refugeesinternational.org/what-does-kenyas-new-refugee-act-mean-for-economic-inclusion/; Mary Wambui, "Kenya Gets $199m for Refugee Transition Plan," *East African*, June 21, 2023, https://www.theeastafrican.co.ke/tea/news/east-africa/kenya-gets-sh28-billion-for-refugee-transition-4277988.

Chapter 8. Here Comes the Money

1. About two-thirds of the $328,441,216 in humanitarian contributions came from fifteen governments, and the other third from national committees of UNICEF and other NGOs (Save the Children, Swiss Solidarity). See "Humanitarian Contributions," OCHA Financial Tracking Service, accessed October 25, 2024, https://fts.unocha.org/countries/178/donors/2022. By the end of October 2022, the European Commission (EC) had mobilized €248 million, and Poland received €144.6 million, almost 60 percent of the total sum. The funds were distributed through the EC's emergency assistance mechanism and allocated to countries receiving the largest numbers of refugees from Ukraine, including Romania, Hun-

gary, Slovakia, and the Czech Republic in addition to Poland. See "Poland: Funding from the EC to Support Those Arriving from Ukraine," European Commission, October 28, 2022, https://ec.europa.eu/migrant-integration/news/poland-funding-ec-support-those-arriving-ukraine_en#:~:text=Poland%20has%20received%20EUR%20144.6,of%20its%20war%20with%20Russia.

2. Samer Saliba and Vittoria Zanuso, *Municipal Finance for Migrants and Refugees: The State of Play* (New York: Mayors Migration Council, 2022), https://mmc-production.s3.amazonaws.com/wp-content/uploads/2023/10/03175127/MMC-Report-Municipal-Finance-for-Migrants-and-Refugees-Pages-2.pdf.

3. Carey Baraka, "Something Big Just Happened in Kenya," *New York Times*, July 14, 2024, https://www.nytimes.com/2024/07/14/opinion/kenya-protests-politics.html.

4. *Rethinking Central Government Policymaking for Local Economic Development: National Recommendations to Revitalize Local Economies in Lebanon*, Municipal Empowerment and Resilience Project (Beirut: MERP, UNDP, and UN-Habitat, October 31, 2022), accessed October 25, 2024, https://www.undp.org/sites/g/files/zskgke326/files/2023-02/Rethinking%20Central%20Government%20Policy%20Making%20for%20LED_Policy%20Paper_EN.pdf.

5. *Rethinking Central Government Policymaking*, 104.

6. *Rethinking Central Government Policymaking*.

7. "Global Cities Fund for Migrants and Refugees," Mayors Migration Council, https://mayorsmigrationcouncil.org/gcf/. The GCF is supported by the Van Leer Foundation, the Conrad N. Hilton Foundation, the IKEA Foundation, Open Society Foundations, and the Robert Bosch Stiftung. It is led by the MMC with six strategic partners: the C40 Cities Leadership Group (C40 Cities), IOM, Metropolis, United Cities and Local Governments (UCLG), UN-Habitat, and UNHCR. See also Samer Saliba, Savarni Sanka, and Helen Elizabeth Yu, *Global Cities Fund for Migrants and Refugees Progress Report* (New York: Mayors Migration Council, December 2023), https://mmc-production.s3.amazonaws.com/wp-content/uploads/2024/04/03165907/Progress-report-under-40.pdf.

8. Saliba and Zanuso, *Municipal Finance for Migrants*, 22–23.

9. Anne Krueger, who coined the term in 1974, said that government restrictions on economic activity give rise to different forms of rents, and people often compete for the rents: "Sometimes, such competition is perfectly legal. In other instances, rent seeking takes other forms, such as bribery, corruption, smuggling, and black markets." Anne O. Krueger, "The Political Economy of the Rent-Seeking Society," *American Economic Review* 64, no. 3 (1974): 291.

10. "EU Support to Refugees in Türkiye," European Commission, accessed October 25, 2024, https://neighbourhood-enlargement.ec.europa.eu/enlargement-policy/turkiye/eu-support-refugees-turkiye_en. See also Sigrid Lupieri, "When 'Brothers and Sisters' Become 'Foreigners': Syrian Refugees and the Politics of Healthcare in Jordan," *Third World Quarterly* 41, no. 6 (2020): 958–975; Gerasimos Tsourapas, "The Syrian Refugee Crisis and Foreign Policy Decision-Making in Jordan, Lebanon, and Türkiye," *Journal of Global Security Studies* 4, no. 4 (2019): 464–481; Luisa F. Freier et al., "Refugee Commodification: The Diffusion of Refugee Rent-Seeking in the Global South," *Third World Quarterly* 42, no. 11 (2021): 2747–2766. For more on the European Commission's Facility for Türkiye, see "The EU Facility for Refugees in Turkey" (factsheet, European Commission, updated December 2024), https://neighbourhood-enlargement.ec.europa.eu/system/files/2023-08/frit_factsheet.pdf.

11. Zeynep Balcioglu, "Stretching the Limits of Authority: Why Do Local Governments Provide for Refugees?" (PhD diss., Northeastern University, 2021).

12. A UNHCR Istanbul official said, "We select municipalities that we want to work with depending on their previous experience, capacity, and willingness to work on a project together." Balcioglu, "Stretching the Limits of Authority," 90.

13. Anonymous municipal official, April 2019, quoted in Balcioglu, "Stretching the Limits of Authority," 90.

14. Balcioglu, "Stretching the Limits of Authority," 91.

15. *The Urban Amplifier: Adapting to Urban Specificities. Report on Humanitarian Action in Urban Crises* (Brussels: ECHO, European Commission, 2018), 10–11, https://ec.europa.eu/echo/files/aid/factsheet/Urban_Report_final_version_printed.pdf.

16. *Urban Amplifier*, 10–11.

17. Saman Rejali, "Race, Equity, and Neo-colonial Legacies: Identifying Paths Forward for Principled Humanitarian Action," *Humanitarian Law and Policy* (blog), International Committee of the Red Cross, July 16, 2020, https://blogs.icrc.org/law-and-policy/2020/07/16/race-equity-neo-colonial-legacies-humanitarian/.

18. "Lebanon 2022: Trends in Reported Funding," UN OCHA Financial Tracking Service, accessed November 24, 2024, https://fts.unocha.org/countries/124/summary/2022.

19. "In 2019, funds were channeled through 75 of 123 appealing partners, primarily to UN and international NGO partners. National NGOs received only 4 percent of the funding under the LCRP." *Lebanon Crisis Response Plan: Annual Report 2019*

(Geneva, Switzerland: UNHCR, 2021), 16, https://reliefweb.int/report/lebanon/lebanon-crisis-response-plan-annual-report-2019.

20. All figures taken from "Lebanon Summary 2015," UN OCHA Financial Tracking Service, accessed October 25, 2024, https://fts.unocha.org/countries/124/summary/2015; "Lebanon Summary 2011," UN OCHA Financial Tracking Service, accessed October 25, 2024, https://fts.unocha.org/countries/124/summary/2011.

21. For more on the World Bank's involvement in Lebanon's Emergency National Poverty Targeting Programme Project, see *Implementation Completion and Results Report*, no. ICR00005534 (Washington, DC: World Bank, 2014), https://documents1.worldbank.org/curated/en/238531641478723882/pdf/Lebanon-Emergency-National-Poverty-Targeting-Project.pdf. The CFF was focused on providing concessional financing to middle-income countries most affected by the presence of large numbers of refugees. Its initial focus was the impact of the Syrian crisis on Jordan and Lebanon, with a primary focus on infrastructure. As of 2020, the CFF had been adapted to address the impacts of current and future refugee crises on a global scale. See *Lebanon Crisis Response Plan, 2017–2020 (2019 Update)* (Geneva, Switzerland: UNHCR, 2019), https://www.undp.org/lebanon/publications/lebanon-crisis-response-plan-2017-2020-2019-update.

22. The Paris Declaration on Aid Effectiveness in 1995 sought to enhance the coordination of aid between official development agencies and partner countries, including by aligning donor support to partner countries and improving mutual accountability. However, despite several subsequent forums and interventions recognizing local governments as the main actors in aid coordination and effectiveness (such as the 2008 Accra Agenda for Action), the Paris Declaration has not succeeded in enhancing aid effectiveness. Many attribute this failure to donors' emphasis on mechanisms of aid delivery rather than the development impact of aid. See Marwa Boustani et al., "Responding to the Syrian Crisis in Lebanon: Collaboration between Aid Agencies and Local Governance Structures" (working paper, IIED, London, 2016), 7–8.

23. *Lebanon Crisis Response Plan 2023* (Beirut: Government of Lebanon and UNHCR, January 2023), https://data.unhcr.org/en/documents/details/100389.

24. Boustani et al., "Responding to the Syrian Crisis," 7–8.

25. Anonymous ex–UNHCR official, email exchange with author, November 2023.

26. See *Syria Refugee Response: UNHCR Institutional and Community Support* (Geneva, Switzerland: UNHCR, 2015), https://www.unhcr.org/lb/wp-content/uploads/sites/16/2017/03/UNHCR-2015_Q4_EN.pdf; and *Syria Refugee Response:*

UNHCR Institutional and Community Support Overview (Geneva, Switzerland: UNHCR, 2017), https://www.unhcr.org/lb/wp-content/uploads/sites/16/2017/03/UNHCR-Institutional-Community-Support-Overview_31May17.pdf.

Chapter 9. Just Give Them Cash

1. "Cash-Based Transfers: Empowering People, Markets and Countries" (factsheet, World Food Programme, November 2020), https://www.wfp.org/publications/wfp-cash-based-transfers-empowering-people-markets-governments-2020; and "Food Assistance," World Food Programme, accessed October 25, 2024, https://www.wfp.org/food-assistance. See also Angus Urquhart et al., *Global Humanitarian Assistance Report 2023* (Bristol, UK: Development Initiatives, 2023), 17, https://devinit.org/resources/global-humanitarian-assistance-report-2023/.

2. Ninette Kelley, interview with author, November 30, 2020. See also "Cash Assistance Gives Refugees the Power of Choice," UNHCR, December 9, 2019, https://www.unhcr.org/en-us/news/stories/2019/12/5b6c40f04/cash-assistance-gives-refugees-power-choice.html.

3. The data on child marriages are unreliable, but see *Child Marriage in the Middle East and North Africa—Lebanon Country Brief* (Amman: UNICEF Middle East and North Africa Regional Office, in collaboration with the International Center for Research on Women, 2017), https://www.unicef.org/mena/media/1806/file/MENA-CMReport-LebanonBrief.pdf.

4. *Lebanon Crisis Response Plan, 2017–2020* (Beirut: Government of Lebanon and the United Nations, 2018).

5. According to the *Lebanon Crisis Response Plan* (p. 37), throughout 2017, the National Poverty Targeting Programme Project launched a recertification exercise targeting enrolled beneficiaries and seeking out others who self-referred. The exercise sought to refine the existing database and identify the estimated 46,000 households living in extreme poverty. This process was to be finalized by the end of 2017. The recertification was based on updated poverty estimations: the lower poverty line is set at $5.70 per capita per day and the higher poverty line at $8.60 per capita per day.

6. UNHCR Global Focus, *2016 Year-End Report, Operation: Lebanon,* https://reporting.unhcr.org/sites/default/files/pdfsummaries/GR2016-Lebanon-eng.pdf. The report states that out of a final budget in 2016 of US$351,079,239, expenditures on "Community Empowerment and Self Reliance" totaled US$11,109,005. Subsequent Global Focus year-end reports indicate an increase in 2017 to US$15.7 million, then a decrease in 2018 to just over US$12 million. See also "Lebanon Host Communities

Support Project," United Nations Development Programme, https://www.undp.org/lebanon/projects/lebanon-host-communities-support-lhsp.

7. Ninette Kelley, interview with author, November 30, 2020.

8. Jad Chaaban et al., *Multi-Purpose Cash Assistance in Lebanon: Impact Evaluation on the Well-Being of Syrian Refugees* (Beirut: American University of Beirut and CAMEALEON, 2020), https://www.nrc.no/globalassets/pdf/reports/camealeon-impact-assessment-of-multi-purpose-cash-assistance-for-syrian-refugees-in-lebanon/camealeon-mpc-impact-assessment.pdf.

9. "UN Plans to Cut Number of Refugees Receiving Cash Aid in Lebanon by a Third, Citing Funding Cuts," *New Arab*, November 2, 2023, https://www.newarab.com/news/un-cut-cash-aid-some-refugees-lebanon-amid-crunch.

10. J. Edward Taylor et al., "Economic Impact of Refugees," *Proceedings of the National Academy of Sciences* 113, no. 27 (2016): 7449–7453, https://doi.org/10.1073/pnas.1604566113.

11. For example, one study compared the outcomes of different aid models in two refugee camps in Kenya: Kakuma (no cash assistance) and Kalobeyei (cash assistance and agricultural programs). Alexander Betts et al., "The Kalobeyei Settlement: A Self-Reliance Model for Refugees?," *Journal of Refugee Studies* 33, no. 1 (2020): 1–21, https://doi.org/10.1093/jrs/fez063. Other studies analyzed the economic impacts of refugees on host-country economies within a ten-kilometer radius of three Congolese refugee camps in Rwanda—Mohamad Alloush et al., "Economic Life in Refugee Camps," *World Development* 95 (2017): 334–347–and more recently, in Kiryadongo settlement: Prankur Gupta et al., "Cash Transfers Amid Shocks: A Large, One-Time, Unconditional Cash Transfer to Refugees in Uganda Has Multidimensional Benefits after 19 Months," *World Development* 173 (January 2024).

12. Elsa Valli, Amber Peterman, and Melissa Hidrobo, "Economic Transfers and Social Cohesion in a Refugee-Hosting Setting," *Journal of Development Studies* 55, no. S1 (2019): 1–20, https://doi.org/10.1080/00220388.2019.1687879.

13. Tina Zintl and Markus Loewe, "More than the Sum of Its Parts: Donor-Sponsored Cash-for-Work Programmes and Social Cohesion in Jordanian Communities Hosting Syrian Refugees," *European Journal of Development Research* 34, no. 3 (2022): 1–20, https://doi.org/10.1057/s41287-022-00536-y.

14. Mohamed Ireg et al., "Five Reasons Not to Use Cash for Work," *Mercy Corps*, March 21, 2024, https://medium.com/mercy-corps-economic-opportunities/five-reasons-not-to-use-cash-for-work-ff983332783e.

15. Zintl and Loewe, "Sum of Its Parts," 1292.

16. Zintl and Loewe, "Sum of Its Parts," 1292–1293. For a discussion of the mixed impact on employment, social cohesion, and household income, see also Markus Loewe et al., *Community Effects of Cash-for-Work Programmes in Jordan* (Bonn: German Development Institute, 2020), https://www.idos-research.de/uploads/media/Study_103.pdf.

Chapter 10. Trash Mountain

1. Bassel F. Salloukh, "The Syrian War: Spillover Effects on Lebanon," *Middle East Policy* 24, no. 1 (2017): 74.

2. "'Cut Off from Life Itself': Lebanon's Failure on the Right to Electricity," Human Rights Watch, March 9, 2023, https://www.hrw.org/report/2023/03/09/cut-life-itself/lebanons-failure-right-electricity.

3. Andrew Maddocks, Robert Samuel Young, and Paul Reig, "Ranking the World's Most Water-Stressed Countries in 2040," World Resources Institute (WRI), August 26, 2015, https://www.wri.org/insights/ranking-worlds-most-water-stressed-countries-2040.

4. According to FAOSTAT database, cited by Hadi Jaafar et al., "Refugees, Water Balance, and Water Stress: Lessons Learned from Lebanon," *Ambio* 49, no. 6 (2020): 1–12.

5. Unnamed expert, interview with author, October 2018, Tripoli.

6. Lebanon is one of twenty-two contracting parties to the Barcelona Convention, adopted in 1995. "UNEP/MAP: The Mediterranean Coastal and Marine Environment," United Nations Environment Programme (UNEP), accessed October 25, 2024, https://www.unep.org/unepmap/node/7619.

7. Abdelazim M. Negm and Noama Shareef, *Waste Management in MENA Regions* (Cham, Switzerland: Springer International, 2019).

8. Michel Soto Chalhoub, "Public Policy and Technology Choices for Municipal Solid Waste Management: A Recent Case in Lebanon," *Cogent Environmental Science* 4, no. 1 (2018): 1–12, https://doi.org/10.1080/23311843.2018.1529853.

9. Peter Ngau and Harro von Blottnitz, *Integrated Solid Waste Management Plan for Nairobi* (Nairobi: Centre for Urban Innovations, 2010), http://www.centreforurbaninnovations.org/content/integrated-solid-waste-management-plan-city-nairobi-kenya.

10. For Addis, see "At Least 35 Dead, Dozens Missing after Ethiopia Landslide at Garbage Dump," NBC News, March 12, 2017, https://www.nbcnews.com/news/world/ethiopia-landslide-garbage-dump-kills-35-dozens-missing-n732396. For Ma-

puto, see Shaun Swingler, "Explosion at Mozambique Rubbish Dump Leaves at Least 17 Dead," *The Guardian,* February 26, 2018, https://www.theguardian.com/global-development/2018/feb/26/explosion-fatal-rubbish-landslide-mozambique-hulene-dump. For Kampala, see Aoife Hilton, "Investigation Ordered into Uganda Landslide That Left 10 Dead," ABC News, August 12, 2024, https://www.abc.net.au/news/2024-08-12/investigation-into-uganda-landslide-ordered/104216414.

11. See Jalal Halwani et al., "Waste Management in Lebanon—Tripoli Case Study," in *Waste Management in MENA Regions,* ed. Abdelazim M. Negm and Noama Shareef (Cham, Switzerland: Springer International, 2019), 228, table 11.2. See also Sara Maassarani, Nabil Mohareb, and Mostafa Abdelbaset, "Proposing a Solid Waste Management Plan in Tripoli, North Lebanon: An Individual Awareness Based Solution," *Regional Science Policy and Practice* 13, no. 3 (2021): 921–943, https://doi.org/10.1111/rsp3.12380.

12. Since 2006, the United States has provided more than $5.5 billion in total foreign assistance to Lebanon, including military assistance. Funding designated as "humanitarian" supports economic growth, workforce employability and productivity, good governance, social cohesion, and access to clean water. "U.S. Relations with Lebanon," US Department of State, accessed July 26, 2024, https://www.state.gov/u-s-relations-with-lebanon/.

13. In a list of 180 countries, the 2018 Corruptions Perceptions Index, produced by Transparency International, ranked Lebanon as the 138th "least corrupt nation"—meaning there are forty-two countries where corruption is worse. "Corruption Perceptions Index 2018," Transparency International, accessed October 25, 2024, https://www.transparency.org/cpi2018.

14. Elizabeth Saleh, "Recycling Policies from the Bottom Up: Waste Work in Lebanon," *Arab Reform Initiative,* January 8, 2021, https://www.arab-reform.net/publication/recycling-policies-from-the-bottom-up-waste-work-in-lebanon/.

15. *Global Waste Management Outlook 2024: Beyond an Age of Waste—Turning Rubbish into a Resource* (Nairobi: UN Environment Programme, 2024), https://www.unep.org/resources/global-waste-management-outlook-2024. "Fair Circularity Initiative: Respecting Rights in Circular Value Chains," Fair Circularity Initiative, accessed October 25, 2024, https://faircircularity.org.

16. Inger Anderson, "Making Rubbish a Resource: End to Wasteful Culture," speech at the launch of the *Global Waste Management Outlook 2024,* February 28, 2024, Nairobi, https://www.unep.org/news-and-stories/speech/making-rubbish-resource-end-wasteful-culture.

17. "The Global Commitment 2022," Ellen MacArthur Foundation, October 31, 2022, https://www.ellenmacarthurfoundation.org/global-commitment-2022/overview.

18. *Breaking the Plastic Wave: A Comprehensive Assessment of Pathways towards Stopping Ocean Plastic Pollution* (Philadelphia: Pew Charitable Trusts and SYSTEMIQ, 2020), https://www.pewtrusts.org/-/media/assets/2020/10/breakingtheplasticwave_mainreport.pdf; Simon Reddy and Winnie Lau, "Breaking the Plastic Wave: Top Findings for Preventing Plastic Pollution," Pew Charitable Trusts, July 23, 2020, https://www.pewtrusts.org/en/research-and-analysis/articles/2020/07/23/breaking-the-plastic-wave-top-findings.

19. WIEGO, https://www.wiego.org.

20. International Alliance of Waste Pickers, accessed October 25, 2024, https://globalrec.org. See also "Waste Pickers," WIEGO, accessed October 25, 2024, https://www.wiego.org/informal-economy/occupational-groups/waste-pickers/.

21. Saleh, "Recycling Policies."

22. Saleh, "Recycling Policies."

Chapter 11. The Smuggling Economy

1. Anne-Marie El-Hage, "The Fight against Smuggling between Lebanon and Syria: All Smoke and Mirrors," *L'Orient-Le Jour,* June 2, 2020, https://today.lorientlejour.com/article/1220202/the-fight-against-smuggling-between-lebanon-and-syria-all-smoke-and-mirrors.html.

2. Until 2019, when President Omar al-Bashir was overthrown, the Sudan government considered Syrians "guests." They could live, work, start a business, and access services like education and health care on an equal footing with Sudanese citizens. See "Syrian Refugees Are No Longer Guests in Sudan," *Al-Monitor,* March 2021, https://www.al-monitor.com/originals/2021/03/sudan-syria-refugees-resident-travel.html#ixzz78KME9dEK. See Tuesday Reitano and Peter Tinti, "Survive and Advance: The Economics of Smuggling Refugees and Migrants into Europe" (ISS paper no. 289, Institute for Security Studies, November 2015), 8, https://issafrica.s3.amazonaws.com/site/uploads/Paper289-2.pdf.

3. Lucia Bird and Tuesday Reitano, "Smugglers' Paradise—Cities as Hubs of the Illicit Migration Business," Mixed Migration Centre, April 7, 2121, https://mixedmigration.org/smugglers-paradise-cities-as-hubs-of-the-illicit-migration-business/; Nicholas Blanford, "Case Study: The Lebanon-Syria Border" (paper presented at the Rethinking International Relations after the Arab Revolutions, Université Saint Joseph, Beirut, April 16, 2016). For an interesting discussion of a

smuggling boss, see Luigi Achilli, "The 'Good' Smuggler: The Ethics and Morals of Human Smuggling among Syrians," *Annals of the American Academy of Political and Social Science* 676, no. 1 (2018): 85–86, https://doi.org/10.1177/0002716217746641; Peter Tinti and Tuesday Reitano, *Migrant, Refugee, Smuggler, Savior* (London: Hurst, 2016).

4. Tine Gade, "Sunni Islamists in Tripoli and the Asad Regime, 1966–2014," *Syria Studies* 7, no. 2 (2015): 20–65. According to Gade, in North Lebanon and on the Syrian coastline "there were more than 50 clandestine ports . . . where one embarked goods on the sea, in arrangement with the customs officials. If they refused to let goods pass, smugglers could kill them" (59).

5. Gade, "Sunni Islamists in Tripoli," 63.

6. El-Hage, "Fight against Smuggling."

7. Achilli, "'Good' Smuggler."

8. See, for example, Romm Lewkowicz, "Informal Practices in Illicit Border-Regimes: The Economy of Legal and Fake Travel Documents Sustaining the EU Asylum System," *Migration Letters* 18, no. 2 (2021): 177–188, https://doi.org/10.33182/ml.v18i2.1189.

9. Bird and Reitano, "Smugglers' Paradise," 155.

10. Achilli, "'Good' Smuggler," 85–86.

11. Reitano and Tinti, "Survive and Advance."

12. Bird and Reitano, "Smugglers' Paradise," 155.

13. According to IOM, the Nigerien authorities estimated that 120,000–150,000 migrants transited Niger in 2016. Most go through Agadez. See "IOM Niger Opens Migrant Information Office in Agadez," IOM, accessed October 25, 2024, https://www.iom.int/news/iom-niger-opensgrant-information-office-agadez. However, Raineri suggests that IOM data about smuggling through Niger are frequently inaccurate. Luca Raineri, "Human Smuggling across Niger: State-Sponsored Protection Rackets and Contradictory Security Imperatives," *Journal of Modern African Studies* 56, no. 1 (2018): 69–88.

14. Raineri, "Human Smuggling across Niger," 69. The smuggler was interviewed by Raineri.

15. Ben Taub, "The Desperate Journey of a Trafficked Girl," *New Yorker*, April 3, 2017, https://www.newyorker.com/magazine/2017/04/10/the-desperate-journey-of-a-trafficked-girl.

16. After Europe's "migration crisis" in 2015, the European Union set up the Emergency Trust Fund for Africa, with pledges of €5 billion, to "address the root causes of instability, forced displacement and irregular migration and to contribute

to better migration management" ("Emergency Trust Fund for Africa," European Union, https://trust-fund-for-africa.europa.eu/index_en). For the period 2021–2024, Niger was slated to receive some €503 million from the EU, in part to control transit migration to Libya ("International Partnerships: Niger," European Commission, https://international-partnerships.ec.europa.eu/countries/niger_en). However, the coup in Niger in 2023 scuttled the plan, as Niger's new government repealed a 2015 law that had been a cornerstone of EU efforts to curb migration, and then cancelled two EU missions working with Niger to fight jihadist militants and stop the movement of people from West Africa toward Europe. See Sophie Douce, "In Post-Coup Niger, Migration Becomes Legal Again," *New Humanitarian,* May 6, 2024, https://www.thenewhumanitarian.org/news-feature/2024/05/06/post-coup-niger-migration-becomes-legal-again.

17. Raineri, "Human Smuggling across Niger," 74.

18. Raineri, "Human Smuggling across Niger," 77–78.

19. "Strengthening Cooperation in the Fight against Migrant Smuggling: The European Union and Niger Launch Operational Partnership to Tackle Migrant Smuggling" (press release, European Commission, July 15, 2022, Brussels), https://ec.europa.eu/commission/presscorner/detail/en/ip_22_4536.

Chapter 12. Comparing the Experiences of Cairo and Tripoli

1. Jennifer Alix-Garcia et al., "Displaced Populations, Humanitarian Assistance, and Hosts: A Framework for Analyzing Impacts on Semi-urban Households," *World Development* 40, no. 2 (2012): 373–386.

2. The political union, which included the occupied Gaza Strip, was led by Egyptian president Gamal Abdel Nasser. After Syria seceded from the union following the 1961 Syrian coup d'état, Egypt continued to be known officially as the United Arab Republic until September 1971, when the union was formally dissolved by Anwar Sadat. See Elie Podeh, *The Decline of Arab Unity: The Rise and Fall of the United Arab Republic* (Liverpool: Liverpool University Press, 2015).

3. *Triangulation of Migrants Stock in Egypt* (Cairo: IOM, 2022), https://egypt.iom.int/sites/g/files/tmzbdl1021/files/documents/migration-stock-in-egypt-june-2022_v4_eng.pdf.

Chapter 13. Egypt

1. "Refugee Context in Egypt," UNHCR, accessed October 25, 2024, https://www.unhcr.org/eg/about-us/refugee-context-in-egypt#:~:text=As%20of%2031%20December%202023,more%20than%2054%20other%20nationalities.

2. According to Egypt's Central Agency for Public Mobilization and Statistics (CAPMAS), in 2016 there were 9.47 million Egyptian expatriates, of whom 6.23 million live in the Arab world, 1.58 million in the Americas, 1.24 million in Europe, 340,000 in Australia, and 46,000 in Africa (mostly in South Africa). See "Egyptian Diaspora," accessed February 24, 2020, http://www.capmas.gov.eg. See also Gerasimos Tsourapas, *Egypt: Migration and Diaspora Politics in an Emerging Transit Country* (Migration Policy Institute, 2018).

3. "Urban Population (% of Total Population)—Egypt," World Bank, accessed October 25, 2024, https://data.worldbank.org/indicator/SP.URB.TOTL.IN.ZS. See also Anda David, Nelly El-Mallakh, and Jackline Wahba, "Internal versus International Migration in Egypt: Together or Far Apart" (working paper no. 1366, Agence Française de Développement, 2019).

4. The New Suez Canal will extend the existing canal by seventy-two kilometers. The government claims it will more than double annual revenues from $5 billion to $12.5 billion by allowing two-way passage through much of the canal, and it will create new employment via new logistics, commerce, and industrial zones. See "The Cost of Progress: We Meet Some of the Thousands of Sinai Villagers Displaced by Suez Canal Expansion," *Vice*, March 3, 2015, https://www.vice.com/en/article/8x7zdz/the-cost-of-progress-we-meet-some-of-the-thousands-of-sinai-villagers-displaced-by-suez-canal-expansion; and "'New Suez Canal' Construction Displaces Over 2,000 People in Egypt," *Middle East Eye*, February 13, 2015, https://www.middleeasteye.net/news/new-suez-canal-construction-displaces-over-2000-people-egypt#:~:text=%27New%20Suez%20Canal%27%20construction%20displaces%20over%202%2C000%20people%20in%20Egypt,-Thousands%20of%20homes&text=At%20least%202%2C000%20Egyptians%20have,Red%20Sea%20and%20Mediterranean%20Sea. See also Mohamed Abdel Shakur et al., "War and Forced Migration in Egypt: The Experience of Evacuation from the Suez Canal Cities (1967–1976)," *Arab Studies Quarterly* 27, no. 3 (2005): 21–39.

5. The International Committee of the Red Cross (ICRC) asked Egypt to respect the fourth Geneva Convention and chartered fourteen ships, between January and September 1957, to transport more than 7,000 people to Greece or Italy as a first step to permanent resettlement. "The ICRC since 1945: The Suez Crisis of 1956," ICRC, accessed October 25, 2024, https://www.icrc.org/en/doc/resources/documents/misc/icrc_suez56.htm.

6. *Statistical Annex 2023* (Geneva, Switzerland: UNHCR, 2023), tables 2 and 3. https://www.unhcr.org/us/global-trends.

7. After 1948, Egypt became responsible for the welfare of two separate Palestinian communities: the 87,000 Palestinians living in Egypt proper and the 200,000 Palestinians living in the Gaza Strip, which was occupied by Egypt. After the 1967 War, the Gaza Strip fell under Israeli control, and some 13,000 additional Palestinians entered Egypt. Oroub el-Abed, *Unprotected: Palestinians in Egypt since 1948* (Washington, DC: Institute for Palestine Studies, 2009).

8. Tsourapas, *Egypt: Migration and Diaspora Politics*.

9. Oroub el-Abed, "The Invisible Community: Egypt's Palestinians," policy brief, *Al-Shabaka*, June 2011, . https://al-shabaka.org/briefs/the-invisible-community-egypts-palestinians/. See also Oroub el-Abed, "The Palestinians in Egypt: Identity, Basic Rights and Host State Policies," *Refugee Survey Quarterly* 28, no. 2–3 (2009): 531–549.

10. The Second Sudanese Civil War, one of the longest civil wars on record, was between the government of Sudan and the Sudan People's Liberation Army, which fought for the independence of southern Sudan. It lasted from 1983 to 2005 and continued the First Sudanese Civil War (1955–72). The civil war engulfed the Nuba Mountains and the Blue Nile, which are still regions of conflict today. Some two million people died in the war, and four million people were displaced. Six years after the end of the war, South Sudan became independent in 2011. The peace did not last, and the civil war in South Sudan started in 2013 and continues today.

11. *UNHCR Statistical Annex 2023* (Geneva, Switzerland: UNHCR, 2023), table 5, https://www.unhcr.org/us/global-trends.

12. "From a Flood to a Trickle: Neighboring States Stop Iraqis Fleeing War and Persecution," Human Rights Watch, 2007, https://www.hrw.org/report/2007/04/17/flood-trickle/neighboring-states-stop-iraqis-fleeing-war-and-persecution.

13. Patrick Kingsley, "Syrian Refugees Suffer Backlash in Egypt after Mohamed Morsi's Removal," *The Guardian*, July 25, 2013, https://www.theguardian.com/world/2013/jul/25/syrian-refugees-suffer-backlash-egypt.

14. Kelsey P. Norman, *Reluctant Reception: Refugees, Migration and Governance in the Middle East and North Africa* (Cambridge: Cambridge University Press, 2021), 43–66.

15. Other reservations included clauses related to personal status, rationing, and social security. A "reservation" is a unilateral statement by a state, when signing, ratifying, accepting, approving, or acceding to a treaty, that excludes or modifies the legal effect of certain provisions of the treaty. Article 2 of the 1969 Vienna Convention on the Law of Treaties," accessed October 25, 2024, https://web.archive.org/web/20050208040137/http://www.un.org/law/ilc/texts/treatfra.htm.

16. *Services for Refugees and Asylum-Seekers Registered with UNHCR in Greater Cairo* (Geneva, Switzerland: UNHCR, December 2019), https://www.unhcr.org/eg/wp-content/uploads/sites/36/2020/01/Merged-brochure-En-December-2019.pdf. See also *Vulnerability Assessment of Syrian Refugees in Egypt* (Cairo: UNHCR, 2017), 20.

17. Ryan Philip, personal communication with the author. Egyptians saw the gigantic Mogamma building as an "icon of red tape and administrative failure," and the extremely trying bureaucratic process was well known. At the end of 2021, as part of Tahrir Square's "facelift," the Mogamma was bought by a consortium of US-Emirati companies whose goal is to turn it into a giant hotel. Amr Emam, "Egypt to Turn Iconic Tahrir Square Building into Luxury Hotel," *Middle East Eye*, December 15, 2021, https://www.middleeasteye.net/news/egypt-turn-its-bureaucracy-icon-luxury-hotel.

18. Both the Refugee Registration Card (blue card), valid for three years, and the Asylum-seeker Registration Card (yellow card), valid for eighteen months, had six spaces for residence permit stickers that indicated renewals every six months at a cost of forty Egyptian pounds. In October 2019, these procedures changed, and henceforth refugees and asylum seekers were issued ID numbers and residence permit cards from the Ministry of Interior. People older than twelve years old got their own card at a cost of E£100 per card, and those under twelve were added as dependents on their guardian's card. Sama Osama, "Egypt Issues New Permit Residence Cards for Refugees and Asylum-Seekers," *Ahram Online*, October 28, 2019, https://english.ahram.org.eg/NewsContent/1/64/354842/Egypt/Politics-/Egypt-issues-new-permit-residence-cards-for-refuge.aspx.

19. The waiting time from being admitted to the United States to getting an immigration court hearing is now about two and a half years. In November 2023, the immigration court asylum backlog (in both the immigration court system and within U.S. Citizenship and Immigration Services) surpassed three million cases. The Transactional Records Access Clearinghouse (TRAC) at Syracuse University tracks immigration into the United States. "Statistical Analysis of Syrian Refugees in Egypt," TRAC, accessed October 25, 2024, https://trac.syr.edu/reports/734/. See also "Mounting Backlogs Undermine U.S. Immigration System and Impede Biden Policy Changes," Migration Policy Institute, February 23, 2022, https://www.migrationpolicy.org/article/us-immigration-backlogs-mounting-undermine-biden. Meeting the standards for asylum is difficult. Denials are issued in about two-thirds of the cases heard by asylum officers (USCIS) and more than half the cases heard by immigration judges. According to TRAC, asylum denial rates increased to record highs in FY 2019, with just over 60 percent of all asylum applications denied.

"Immigration Court Backlog Tool," TRAC, accessed October 25, 2024, https://trac.syr.edu/immigration/reports/590/.

20. For example, in 2010, the Egyptian government deported Sudanese men who had been granted refugee status by UNHCR ("Egypt: Don't Deport Darfur Refugees to Face Persecution," ReliefWeb, accessed October 25, 2024, https://reliefweb.int/report/egypt/egypt-dont-deport-darfur-refugees-face-persecution), and more recently there have been ongoing reports of Eritreans being deported back to Eritrea. See also Nour Abdel Aziz, "Out of Sight, Out of Rights: Rejected Asylum Seekers and Closed-Files Individuals in Egypt" (master's thesis, American University in Cairo, 2018).

21. Nour Abdel Aziz, *Surviving in Cairo as a Closed-File Refugee: Socio-economic and Protection Challenges* (London: International Institute for Environment and Development, 2017).

22. These were Afghanistan, Eritrea, Ethiopia, Iraq, Nigeria, Somalia, South Sudan, Sudan, Türkiye, and Yemen. Syrians automatically receive asylum status, so they are not included in these numbers. *2022 Statistical Annex* (Geneva, Switzerland: UNHCR, 2022), tables 9 and 10, https://www.unhcr.org/sites/default/files/2023-06/global-trends-report-2022.pdf.

Chapter 14. Drops in the Bucket

1. In June 2022, the government destroyed or removed the famous wooden houseboats that had lined a section of the Nile's western bank since the 1800s. Many Cairenes loudly objected to this act of destruction. The authorities wanted to replace residential houseboats with floating cafés and restaurants "in line with government plans to modernize—and monetize—much of Cairo by handing it over to private developers or the military, bulldozing several historic neighborhoods to build new high-rises, roads, and bridges." Vivian Yee and Nada Rashwan, "Egypt Destroys Nile Houseboats, Washing Away a Living Lore," *New York Times,* June 29, 2022. See also "In Ongoing Campaign of Demolition Intensifying across Cairo, Iconic and Unique Houseboats Find No Safe Port," *Cairo Observer,* July 2, 2022, https://cairobserver.com/post/688692185875529728/in-on-going-campaign-of-demolition-intensifying#.YtivxS-B1hA.

2. Regina Kipper and Marion Fischer, *Cairo's Informal Areas between Urban Challenges and Hidden Potentials. Facts. Voices. Visions.* (Cairo: GTZ, 2009), 15, https://www.citiesalliance.org/sites/default/files/2019-07/CairosInformalAreas_fulltext.pdf.

3. David Sims, *Understanding Cairo: The Logic of a City Out of Control* (Cairo: American University in Cairo Press, 2012), 253–254.

4. As of 2023, by Statista.com estimates. "Total Population of Egypt from 2018 to 2028," Statista, accessed October 26, 2024, https://www.statista.com/statistics/377302/total-population-of-egypt/. The national census of April 2017 put Egypt's population at 94,798,827 citizens living in Egypt and another 9.4 million Egyptian expatriates. The 2006 census put Cairo's population at sixteen million inhabitants, but experts believe the actual number was closer to twenty million. *Migration Booklet in Egypt 2018* (Cairo: Central Agency for Public Mobilization and Statistics, 2019), https://www.capmas.gov.eg/Admin/News/PressRelease/201991215340_Migration%20Booklet%20Eng.pdf. (This contains summary statistics from Egypt's 2017 census and other sources incl. UNHCR and surveys.)

5. Sims, *Understanding Cairo*, 46.

6. Sims, *Understanding Cairo*, 46–50.

7. Sims, *Understanding Cairo*, 51.

8. Sims, *Understanding Cairo*, 52.

9. Sims, *Understanding Cairo*, 62. See also Marwa A. Khalifa, "Evolution of Informal Settlements Upgrading Strategies in Egypt: From Negligence to Participatory Development," *Ain Shams Engineering Journal* 6, no. 4 (2015), https://doi.org/10.1016/j.asej.2015.04.008.

10. Elena Piffero, "Beyond Rules and Regulations: The Growth of Informal Cairo," in *Cairo's Informal Areas: Between Urban Challenges and Hidden Potentials*, ed. Regina Kipper and Marion Fischer (Cairo: GTZ, 2009), 22–25.

11. 'Ashwa'iyyat, the plural for 'ashwa'iyya (lit. "haphazard") refers to slums or informal communities in Egypt. Asef Bayat and Eric Denis, "Who Is Afraid of Ashwaiyyat? Urban Change and Politics in Egypt," *Environment and Urbanization* 12, no. 2 (2000): 111.

12. The 5.9 earthquake occurred on October 12, 1992, centered near the village of Dahshur, eighteen kilometers south of Cairo. It caused more than 500 fatalities and 6,500 injuries, and damaged or destroyed thousands of buildings. P. C. Thenhaus, M. Çelebi, and R. V. Sharp, "The October 12, 1992, Dahshur, Egypt, Earthquake," *Earthquakes and Volcanoes* (USGS) 24, no. 1 (1993): 27–31, https://pubs.usgs.gov/publication/70169014.

13. Heba Elhanafy, "Cairo's Informal Highrise Market," *Charter Cities Institute* (blog), November 12, 2020, https://chartercitiesinstitute.org/blog-posts/cairos-informal-highrise-market/.

14. Deen Sharp, "Haphazard Urbanisation: Urban Informality, Politics and Power in Egypt," *Urban Studies* 59, no. 4 (2022): 738.

15. Ryan Philip, "Getting By on the Margins," Cairo, Egypt Case Report (Refugees in Towns Project, Tufts University, 2018), https://refugeesintowns.net/all-reports/cairo-2018.

Chapter 15. The Bus to 6th of October

1. *Mofwadiyeh* means the "commission," but when refugees use the term they mean UNHCR.

2. The New Administrative Capital (NAC) is part of an initiative called Egypt Vision 2030, which President el-Sisi began in 2015. There are very few people living in the NAC, and the project is heavily criticized both because of its reputation as a "city for the rich" and because of the government's troubles in funding its construction. See Robert Draper, "Egypt's Audacious Plan to Build a New Capital in the Desert," *National Geographic,* October 19, 2022; and Declan Walsh and Vivian Yee, "A New Capital Worthy of the Pharaohs Rises in Egypt, but at What Price?," *New York Times,* October 8, 2022, https://www.nytimes.com/2022/10/08/world/middleeast/egypt-new-capital.html.

3. According to Natalie Cowling, "Biggest Shopping Centers in Africa in 2023, by Floor Area," Statista, April 5, 2024, https://www.statista.com/statistics/1426769/biggest-shopping-centers-in-africa-by-floor-area/.

4. Extrapolating from the 2006 census. Ibrahim Rizk Hegazy and Wael Seddik Moustafa, "Toward Revitalization of New Towns in Egypt: Case Study: Sixth of October," *International Journal of Sustainable Built Environment* 2, no. 1 (2013): 14.

5. I could find no substantive information on the number of Syrians living in Egypt before 2011.

6. UNHCR put the total count at twenty-eight, of whom eleven were under twelve years old. Other sources have reported as many as 156 deaths. Natalie Forcier points out that "the discrepancy may be attributed to the large number of protest participants who were closed file refugees and therefore not 'individuals of concern' to UNHCR." Natalie I. Forcier, *Divided at the Margins: A Study of Young Southern Sudanese Refugee Men in Cairo, Egypt* (Cairo: Center for Migration and Refugee Studies, American University of Cairo, 2009), 6, https://fount.aucegypt.edu/faculty_journal_articles/5009. See also Fateh Azzam et al., "A Tragedy of Failures and False Expectations: Report on the Events surrounding the Three-Month Sit-in and Forced Removal of Sudanese Refugees in Cairo, September–December 2005" (working pa-

per, Forced Migration and Refugee Studies Program, American University in Cairo, June 2006).

7. In Baghdad, among the dead was Sergio Vieira de Mello, the UN High Commissioner for Human Rights and the head of the UN mission in Iraq. See "Remember the Fallen," United Nations, accessed October 26, 2024, https://www.un.org/en/memorial/algiers2007.shtml.

8. UNHCR international officer based in Somalia, personal communication with author, July 2023.

9. Stephen Grey and Amina Ismail, "In Cairo, Ethiopia's Oromos Lose Hope with U.N. Refugee Agency," Reuters, December 6, 2016, https://www.reuters.com/article/us-europe-migrants-egypt-oromos/in-cairo-ethiopias-oromos-lose-hope-with-u-n-refugee-agency-idUSKBN13V1FC.

10. *Annual Results Report 2022, Egypt* (Geneva, Switzerland: UNHCR, 2022), 9, https://reporting.unhcr.org/sites/default/files/2023-06/MENA%20-%20Egypt.pdf.

11. Rochelle Davis et al., "Sudanese and Somali Refugees in Jordan: Hierarchies of Aid in Protracted Displacement Crises," *Middle East Report* 279 (July 2016): 2–10. See also Ryan Philip, "Getting By on the Margins," Cairo, Egypt Case Report (Refugees in Towns Project, Tufts University, 2018), https://refugeesintowns.net/all-reports/cairo-2018.

12. This change occurred after the government and UNHCR adopted the "One Refugee" approach, which sought to ensure equal access to protection, services, and humanitarian assistance for Africans, Iraqis, and Yemenis registered with UNHCR. In Egypt, USAID's Office of Food for Peace provided funds for WFP to reach an additional 24,000 registered refugees identified as "most vulnerable." The refugees receive a monthly food voucher to purchase food at fifty contracted retailers. "WFP Expands Food Assistance in Egypt to Include Refugees from Multiple Countries," World Food Programme, May 30, 2019, https://www.wfp.org/news/wfp-expands-food-assistance-egypt-include-refugees-multiple-countries.

13. Refugees and aid agency staff, personal communications with author, Cairo, 2018.

14. *Egypt Response Plan for Refugees and Asylum-Seekers from Sub-Saharan Africa, Iraq & Yemen 2020* (6th of October City, Egypt: UNHCR, October 6, 2020), https://reliefweb.int/report/egypt/egypt-response-plan-refugees-and-asylum-seekers-sub-saharan-africa-iraq-yemen-2020; "Egypt 2020," OCHA Financial Tracking Service (FTS), accessed October 26, 2024, https://fts.unocha.org/countries/66/summary/2020.

15. About $2.5 million went to "UN agencies and NGOs (Confidential)." This probably includes international NGOs that work as UNHCR's implementing partners, such as Plan International. "Egypt 2022," OCHA Financial Tracking Service, accessed October 26, 2024, https://fts.unocha.org/countries/66/sectors/2022.

16. *Global Humanitarian Assistance Report 2023* (Wilmington, DE: Development Initiatives, 2023), 69, https://devinit-prod-static.ams3.cdn.digitaloceanspaces.com/media/documents/GHA2023_Digital_v9.pdf.

17. "Egypt: Durable Solutions (November 2022)" (factsheet, UNHCR, December 1, 2022), https://reliefweb.int/report/egypt/unhcr-egypt-durable-solutions-november-2022.

18. *UNHCR Fact Sheet—Egypt,* December 2024, https://www.unhcr.org/eg/wp-content/uploads/sites/36/2025/01/UNHCR-Egypt-Factsheet_DEC-2024.pdf.

19. Bram J. Jensen, *Kakuma Refugee Camp: Humanitarian Urbanism in Kenya's Accidental City* (London: Zed Books, 2018).

20. Ex–UNHCR community officer in Cairo, personal communication with author.

21. "Food Assistance," UNHCR Egypt, accessed October 26, 2024, https://help.unhcr.org/egypt/en/food-assistance/.

22. "Women's Rights," CARE Egypt, accessed October 26, 2024, https://care.org.eg/women-rights/.

Chapter 16. Refugee Entrepreneurs

1. Health or medical tourism is a well-established phenomenon. See I. Glenn Cohen, "Medical Outlaws or Medical Refugees? An Examination of Circumvention Tourism," in *Risks and Challenges in Medical Tourism: Understanding the Global Market for Health Services. Controversies in the Exploding Industry of Global Medicine,* ed. Jill Hodges (Santa Barbara, CA: Praeger, 2012), 207–229.

2. Joseph Daher, *Syrian Entrepreneurs and Investors in Egypt and Their Relations with Syria* (Fiesole, Italy: European University Institute, 2023).

3. *Market Systems Analysis for Syrian Refugees in Egypt* (Geneva, Switzerland: International Labour Organization, 2018), 10–11, https://www.ilo.org/sites/default/files/2024-07/Market%20Systems%20Analysis%20for%20Syrian%20Refugees%20in%20Egypt.pdf.

4. Alcohol is rarely served throughout the Middle East because Islam forbids the consumption of alcohol. In most Muslim countries non-Muslims are permitted to purchase alcohol, and it is usually served in high-end hotels and restaurants. In

Egypt, prior to 2013, the Islamic revival led to a resurgence in the practice and public expression of Islam among a broad spectrum of Egyptians. See Aaron Rock-Singer, *Practicing Islam in Egypt: Print Media and Islamic Revival* (Cambridge: Cambridge University Press, 2019).

5. Daher, *Syrian Entrepreneurs and Investors*, 8. See also *Jobs Make the Difference: Expanding Economic Opportunities for Syrian Refugees and Host Communities* (Geneva, Switzerland: UN Development Programme, International Labour Organization, and World Food Programme, 2017), https://www.jobsmakethedifference.org/full-report; Valentina Primo, "The Syrian Entrepreneurs Starting New Lives in Egypt," BBC News, October 1, 2015, https://www.bbc.com/news/business-34380016.

6. Daher, *Syrian Entrepreneurs and Investors*, 8. See also "Egypt Cracks Down on Syrian Businesses Allegedly Tied to Brotherhood," Al-Monitor, September 30, 2020, https://www.al-monitor.com/originals/2020/09/egypt-syrian-funds-muslim-brotherhood-crackdown.html.

7. *Urban Planning & Infrastructure in Migration Contexts: Damietta Spatial Profile, Egypt* (Nairobi: UN-Habitat, 2022), https://www.3rpsyriacrisis.org/wp-content/uploads/2023/06/damietta_spatial_profle-min.pdf.

8. *Market Systems Analysis*, 5.

9. *Market Systems Analysis*, 19n11. The study estimate was based on experts' views and ILO field research. The study data from the Cairo Chamber of Commerce confirmed only 550 registered enterprises.

10. Ola Noureldin, "Syrian Immigrants Spur Economic Revival," American Chamber of Commerce in Egypt, April 2019, https://www.amcham.org.eg/publications/business-monthly/issues/280/April-2019/3843/syrian-immigrants-spur-economic-revival. See also Primo, "Syrian Entrepreneurs Starting New Lives."

11. Conversation with the author, September 2018. We did not find this view to be widely shared by the Syrians, who tend to have a low opinion of Egyptians and consider themselves better educated. For more on the views of Egyptians about refugees in general, see Kelsey P. Norman, *Reluctant Reception: Refugees, Migrants and Governance in the Middle East and North Africa* (Cambridge: Cambridge University Press, 2020), chap. 6.

12. Primo, "Syrian Entrepreneurs Starting New Lives."

13. The petitions were brought in 2011 and again in 2016. For an interesting discussion, see Kirstine Strøh Varming, "Urban Subjects: Somali Claims to Recognition and Urban Belonging in Eastleigh, Nairobi," *African Studies* 79, no. 1 (2020): 1–20, https://doi.org/10.1080/00020184.2020.1747935.

14. Anna Lowenhaupt Tsing, *The Mushroom at the End of the World: On the Possibility of Life in Capitalist Ruins* (Princeton, NJ: Princeton University Press, 2015), chap. 1.

Chapter 17. "Money Has Come"

1. There is much debate about how remittances affect economic growth in poor countries, and recent work shows substantial regional variation. One study found that remittances enhance growth in Asia but not in Africa. Riyazuddin Khan et al., "How Foreign Aid and Remittances Affect Poverty in MENA Countries?" *PLoS One* 17, no. 1 (2022); Stuart S. Brown, "Can Remittances Spur Development? A Critical Survey," *International Studies Review* 8, no. 1 (2006): 55–76.

2. However, according to the World Bank, "flows to the Middle East and North Africa fell for the second year, declining by 5.3% mainly due to a sharp drop in flows to Egypt." "Remittance Flows Continue to Grow in 2023 albeit at Slower Pace" (press release 2024/040/SPJ, World Bank, December 18, 2023), https://www.worldbank.org/en/news/press-release/2023/12/18/remittance-flows-grow-2023-slower-pace-migration-development-brief. See also *Resilience: COVID-19 Crisis through a Migration Lens*, Migration and Development Brief 34 (Washington, DC: World Bank Group, 2011); Mohammed Soliman, "Egypt's Informal Economy: An Ongoing Cause of Unrest," *Journal of International Affairs* 73, no. 2 (2020): 185–193.

3. Much of the research on debt and migration focuses on return migration. For a review, see Maryann Bylander, *Debt and the Migration Experience* (Bangkok: International Organization for Migration, 2019), https://publications.iom.int/system/files/pdf/debt_and_the_migration_experience_insights_from_southeast_asia_2.pdf. Our 2011 study of the migration of Africans to Israel also explores the problems of debt and remittances. See Rebecca Furst-Nichols and Karen Jacobsen, *African Migration to Israel: Debt, Employment and Remittances* (Medford, MA: Feinstein International Center, 2011), https://fic.tufts.edu/wp-content/uploads/migration-israel.pdf.

4. Amanda Poole, "Ransoms, Remittances, and Refugees: The Gatekeeper State in Eritrea," *Africa Today* 60, no. 2 (2013): 67. The situation Poole describes in Eritrea has only worsened since 2013. Eritrea's population is unknown, as the country has never held an official national census. Estimates range between 3.6 to 6.7 million. At least 200,000 people are in active military service, and all able-bodied adults are required to work for a period in unsalaried national service. See also Fikrejesus Amahazion, "Understanding Remittances in Eritrea: An Exploratory Study," *International Journal of African Development* 5, no. 2 (2019): 13–22.

5. Anna Lindley, *The Early Morning Phone Call: Somali Refugees' Remittances* (New York: Berghahn Books, 2010). See also Laura Hammond, "Obliged to Give: Remittances and the Maintenance of Transnational Networks between Somalis at Home and Abroad," *Bildhaan: An International Journal of Somali Studies* 10 (2010): 125–151.

6. Ryan Philip, personal communication with author, 2018. See also Karen Jacobsen, Maysa Ayoub, and Alice Johnson, "Sudanese Refugees in Cairo: Remittances and Livelihoods," *Journal of Refugee Studies* 27, no. 1 (2014): 145–162.

7. Banks and businesses use KYC guidelines to verify the identity, suitability, and risks of a current or potential customer in order to identify suspicious behavior such as money laundering and financial terrorism. KYC involves customer identification (usually four forms of identifying information) and customer due diligence, which involves screening steps to ensure that clients do not appear on government sanction lists, politically exposed person (PEP) lists, or lists of suspected or known terrorists. See "Understanding the Steps of a 'Know Your Customer' Process," Dow Jones, accessed October 26, 2024, https://www.dowjones.com/professional/risk/glossary/know-your-customer/.

8. "Opening a Bank Account in Egypt," Expat.com, accessed October 26, 2024, https://www.expat.com/en/guide/africa/egypt/14268-opening-a-bank-account-in-egypt.html.

9. See "5 Ways to Send Money to Offshore Workers (Cheaper than PayPal)," Time Doctor, accessed October 26, 2024, https://www.timedoctor.com/blog/5-ways-send-money-offshore-workers-cheaper-paypal/. On WorldRemit, see "A Former Refugee Is Shaking Up the $441B Remittances Industry," NBC News, December 25, 2017, https://www.nbcnews.com/news/world/former-refugee-shaking-441b-remittances-industry-n827361. M-Pesa is a mobile banking service that allows users to store and transfer money through their phones. Safaricom, the largest mobile phone operator in Kenya, launched M-Pesa in Kenya in 2007 as a way for the "unbanked" poor population to have access to financial services. (*M* stands for mobile and "Pesa" means money or payment in Kiswahili). Julia Kagan, "What Is M-Pesa?," Investopedia, June 21, 2023, https://www.investopedia.com/terms/m/mpesa.asp.

10. See Mohammed L. Qorchi, "Hawala," *Finance and Development* 39, no. 4 (2002), https://www.imf.org/external/pubs/ft/fandd/2002/12/elqorchi.htm; and Samuel Munzele Maimbo, *The Money Exchange Dealers of Kabul: A Study of the Hawala System in Afghanistan* (Washington, DC: World Bank, 2003).

11. According to Anna Lindley, "*xawilaad* means 'transfer of debt.'" Anna Lindley, "Between 'Dirty Money' and 'Development Capital': Somali Money Transfer

Infrastructure under Global Scrutiny," *African Affairs* 108, no. 433 (2009): 519–539. See also Jonathan G. Ercanbrack, "An Introduction to the Concept and Origins of Hawala," *Journal of the History of International Law* 10 (2008): 83–118.

12. Nikos Passas, "Demystifying Hawala: A Look into Its Social Organization and Mechanics," *Journal of Scandinavian Studies in Criminology and Crime Prevention* 7, supp. 1 (2006): 46–62; Froilan Malit Jr., Mouawiya Al Awad, and George Naufal, "More than a Criminal Tool: The Hawala System's Role as a Critical Remittance Channel for Low-Income Pakistani Migrants in Dubai," *Remittance Review* 2 (October 2017).

13. Samuel Munzele Maimbo, "Challenges of Regulating and Supervising the Hawaladars of Kabul," in *Regulatory Frameworks for Hawala and Other Remittance Systems*, ed. International Monetary Fund (Washington, DC: IMF, 2005), https://www.elibrary.imf.org/display/book/9781589064232/ch07.xml#ch07fn06.

14. Khaled Sharif et al., "Management, Control and Governance of Hawala Networks in the Gulf Cooperation Council Region," *Asian Academy of Management Journal of Accounting and Finance* 12, no. 2 (2016): 65–93.

15. Hassan, conversation with Ryan Philip, February 22, 2019

16. Lindley, "'Dirty Money' and 'Development Capital,'" 526.

17. UN Security Council Resolution 2023 (2011) demands that Eritrea halt the tax, which Eritrea has resisted. See DSP-groep Amsterdam, *The 2% Tax for Eritreans in the Diaspora* (Tilburg, Netherlands: Tilburg University, 2017).

18. Amanda Poole, "Ransoms, Remittances, and Refugees: The Gatekeeper State in Eritrea," *Africa Today* 60, no. 2 (2013): 74. See also Amahazion, "Understanding Remittances in Eritrea," 13.

19. Liza Rose Cirolia et al., "Remittance Micro-worlds and Migrant Infrastructure: Circulations, Disruptions, and the Movement of Money," *Transactions of the Institute of British Geographers* (2021); Neil C. M. Carrier, *Little Mogadishu: Eastleigh, Nairobi's Global Somali Hub* (New York: Oxford University Press, 2016).

20. Haroun Rahimi, "Hawala as Credit: Recognizing How Hawala Supports the Business Climate in Afghanistan," *Journal of Money Laundering Control* 23, no. 1 (2020). See also Prem Mahadevan, Maria Khoruk, and Alla Mohamad Mohmanzaï, "A New Exodus: Migrant Smuggling from Afghanistan after the Return of the Taliban" (SOC ACE research paper no. 23, University of Birmingham, 2023), https://globalinitiative.net/wp-content/uploads/2022/06/SOCACE-RP23-NewExodus-27Oct23.pdf.

21. Remittance costs averaged above 6.3 percent in 2024, more than double the SDG target of 3 percent by 2030. The average cost was lowest in South Asia, at

5.1 percent, while Sub-Saharan Africa continued to have the highest average cost, at 7.7 percent. *Remittance Prices Worldwide Quarterly*, no. 49 (March 2024), https://remittanceprices.worldbank.org/sites/default/files/rpw_main_report_and_annex_q124_final.pdf.

22. Whitehead Zikhali, "Changing Money, Changing Fortunes: Experiences of Money Changers in Nkayi, Zimbabwe," *Canadian Journal of African Studies* 56, no. 1 (2020): 199–216. See also Natasha Venables, "Finding Home in Uncertainty: Returnees, Reintegration, and Reconciliation," Harare, Zimbabwe Case Report (Refugees in Towns Project, Tufts University, 2020), https://refugeesintowns.net/all-reports/harare.

Chapter 18. Ard al-Lewa

1. For example, Veronika Fajth et al., "How Do Refugees Affect Social Life in Host Communities? The Case of Congolese Refugees in Rwanda," *Comparative Migration Studies* 7, no. 1 (2019); Estella Carpi, "Towards a Neo-cosmetic Humanitarianism: Refugee Self-Reliance as a Social-Cohesion Regime in Lebanon's Halba," *Journal of Refugee Studies* 33, no. 1 (2020).

2. *Global Trends 2018* (Geneva, Switzerland: UNHCR, 2018), table 5. See also Hazel Hadden, "For Eritreans, Egypt Is the New Route to Europe," IRIN, June 6, 2016, https://www.refworld.org/docid/5757bb6d4.html.

3. Ryan Philip, "Getting By on the Margins," Cairo, Egypt Case Report (Refugees in Towns Project, Tufts University, 2018), 18, https://refugeesintowns.net/all-reports/cairo-2018.

4. During the month of Ramadan, it's illegal for restaurants and bars to serve alcohol to anyone, including foreigners. "Drinking Alcohol Is Always an Open Secret in Egypt," *Vice*, August 19, 2016, https://www.vice.com/en_us/article/4xbbqj/drinking-alcohol-is-always-an-open-secret-in-egypt.

5. Amanda Elizabeth Siino, "Livelihood Strategies of Displaced Independent Eritrean Youths in Cairo: Examining Agency and Vulnerability" (master's thesis, York University, Toronto, Ontario, July 2018), 77–79, https://yorkspace.library.yorku.ca/server/api/core/bitstreams/6551e068-b325-4d8f-9b5b-151b6132d7d7/content.

6. Putnam argues that the increased ethnic diversity resulting from immigration challenges social solidarity and inhibits social capital, leading people to "withdraw from collective life, . . . to withdraw even from close friends, . . . [and] to volunteer less," and that trust (even of one's own race) is lower, altruism and community cooperation rarer, friends fewer. Robert D. Putnam, "E Pluribus Unum: Diversity and

Community in the Twenty-First Century—the 2006 Johan Skytte Prize Lecture," *Scandinavian Political Studies* 30, no. 2 (2007).

7. Karen Jacobsen et al., *Remittances to Transition Countries: The Impact on Sudanese Refugee Livelihoods in Cairo* (Cairo: Center for Migration and Refugee Studies, American University in Cairo, 2012); Philip, "Getting By on the Margins." These racist stereotypes, including those regarding black women and their bodies, have been well documented in Egypt. See, for example, "Fleeing War, Poverty, African Migrants Face Racism in Egypt," Al Jazeera, January 2, 2020, https://www.aljazeera.com/news/2020/1/2/fleeing-war-poverty-african-migrants-face-racism-in-egypt#:~:text=Racism%20has%20roots%20in%20Egyptian,cleaners%20in%20films%20for%20decades.

8. Ryan Philip and Karen Jacobsen, "The Cowardly Man Raises His Children: Refugee Gang Violence and Masculine Norms in Cairo" (Refugees in Towns Project, Tufts University, 2018), 16.

9. The World Health Organization's Eastern Mediterranean region has a population of nearly 745 million people, including twenty-one member states and the Occupied Palestinian Territory. "About Us," World Health Organization, 2025, https://www.emro.who.int/entity/about-us/index.html. See also Maha El-Adawy et al., "Addressing Violence against Women in the Eastern Mediterranean Region," *Eastern Mediterranean Health Journal* 27, no. 5 (2021).

10. Ainav Rabinowitz, "The Renewed Fight to Prevent Domestic Violence in Egypt," Wilson Center, Middle East Women's Initiative, January 26, 2023, https://www.wilsoncenter.org/article/renewed-fight-prevent-domestic-violence-egypt.

11. Philip and Jacobsen, "Cowardly Man Raises His Children."

12. As Philip notes ("Getting By on the Margins," 16n24): "Egypt has four categories of schools: standard Egyptian public schools are the lowest ranked and least valued, Egyptian 'language schools' are public but with a slightly higher reputation, private schools are sought after but expensive, and most desirable are the very expensive international schools where the primary language of instruction is English."

13. Philip, "Getting By on the Margins." The harassment and bullying of African refugee children in schools and on the streets does not show up much in the annual vulnerability assessments conducted by UNHCR and WFP. See, for example, Heba El Laithy and Dina Armanious, *Vulnerability Assessment of Refugees in Egypt: Risks and Coping Strategies* (Cairo: UNHCR, April 2019), https://www.unhcr.org/eg/wp-content/uploads/sites/36/2021/01/Vulnerability-Assessment-of-Refugees-in-Egypt-Risks-and-Coping-Strategies-April-2019.pdf.

14. Four Faysel schools offer the Sudanese and Egyptian curriculum from kindergarten to high school, and one technical school provides training in carpentry, plumbing, and electrical skills. Extracurricular activities include music, art, and sports. "About Us," Faysel Community School, accessed October 26, 2024, https://www.faisel-school.education/about.html.

15. Iman El-Mahdi, "Sudanese Women on the Move in Cairo Defy Stereotypes" (policy brief, Baker Institute of Public Policy, Rice University, March 21, 2023), https://www.bakerinstitute.org/sites/default/files/2023-04/BI-Brief-032123-CME%2BSudaneseCairo.pdf.

16. Kate Pincock et al., "The Rhetoric and Reality of Localisation: Refugee-Led Organisations in Humanitarian Governance," *Journal of Development Studies* 57, no. 5 (2021).

17. Pincock et al., "Rhetoric and Reality."

18. Zeynep Sahin Mencutek, "Refugee Community Organisations: Capabilities, Interactions and Limitations," *Third World Quarterly* 42, no. 1 (2021): 181–199.

19. Mencutek, "Refugee Community Organisations."

Epilogue: Strengthening Host Cities

1. The solar plant was funded by the government of Germany through the KfW Development Bank at a cost of €15 million (US$17.5 million). The project also provided employment and training to local Jordanian workers and to seventy-five Syrian refugees as part of a cash-for-work scheme. Marwa Hashem, "Jordan's Zaatari Camp Goes Green with New Solar Plant," UNHCR, November 14, 2017, https://www.unhcr.org/us/news/stories/jordans-zaatari-camp-goes-green-new-solar-plant.

2. There are so many examples of community organizations in host cities that it seems unfair to single out any one. For a sampling, see the case reports in the Refugees in Towns Project, Fletcher School, Tufts University, accessed October 26, 2024, https://refugeesintowns.net.

3. Nicole C. Brambila, "Five Things to Know about Denver's New WorkReady Program," *Denver Gazette*, June 19, 2024, https://denvergazette.com/news/immigration/denver-workready-program-immigrants/article_9d9dac38-2e6b-11ef-9c6e-63dec980c729.html.

4. The case reports for my Refugees in Towns project are written by refugees with direct experience of living in host cities. Their insights show how diverse a city's response can be: within the same city, some neighborhoods are much more tolerant and supportive of refugees than others. See Refugees in Towns Project.

5. Peter William Walsh, "Q&A: The UK's Former Policy to Send Asylum Seekers to Rwanda," Migration Observatory, July 25, 2024, https://migrationobservatory.ox.ac.uk/resources/commentaries/qa-the-uks-policy-to-send-asylum-seekers-to-rwanda/.

Postscript: Update on Mahmoud and Hassan

1. The armed coalition was led by an Islamist militant group, Hayat Tahrir al-Sham, supported by the Turkish-backed Syrian National Army (SNA). See "Conflict in Syria," Council for Foreign Relations, December 11, 2024, https://www.cfr.org/global-conflict-tracker/conflict/conflict-syria.

Index

Abdullah, Ahmad Mohamed (Abu Islam), 254
Abed, Oroub al-, 178
Abidjan, Côte d'Ivoire, xii
Abou Ali River, 138, 139
Abu Islam, 254
Abuja, Nigeria, 206–207
Abu Nidal Organization, 178
Accra, Ghana, 107, 108–109
Achlli, Luigi, 159
Addis Ababa, Ethiopia, 146
advocacy groups, 49–50, 264, 266
affordable housing, 14–15
Afghanistan, 9, 35, 44, 61, 232, 236–238, 242
Africa, 5; cities of, 37–38; displaced populations in, 5; rural bias in, 17; smuggling through, 159–164. *See also specific countries*
African National Congress (ANC), ix, 98–99
African Union Convention for the Protection and Assistance of Internally Displaced Persons in Africa (Kampala Convention), 21–22
Afrikaner Nationalist Party, ix
Agadez, Niger, 160–164
agricultural land, 41, 137, 192, 197, 269
Ahlam, Umm, 154

Ahmed, Ismail, 235
aid agencies. *See* humanitarian agencies
aid workers: housing needs of, 79; impact of, on cities, 77, 167–168; local hires and, 212–213; segregation of, 209, 211
Ain al-Hilweh camp, 101
Ain Shams, 192
Akkar governorate, 79–82
Akkarouna, 92
alcohol consumption, 248–250
Alexandra (Johannesburg), x
Alexandria, Egypt, 40, 199–200
Alfi, Ahmed, 228
Algeria, 106
Alix-Garcia, Jennifer, 96
Allston, Massachusetts, 246
American Community Survey, 35
Amman, 39, 106, 112, 210
anti-immigrant policies, 268
apartheid, ix–xi
apartment buildings, 83, 170–171, 192, 195, 198–199
Arab-Israeli War, 176, 178
Ard al-Lewa, 16, 194, 202, 204, 239, 244–259
area-based approach, 91–93, 126–127, 137

313

INDEX

armed conflicts, 14, 37, 41, 61, 65–66, 173, 231, 270
'ashwa'iyyat, 197–199, 245–246. *See also* informal settlements
Asia, 5; cities of, 38; displaced populations in, 5. *See also specific countries*
Assad regime, 70, 156, 181, 271
Aswan High Dam, 176
asylees, 22
Asylum and Migration Fund (AMF), 113
asylum decisions, 22, 185–187
Asylum-seeker Certificate "white paper," 183, 186
Asylum-seeker Registration Card "yellow card," 183, 185
asylum seekers, 22, 30, 57, 60, 167, 183, 185–187, 267
Athens, Greece, 37
ATM cards, 128, 129, 132
Augusta, Maine, 40
Australia, 18, 35

Baghdad, 39, 180, 209
Bain, 30
Balcioglu, Zeynep, 115, 116
Balkan wars, 5, 17
Bangladesh, 9, 27, 36, 48, 80, 104–106
banks, 27, 193, 230, 233–235, 239
bars, 248–249
Beddawi. *See* Jabal Beddawi (or "Beddawi")
Beddawi camp, 76, 86, 94, 95, 101–104, 147
Beirut, 7, 19, 39, 54, 55, 73, 82–83, 100, 101, 103, 120, 127, 138, 142–143, 149, 151
Beqaa, 64, 66, 89
bilateral funding, 29, 112

bimodal pattern, of refugee movement, 37–39
black market. *See* underground economy
"Black September" crisis, 103, 178
"blue card," 183, 185
Blue Nile, 179, 195
Bogotá, Colombia, 39, 48
Boo, Katherine, 149
border cities, 5, 15, 18, 37–40, 48, 80–81, 90, 265, 269. *See also specific cities*
borders: and camps, 97; closed, 9; crossing, 21, 64, 153–154; tightening (hardening) of, 57, 61, 64, 71, 269–270
Bosnians, 17–18
Bossaso, Somalia, 160
Boston, Massachusetts, 23, 40, 235, 246
Bourj al-Barajneh camp, 103
BRAC International, 27
Brazil, 39, 49, 80
brokerage services, 221–222
Brookline, Massachusetts, 246
Buduburam camp, 106–109
building permits, 83
burden sharing, 98, 115
Bureau for Humanitarian Assistance (USAID), 29
Burlington, Vermont, 17
Burma. *See* Myanmar (Burma)
business sector, 222–226

cadastral maps, 44
Cairo, xiv, 7, 19; Ard al-Lewa neighborhood of, 244–259; compared with Tripoli, 167–172; downtown area, 194; field research for, 171–172; formal city of,

INDEX

191–196; government of, 190–191; hawala networks in, 236–241; housing in, 193–196; humanitarian funding in, 213–215; informal settlements in, 50, 190–191, 196–199; neighborhoods of, 8, 189–204; non-Muslim refugees in, 16; population of, 167–168; refugee arrival in, 9; refugee neighborhoods in, 199–204; satellite cities of, 200, 203–213; schools in, 255–256, 257; sexual violence against women in, 252–255; size of refugee population in, 187
Cairo Agreement (1969), 100, 101, 103
Calais, France, 46
Cambodian refugees, xi, 97–98
Camp David Accords, 178, 193
camps. *See* encampment policies; refugee camps
Canada, 5, 18, 35, 125, 222
Capernaum, 126–127
capital cities, 18, 23, 37–40, 48, 104, 167, 206, 259, 269. *See also specific cities*
capitalism, 229. *See also* entrepreneurs
CARE, 26, 92
Care Egypt, 218
cash assistance, 125–137, 217; benefits of, 128–129; impact on cities of, 135–137; in Lebanon, 130–135; limits on, 133–135; targeting of, 134
cash for work (CfW) programs, 130, 136–137
Catholic Relief Services, 26, 29, 256
census, 34–35, 44; Egypt, 191; Jordan, 31; Lebanon, 64; undercounts, 33–34, 36, 191
Central America, 158, 232. *See also specific cities*

childcare, 251–252
child marriages, 130
children: refugee, 16, 33–34, 183, 187, 244, 251–252, 255–257; schools for, 12, 16, 63, 107, 131, 183, 217, 255–257
China, 49, 95
Chinatowns, 7
Christians, 7, 66, 75, 103, 176–177, 204, 214, 248
cities: citizens' response to refugees in, xiii–xiv, 11–14; co-nationals in, xv, 7, 8, 204, 220, 222, 265, 268–269; displacement history of, 11–12; flooding in, 15, 141; growth of, 37–51, 100; humanitarian assistance for, 17, 112–113; humanitarian influxes into, 3–19; impact of smuggling on, 156–160; informal settlements in, 7–8, 37–51, 83–87, 190–191, 196–199; leadership of, 13; migration in and out of, 3; neighborhood effect in, 7–8; politics in, 49–50; in poor countries, 4–7; primary, 37–39, 167; problems with counting refugees in, 34–36; refugees in, xi–xv, xvi; secondary, 38, 40, 48, 167; urban core of, 40. *See also* host cities; *specific cities*
citizens. *See* host population; local residents
citizenship, 33, 59, 258; 187; for Palestinians, 178; for refugee children, 33–34
city budgets, 24, 111–112; 190
city governments, 23–24; aid agencies and, 122–123; Cairo, 190–191; confrontations between residents and, 49; fiscal transfers to, from national government, 111–112; funding for, 115–118, 122, 264; rent

315

INDEX

city governments (cont.)
  seeking by, 115; response of, to refugees, 264; revenue sources for, 110–112
city neighborhoods. *See* neighborhoods
civil society, 16, 112, 121, 149, 258, 269
climate change, 4, 15, 21–22, 40, 231, 269
"closed files," 185–187
co-ethnics, 7, 62
Colombia, xi, 31, 39, 48
combatants, 97–98
commercial property developers, 41
community organizations, 16, 149, 168, 172, 255–259, 265–266
community support projects (CSPs), 89, 91–92
co-nationals, xiv–xv, 7, 8, 76, 169, 204, 220, 222, 265, 268–269
concessional financing, 11, 264; Concessional Financing Facility (CFF), 120
conflict hypothesis, 249–250
conflicts. *See* armed conflicts
conflict zones, 35, 38, 39, 44
Congolese refugees, 7, 39, 107, 185, 195
contact hypothesis, 249
Convention for the Protection of the Marine Environment, 145
Convention Relating to the Status of Refugees (Refugee Convention, 1951), 21, 22, 25, 70, 119, 182, 183; Article 1(A), 21
co-religionists, 7
corporate social responsibility, 11
corruption, 111, 143, 146, 148–149, 155–156, 161–162, 197, 213, 226, 241
counterfeit documents, 159

COVID-19 pandemic, 54, 73, 112, 124, 171, 176, 230, 253, 271
Cox's Bazar, Bangladesh, 48, 104
credit-hawala, 242
crime, xvi, 13, 18, 49, 83, 126, 186, 208, 212, 249; criminal justice, 26; criminals, 50, 108, 129, 159, 187, 234, 242
cross-border trade (business) 74, 220, 221–222, 241, 265
cross-sector cash, 129–130, 132
Cyprus, 154, 178

Dadaab, Kenya, 39, 93, 104, 109, 171
Dahshur, 198
Damietta, Egypt, 200, 223, 225–226
Danish Refugee Council, 27
Dar es Salaam, 18, 37
Darfur (Sudan), 39, 43–44, 46, 48, 96, 179, 195, 221
Death and Life of American Cities, The (Jacobs), 14
debt: foreign, 73; migration, 60, 163–164, 220, 231; repayment, 129, 220
decolonization, of humanitarian assistance, 117–118
defensive asylum, 60
Democratic Republic of the Congo (DRC), 9, 39, 44, 48, 61, 97, 158, 232
demographic impact, of refugees, 15–16, 20, 30–36
Denmark, 29, 145
Denver, Colorado, 267–268
deportation, 37, 73, 181, 186–187, 210
desert cities, 205–213
detention, 181, 186; centers, 62
development agencies, xv, 16, 26, 28, 91–93; 122–124, 145, 148, 238, 269

development funds, 109, 110, 120, 124, 148
development industry, 26–28
Dhaka, Bangladesh, 104
diaspora, xv, 8, 68, 169, 176, 232, 240–241, 265; near-diaspora, 23
digitalization, 128, 184; banking, 233, 235. *See also* fintech (financial technologies)
disasters, 3, 9, 20, 22, 25, 41, 44, 128, 264, 269–270
diseases, infectious, 15
displacement: causes of, 20–21; in cities, 3; definition of, 20–21; Egypt's history of, 174–182; experiences of, xiii–xiv; flows of, 173; humanitarian assistance for, 121–122; Lebanon's history of, 68–70; vs. migrants, 23; stages of, 37; statistics on, 5, 6, 30–36; trauma experienced by, 41
Displacement Tracking Matrix (IOM), 31–32
Djibouti, 160
domestic violence, 254
donor countries, 10, 16–17, 25, 27–29
donor funding, 88, 110–124; applications for, 115–116; bureaucratic requirements for, 116; to cities, 112–113, 116–117; control over, 119–121; earmarked, 29, 88, 111, 121, 137, 213; from industry, 11; of NGOs, 117–118; pledging conference, 10. *See also* humanitarian assistance
drainage, 15, 89
drinking, 248–250
drug smuggling, 155
Dunkirk, France, 46

earmarked funding, 29, 88, 111, 121, 137, 213
earthquakes, 3, 9, 198
Eastleigh (Nairobi), 131, 170, 228–229, 242
education, 17, 25–26, 28, 63, 114, 129, 134, 163, 168, 178, 183, 213, 215, 217, 242, 255–256, 262. *See also* schools
Egypt: Alexandria, 40; asylum seekers in, 186; banking in, 233; bureaucracy in, 226–227; corruption in, 226; domestic situation in, 175; economy of, 193–194; Free Officers revolution, 177, 192; humanitarian funding in, 213–215; infrastructure, 193–194; internal displacement in, 176; January 25 Revolution, 175, 181; migration and displacement history in, 174–182; nationalism in, 177; Palestinians in, 177–179; political situation in, 177–178, 181–182, 227–228; population of, 169; refugee context in, 173–188; refugee policy of, xi, 169–170, 182–188; refugees in, 53, 167–182, 185, 199–200; refugee women in, 250–255; remittances to, 230; resettlement in, 215–219; schools in, 255–257; sharia law in, 248; smuggling routes to, 154; Syria and, 168; Syrian businesses in, 222–228; Syrian refugees in, 168–171, 173–175, 180–182, 185, 199–200; urban development in, 205–213. *See also* Cairo
Egypt Response Plan (ERP), 214
electricity, 45, 81, 85, 86, 92, 141, 198
emergency phase, 9, 110, 122, 173

INDEX

employment, 67; in Lebanon, 71–72; opportunities, 220–229, 267–268; work permits, 71–72, 183
encampment policies, xi, 11, 46, 94–100, 217, 262–263; Kenya encampment policy, 171, 185
energy, 12, 15–16, 81, 263
entrepreneurs, 18, 160, 197, 220–229, 261, 267
environmental impact, 15, 49, 141, 269
Erbil, Iraq, 39
Eritrea, 232, 231–232, 240–241; Eritrean diaspora, xvi–xvii, 7, 16, Eritrean hawala, 240–241; Eritrean Liberation Front, 240; Eritrean national service, 231; Eritrean refugees, 39, 107, 154, 171, 174–175, 179–180, 186, 204, 247–248, 250–252, 256
Ethiopia, 146, 158, 173, 231–232, 240, 270
Ethiopian diaspora, xvii; Ethiopian refugees, 39, 48, 154, 171, 174–175, 179–180, 186, 204, 212, 247–248, 256
ethnic neighborhoods, 7–8. *See also* neighborhood effect
Ettijahat, 255
Europe: cities, 4; desire to move to, 57–59; informal settlements in, 46; migration crisis in, 53; refugees to, 4–5, 18, 38, 39; resettlement in, 59–60; Schengen visa for, 59; smuggling routes to, 154. *See also specific countries*
European Civil Protection and Humanitarian Aid Operations (ECHO), 116–117
European Union, xii, 17, 25, 28; donations by, 29; efforts to stop smuggling by, 162; humanitarian assistance from, 113–114, 148
evictions, 43, 50, 195–196
expatriate staff, 77, 79, 167–168, 209, 211
exploitation, 72, 215; in smuggling industry, 163–164

faith-based organizations, 16, 26
family connections, 8, 106, 268–269
Fargo, North Dakota, 17
Fashir, al-, Sudan, 39
Fatah al-Islam, 101, 103
favelas, 49
Faysel Community Schools, 256
female genital mutilation (FGM), 254
fertility rates, 47
field research: in Cairo, 171–172; in Tripoli, 55
financial infrastructure, 238, 240, 241
financial institutions, 233–235
financial linkages, 193, 230–243
Financial Tracking Service (UN), 120
fintech (financial technologies), 233, 235. *See also* digitalization
First World War, 69
fiscal autonomy of cities, 111–112
flooding, 15, 141, 269
food assistance, 128, 130, 131, 133, 213–214, 217
food service business, 222–227
foreign aid. *See* donor funding; humanitarian assistance
France, 5, 46, 69
Fuji Optical, 30

Gaddafi, Muammar, 160
Gade, Tine, 155, 155–156
gangs, 129; criminal 50; street, 49, 255

INDEX

garbage, 138–152; garbage incineration, 145; garbage removal, 15, 81, 83
Gaza, 103, 122, 133, 168, 173, 264, 270
Gazientiep, Türkiye, 39
Gemayel, Amine, 103
General Electric, 17
genocide, Rwandan, 9
gentrification, 47, 79, 246
Germany, 5, 13; aid from, 29, 119, 136, 214; Nazi, 9–10; waste management in, 145
Gezira Island (Cairo), 189
Ghana, 106, 107, 108–109
Giza (Cairo), 189, 190, 200, 206, 207, 227
Global Cities Fund for Migrants and Refugees (GCF), 113
Global Commitment, 150
governance, 24, 28, 53, 80–81, 258–259
Greater Cairo, 23, 167, 190–200
Greater Tripoli, 74–75, 82, 96, 102, 111, 122; informal settlements in, 86–87
Greece, 13, 39, 53, 154
Greek Campus, 228
Gulf States, 160, 193, 237

Haiti, 35; earthquake in, 9
Halba, Lebanon, 75, 77, 79–82, 89–90
Harare, Zimbabwe, 242–243
harassment, 183, 215, 226, 250, 252–254, 256
Haret al-Jdideh, 87
Hariri, Rafiq al-, 65, 70
Hartman, Susan, 17
hashish, 155
hawala, 170, 229, 236–243, 269

Hay al-Ashr (Cairo), 172, 194, 195, 204, 237, 256
Hay al-Tanak (Tripoli), 86–87, 92, 141, 147
health services, 12, 16, 107, 131, 153–154, 183, 217
health tourism, 221–222
Hezbollah, 65–66, 68, 70, 103, 156
hierarchies of aid, 213
High Relief Commission, 131
home countries, xiv, 5, 12, 231; linkages with, 193, 221, 230–243; return to, 34, 61, 187
Homs, Syria, 74, 101, 156
Horn of Africa, 179–180
hospitality industry, 61
Hossary Square (Cairo), 223
host cities: area-based approaches in, 91–93, 126–127; housing in, 13–15, 41–46, 79–93, 193–196, 261; impact of humanitarian assistance on, 10, 135–137; impact of humanitarian influx on, 12–18, 125–126; impact of refugee camps on, 104–109; informal money transfers and, 241–243; neighborhood effect in, xiv–xv, 7–8, 244; positive outcomes for, 16–17; responses to refugees in, 11–13; strengthening, 261–270. *See also specific cities*
host countries, 5; donor funding and, 29, 110–124; internal variations in, xiii; international assistance for, 11, 16–17; refugee camps in, 105–106; revenue sources in, 110–112. *See also specific countries*
host governments: concessions for, 113–114; encampment policies of, xi, 11, 46, 94, 96–100, 169–171, 185, 262–263; refugee camps and, 107,

INDEX

host governments (*cont.*)
109; as rent seekers, 113–114;
response to refugees by, xiv, 4. *See also* city governments; national governments

host population: cash assistance and, 135; challenges of, 88; definition of, 23, 265; humanitarian assistance for, 10, 107, 122, 124, 127, 214, 262; impact of refugee camps on, 96, 107–108; response of, to refugees, 125–127, 136, 244, 249, 250, 261–262, 264–266, 270; support for, 88–89; sympathy for new arrivals, xiii, xv, 11, 75, 125, 244, 264–265. *See also* local residents

housing, 13–15; aid agencies demand for, 10, 15, 163, 262; in Cairo, 193–196; diaspora support with, xv, 83; funds for, 89–90; impact of refugees on, 13–15, 18, 75, 79–82, 158, 261; informal, 45–47, 83–87, 187, 190, 196–199; new construction of, 77; humanitarian programs and, 88–93; Lebanon's Housing Law (1965), 82; public, 193; shacks, 41–43, 45, 47; in Tripoli, 75–77, 79–82. *See also* rent

Houston, Texas, 15

humanitarian agencies, 10, 16–17, 24–26, 28; collaboration with city governments, 122–123; funding of, 88; housing programs by, 88–93; in large cities, 167–168; staff of, 77, 79, 167–168, 209, 211–213. *See also specific agencies*

humanitarian assistance, xii, xiv, 10–11, 28–30, 88–93, 110–124, 262; applications for, 115–116; architecture of, 29; area-based approaches to, 91–93, 126–127; beneficiaries of, 121–122; in Cairo, 213–215; cash programs, 125–137, 217; changes in, xv; decolonization of, 117–118; from donor countries, 10–11, 16–17, 112–124; hierarchies of, 213; to host population, 107, 122, 124, 135, 262; in Lebanon, 118–124; long-term, 90–91; unearmarked, 29; for waste management, 148

humanitarian gaze, 32

humanitarian industry, 10, 24–28; as colonizing force, 117–118; impact of, in host cities, 10, 77, 262; localization agenda in, 258

humanitarian influxes: into cities, 3–19; definition of, 3, 22; impact on host cities, 12–18, 125–126; versus other urban migration, 8–12, 261–263

Human Rights Watch, 24, 73

human smuggling, 153–164, 247, 268, 269

Hungary, 38

hunkering down theory, 249–250

Hussein, Saddam, 180

IKEA, 29–30

illegal workers, 14

illicit economy. *See* underground economy

immigrants. *See* migrants

immigration. *See* migration

implementing partners, 117, 182, 217–218, 258

Independent Municipal Fund, 111–112

inflation, 135–136

informal economy, 43, 111, 149, 187–188, 221–222, 226–227; smuggling, 153–164

INDEX

informal housing, 45–46, 187, 190
informal money transfers, 230–243; hawala, 236–241; implications of, for cities, 241–243
informal settlements, 7–8, 37–51, 196–199; in Cairo, 190–191; clearing of, 50–51; concept of, 45–46; flooding in, 15; impact on cities, 47–51; in Lebanon, 83–87; vs. refugee camps, 46; in Sudan, 41–44; in Tripoli, 76; urban growth and, 44–45
informal tented settlements, 84, 87, 88
infrastructure, 12–17, 49, 81, 83, 141; Egypt, 193–194, 227; funding for, 122, 124, 131, 148, 168, 193, 198–199, 215, 262, 263; lack of, in informal settlements, 198; projects, 89
in-kind assistance, 128, 130
Inter-American Development Bank, 27
inter-census surveys, 35–36
intergovernmental funding, 111–112
Internal Displacement Monitoring Center (IDMC), 32
internally displaced people (IDPs), xi–xii, 3; after natural disasters, 9; definition of, 21; in Egypt, 169, 176; experiences of, xiii–xiv; in Lebanon, 68–69; movement patterns of, 39; resettlement for, 60; statistics on, 31–32; in Sudan, 41–44, 46; in Syria, 53
internal migration, 176
International Alliance of Waste Pickers, 150
International Committee of the Red Cross, 100
international development industry, 26–28

International Finance Corporation, 30
international humanitarian resources, 10–11, 16–17. *See also* humanitarian assistance
International Labour Organization (ILO), 226, 227
International Monetary Fund (IMF), 238
international nongovernmental organizations (INGOs), 24, 26, 27, 214
International Organization for Migration (IOM), 25, 31–32, 46, 162–163, 169
international refugee law, xiv, 21, 97
International Rescue Committee (IRC), 24, 26, 30, 132
international sanctions, 237–238, 242
Iraq, 39, 44, 232; refugee camps in, 67, 94, 96; refugees from, 63, 180; refugees in, 53
Irbid, Jordan, 39
Islamic Development Bank Group, 10–11
Islamic law (sharia), 179, 248
Israel, 65, 66, 68, 103, 178
Istanbul, Türkiye, 7, 39, 115
Italy, 5, 13, 39
Izmir, Türkiye, 159

Jabal Beddawi (or "Beddawi"), 74, 75, 76, 77, 94, 102, 147, 157
Jacobs, Jane, 14
Japan, earthquake in, 9
jobs, 13, 14, 67. *See also* employment
Johannesburg, South Africa, ix–x, xvi–xvii, 7, 9, 228
Jordan, 10, 106; Black September in, 178; border cities, 39; cash

INDEX

Jordan (*cont.*)
assistance in, 136–137; Compact, 114; Egyptians in, 176; humanitarian funding to, 114; informal settlements in, 45; refugee camps in, 67, 94, 96, 98, 263; refugees in, 31, 33, 36, 39, 53; UNHCR protests in, 210
Just Family Law, 254

Kabul, Afghanistan, 236
kafala system, 71
Kakuma camps, Kenya, 39, 93, 96, 104, 107, 109
Kalobeyei Integrated Settlement, Kenya, 107
Kampala, Uganda, 17, 146, 147, 257–258
Kampala Convention, 21–22
Kelley, Ninette, 118, 129, 131–132, 153
Kenya, 39, 57, 93, 104, 105, 107, 109; encampment policies, 171; government corruption in, 111; refugee policies of, 185; refugees in, 170–171; waste management in, 145–146
Khartoum, Sudan, xii, 39, 41–44, 154
know your customer (KYC) requirements, 233, 235
Kruger Park, South Africa, x

Labaki, Nadine, 126
labor market, 109, 176
Lagos, Nigeria, 50, 206–207
Lampedusa, Italy, 13, 39
land commodification, 41
land encroachment, 49
landfills, 139–140, 142–147; Dandora, 146; Kiteezi, 147; Naameh, 143

landlords: in Cairo, 195–196; housing programs and, 88–91; predatory behavior by, 81–82, 84, 187
land speculation, 41
Latin America, 5, 38
LavaJet, 143
Lebanon, xi, 10, 23, 35, 39; border between Syria and, 74–75; camps in, 94; cash assistance program in, 130–135; civil war in, 65, 66, 68, 69, 74, 78, 103, 142, 153; development aid for, 120, 124; diaspora, 68, 176; domestic situation in, 65–66, 73, 118; economy of, 66–67, 73, 130; encampment policies, 96, 99–100; government response to refugees in, 70–73; historical context of, 67–70; humanitarian funding to, 118–124, 141; informal settlements in, 45, 46, 83–87; Internal Security Forces, 101; migration and displacement in, 68–70; Northern region, 74, 79–82; Palestinians in, 66, 67, 69, 86, 100–104; political situation in, 66; refugee context in, 63–73; refugee policies in, 64, 67, 70–73, 169–170; refugees from, 68–69; remittances to, 230; Syria and, 69–70, 168; Syrian refugees in, 53, 74–93, 96, 99–100, 118–119, 146–152, 169–170; urban policies in, 81–82; waste management in, 138–152. See also Tripoli, Lebanon
Lebanon Crisis Response Plan (LCRP), 121, 124
Lesvos, 13
Levantine Christians, 177
Lewiston, Maine, 17
Liberia, 108; First Liberian Civil War, 108; Liberian refugees, 108–109

INDEX

Libya, 25, 193; smuggling through, 159–160
Lindley, Anna, 232
"Little Eritrea," 7
"Little Somalia," 7
local authorities. *See* city governments; municipal authorities
localization agenda, 258
local residents: resentment of, toward refugees, 125–127, 136; responses of, to refugees, xiii–xiv, xv, 11–14, 69, 72, 75, 125–127, 261–262; sympathetic, 265–266. *See also* host population
Lutheran World Relief, 26

Madinat Nasr (Nasr City, Cairo), 192–193
Mafraq, al-, Jordan 39, 263
Mahfouz, Naguib, 191
Makoko, Nigeria, 50–51
Malawi, x
Mall of Arabia, 207
Malta, 39
Mandela, Nelson, ix, 98–99
Maputo, Mozambique, 146
Mardini, Hossam, 223–224
Martin, Diana, 100
MasterCard Foundation, 30
mayors, 13, 23
Mayors Mitigation Council (MMC), 112–113, 137, 264, 268
Médecins Sans Frontières (MSF), 27
Medellín, Colombia, 39
media coverage: of informal settlements, 50, 51; of refugees, 13
megalopolis, 7, 18, 19, 38, 40, 167
MercyCorps, 27
Mexico, 234
Miami, Florida, 15

microbuses, 205–206
micro businesses, 47
microcredit, 28
Microsoft, 30
Middle East, 5; cities of, 37–38; displaced populations in, 5; Egyptian diaspora in, 176. *See also specific countries*
migrant camps. *See* refugee camps
migrants: to cities, 3; compared with refugees, xiv; definition of, 22–23; vs. displaced people, 23; in Egypt, 169; long-standing, 265; population characteristics, 12; scapegoating of, 18; services for, 220–221; in South Africa, x; undocumented, 60–61, 71–72, 102–103, 164, 179, 186–188
migration: data, 34–36; Egyptian history of, 174–182; in Lebanon, 68–70; loans for, 231; policies on, 268; rural-urban, 40, 169, 175, 176
migration agencies, 25
migration debt, 60, 163–164, 220, 231
migration industries, 220–221
migration loans, 231
military services, 231
Mina, al- (Tripoli), 58, 74, 77, 79, 86
mobile banking, 233, 235
Mogadishu, Somalia, 44, 77, 170, 209–210
Mogamma al-Tahrir (Cairo), 183–184
Moldova, 38
money transfer: hawala system, 236–241; industry, 233–235; informal, 236–243
Morsi, Mohamed, 181, 254
Mosul, Iraq, 39
Mouakeh, Khaldoun al-, 225
Mozambique, x, xi, 146
M-PESA, 233, 235

INDEX

Mubarak, Hosni, 179, 181
multinational corporations, 28–30
municipal authorities, 13, 23, 49, 190–191; aid agencies and, 122–123; autonomy of, 111–112; funding for, 122
Muslim Brotherhood, 181, 198
Myanmar (Burma), 9, 18, 61, 232
Mytilene, Greece, 39

Naba'a, al- (Beirut), 82–83
Nahr al-Bared Palestinian camp, Lebanon, 101–102
Nairobi, Kenya, 7, 18, 104, 145–146, 170–171, 228–229, 242
Nakba, 178
Nasr City (Cairo), 172, 192–197, 200, 204
Nasser, Gamal Abdel, 176–178, 192, 193
national governments, 4, 24; donor funding and, 120–121, 264; encampment policies, xi, 11, 46, 94, 96; fiscal transfers from, to cities, 111–112; international assistance for, 11; refugee policies of, 12, 24, 169–170, 182–188; as rent seekers, 116
National Poverty Targeting Programme, 131, 132
Nazi Germany, 9–10
near-diaspora, 23
Neighborhood, Development and International Cooperation Instrument—Global Europe, 113
neighborhood effect, xiv–xv, 7–8, 244
neighborhoods: Ard al-Lewa, 244–259; area-based approaches to helping, 91–93, 126–127; of Cairo, 189–204; impact of refugees on, xiv–xv, 7–8, 125–127, 168, 244; local citizens in, 125–127; social cohesion of, 15–16, 136, 168, 244–259, 262; social transformation of, 82–83; tensions within, 248–250; in Tripoli, 76, 82–83
Netherlands, 5, 29
networks, 221
New Administrative Capital, 207
"New Cities," Egypt, 199, 207
New Damietta, Egypt, 225–226
New Suez Canal, 176
Niemeyer, Oscar, 78
Niger, 160–164
Nigeria, 50, 206–207; Nigerians, 195
nongovernmental organizations (NGOs), xii, xv, 24, 26, 27; funding for, 117–120; international, 24, 26, 27, 214; in Lebanon, 118–119; smuggling and, 162–163
Nordic countries, 13
Norman, Kelsey, 182
North America: cities, 4; resettlement in, 59–60
North Lebanon, 74–75, 79–82
Norway, 29
Norwegian Refugee Council (NRC), xii, 32, 88–89, 91
Nuba Mountains, Sudan, 195
Nyala, Sudan, 39, 46, 96

Obock, Djibouti, 160
Obour, al-, Egypt, 200
Occupancy Free of Charge (OFC) program, 88–89, 91
Omdurman, Sudan, 41–44, 47
OpAntiSH (Operation Anti-Sexual Harassment), 253
Open Society Foundations, 27
Ottoman Empire, 69, 177

INDEX

out-groups, 249–250
own-source revenues (OSRs), 110–111, 123
Oxfam, 26

Pakistan, xi, 18
Palestine Liberation Organization (PLO), 69, 100, 103, 178
Palestinian refugees, 33, 36, 64, 96; camps, 94–96, 100–104, 170, 262–263; in Egypt, 168, 173–179; gatherings, 86; humanitarian assistance for, 122; in Lebanon, 66–69, 86, 100–104; refugee policies for, 185
Partnership for Prospects program, 136
Pasha, Muhammad Ali, 177
patronage politics, 161–162
PayPal, 233
peri-urban land, 43, 44–45, 117, 190, 197. *See also* informal settlements
persecution, xi, xiv, 3, 9, 12, 20, 22, 53, 57, 61, 176, 179, 266, 270
Personal Status Law (PSL), 254
Philip, Ryan, xix, 19, 172
place attachment, 61
plastics, 142, 150
Poland, 5, 15, 38, 79, 110
political activism, 107, 108–109, 253–254
political mobilization, xiv, 12, 49–50
Pol Pot regime, xi
popular urbanization, 51
population data, 32–36, 112
population registries, 34
port cities, 37, 40, 225–226. *See also specific cities*
Port Said, Egypt, 176
poverty, in Lebanon, 66–67, 73, 130–131

primary cities, 37–39, 167. *See also specific cities*
private sector, 16–17; funding, 26, 28–30; humanitarian industry and, 11; Private Sector Partnerships, 29
property developers, 41, 81–82
property prices, 14–15
protests, 16, 50, 143, 181, 208–211, 212–213, 253–255, 261. *See also* political activism
Protocol Relating to the Status of Refugees (1967), 21, 22, 25, 70, 119
Przemysl, Poland, 38
PS4R (Private Sector for Refugees), 30
public health, 15, 49. *See also* health services
public housing, 193
public-private partnerships, in waste management, 148
public schools. *See* schools
public services, 15–17, 24, 81, 83, 131, 141; in Egypt, 183, 217–218; funding for, 122; lack of, in informal settlements, 86, 198; in Tripoli, 141–142. *See also* infrastructure
Putnam, Robert, 249

Qatar Airways, 30

Rachid Karame Fairground, 77–78, 123
Raineri, Luca, 161, 162
ransom money, 156, 231
real estate developers, 198–199
recycling, 142, 143
Refugee Act (Kenya), 109
refugee agencies, 25, 137, 167, 172, 247. *See also* humanitarian agencies; United Nations High Commissioner for Refugees

refugee camps, xi, xiv, 5, 94–109; impacts of, 96, 104–109, 262–263; vs. informal settlements, 46; in Lebanon, 94; local residents and, 107–108; location of, 96; management of, 98; movement on and off, 104, 106; in/near Tripoli, 96; Palestinian, 94, 95, 96, 100–104, 170, 262–263; policies on, xi, 11, 46, 67, 94, 96, 98–100, 169–171, 185, 262–263; reasons for, 97–99; resources provided by, 106–107; security issues on, 103; turned into urban settlements, 107, 109; UNHCR and, 97–99. *See also specific camps*

refugee community organizations (RCOs), 255–259

Refugee Convention. *See* Convention Relating to the Status of Refugees

refugee entrepreneurs, 220–229, 261, 267

Refugee Registration Cared "blue card," 183, 185

refugees, xi–xvi, 3; actions of, 17–18; assets of, 266–267; attitudes toward, xiii–xv, 11–14, 69, 72, 75, 125–127, 136, 261–262, 264–266; banking by, 233–235; children, 16, 33–34, 244, 251–252, 255–256, 257; compared with migrants, xiv; counting of, 33–34, 36, 191; definition of, 21–22, 57, 60; deportations of, 73; determination process for, 57; diversity of, 266–267; in Egypt, 168–169, 171, 173–188, 195–196, 199–204; in Europe, 4–5; experiences of, xiii–xiv, 4; flows of, 9–10, 37–39, 173; harassment of, 250; housing for, 79–82, 88–93, 195–196; humanitarian assistance for, 10–11, 25, 28, 88–93, 112–124, 125–137, 217–219, 262; impact of, 79–82, 125–126, 244, 261–270; in Lebanon, 63–73; from Lebanon, 68–69; policies on, 12, 24, 169–170, 182–188; population characteristics, 12; protections for, 21–22; registration of, 65, 71, 183–184; research on, xi–xiii; resettlement of, 59–60, 215–219, 271; return home by, 61; risk factors for, 215, 217; scapegoating of, 18; smuggling of, 59, 60–61, 153–164; statistics on, 30–36, 64, 261; stuck in cities, reasons for, 57–62; unequal treatment of, 213; unregistered, 33–34, 268–269; women, 250–255; work policies toward, 12, 71–72, 183, 218, 267. *See also specific nationalities*

Refugees Act (South Africa), 99

refugee status determination (RSD) interviews, 60

Refugee Voices, 208

Regional Refugee and Resilience Plan (3RP), 213–214

remittances, 193, 230–232; informal money transfers and, 236–243; money transfer industry and, 233–235

rent: control, 189, 193, 196; costs, 47, 76, 79–80, 84, 87–89, 123, 125, 129, 135, 194–196; seeking, 113–116, 155

rents (from aid agencies), 123, 163, 194–196. *See also* housing

resettlement, 31, 59–60, 61, 67, 71, 208, 215–216, 271

residence permits, 72, 183–184, 186

INDEX

Rio de Janeiro, Brazil, 39
Rohingya refugees, 9
Romania, 38, 286
Rosto (Cairo), 223–224, 227, 229
rural-urban migration, 40, 169, 175, 176
Russia, 5; invasion of Ukraine by, 4, 38, 79; refugees in, 38
Rwanda, 268; genocide, 9

Sadat, Anwar al-, 178, 193, 206, 207
Saleh, Elizabeth, 149
Samuel, Akinrolabu, 50
sanadiq (informal savings groups), 256–257
sanctions, 237–238, 242
sanctuary cities, 268
Sandton (Johannesburg), ix–x
sanitation systems, 12, 15, 81, 86, 88, 92, 131, 140, 146, 198
San José de Cúcuta, Colombia, 39
Santa Marta, Colombia, xii
Saqba, Syria, 225
satellite cities, of Cairo, 200, 203–213
Saudi Arabia, 248
Schengen visa, 59
schools, 12, 16, 63, 107, 131, 183, 217, 255–257
sea dumping, 143, 144–145
secondary cities, 38, 40, 48, 167. *See also specific cities*
Second World War, 36
sector-specific cash, 129
security problems, 15–16, 49, 97–98, 103, 263
Serbia, 13
sexual harassment, 250, 252–254
Shabaab, al-, 57, 170
shantytowns, 76. *See also* informal settlements

sharia law, 179, 248
Sharkia, al-, Egypt, 200
Sharp, Deen, 45, 199
Shatila camp, Lebanon, 100, 103
Sheikh Zayed City, Egypt, 207, 227, 251
Shirika Plan, 93, 109
Sibai, Yusif al-, 178
Sicily, 13
Sidon, Lebanon, 103
SIM cards, 34, 235
Sims, David, 191, 193, 196, 199
Sinai Peninsula, Egypt, 176
Sisi, Abdel Fattah el-, 175, 181, 199, 227
Six-Day War, 176
6th of October City, Egypt, 200, 204, 206–208, 211–212, 271; establishment of, 207–208; refugee entrepreneurs in, 222–224; UNHCR in, 208–213
Slovakia, 38
Slumdwellers International, 50
slum lords, 81
slums, xiv, 7, 35, 44, 50–51, 83, 194. *See also* informal settlements
small businesses, 28, 47
smugglers, 59–61, 64
smuggling, 153–164, 247, 268–269; in Agadez, 160–164; hub towns, 160–164; impact on cities of, 156–160; revenue from, 158–159; routes and networks, 156, 157–158
social cohesion: impact of cash assistance on, 136; of neighborhoods, 15–16, 136, 168, 244, 245–259, 262; programs to support, 131
social media, 13, 16, 50
social transformation, of neighborhoods, 82–83

INDEX

Solidarités International, 92
solid waste, 89, 122, 138–152
Somalia, 9, 36, 44, 57, 160, 230, 232
Somali refugees, 18, 59, 179–180, 185, 194, 232
Sony, 30
South Africa, ix–x; apartheid, ix–xi; census data, 35; encampment policies, 98–99; refugee policy of, xi; UNHCR protests in, 210
South Sudan, 9, 39, 44, 107, 230; refugees from, 179, 195, 204; remittances to, 232; return to, 61
Soweto, South Africa, ix
Spain, 5
spatial landscape, 77–78
St. Andrew's Refugee Services (Cairo), 214
statelessness, 6, 25, 33, 87, 177, 179, 187
state protection rackets, 161–162
statistics, xiii, 30–36, 64
Sudan, 9, 25, 105, 248, 270; civil war in, 44, 173; IDPs in, 41–44, 46; refugees in, 177; remittances to, 232; return to, 61; Second Sudanese Civil War, 179; smuggling through, 154
Sudanese refugees, 16, 169, 171, 173, 175, 179, 182, 185, 186, 194, 195, 204
Suez Canal, 176; Suez Canal Zone, 196
Suez Crisis, 176–177
Sultanbeyli, Istanbul, 115
Sweden, 5, 29
Syria, xv, 4, 9, 232; border between Lebanon and, 74–75; civil war in, 53, 65, 70; Egypt and, 168; Lebanon and, 69–70, 168; return to, 61, 73
Syrian Arab Red Crescent, 69

Syrian Businessmen Association (Cairo), 225
Syrian cuisine, 223–224
Syrian refugees, 10, 53, 270; in 6th of October City, 208; businesses by, 222–228; in camps, 94–96; in Egypt, 168–171, 173–175, 180–182, 185, 199–200; humanitarian assistance for, 114, 121–122, 213–215; impact of, on waste problem, 146–152; in Jordan, 31, 33, 36; in Lebanon, 63–73, 96, 99–100, 118–119, 146–152, 169–170; movement of, 39; return home by, 73; rights and protections for, 71–72; smuggling of, 153–154; in Tripoli, 15–16, 57–62, 244; in Türkiye, 58

Tanzania, 97, 105
targeting problem, 133
Tartus, Syria, 74
taxes, 45, 110, 111, 155, 229, 262; diaspora tax, 240; tax base, 49, 267
temporary residence permits, 72
Texas, 4
Thailand, xi
Toms, 30
townships, in South Africa, ix, x–xi
trade, cross-border, 221–222
trade-in-aid, 135
traffic congestion, 49, 78, 192, 194, 206, 251
trafficking, 155, 156, 162, 187, 215. *See also* human smuggling
transit cities, 19, 54, 158, 252, 269; refugees stuck in, 54, 57–62, 162
transit countries, 18, 155, 268
transportation, 12, 16, 194, 205–206

INDEX

trash, 143–145, 146; Trash Mountain, 138–140
Tripoli, Lebanon, xiv, 18–19, 53–55; al-Mina port, 58; area-based projects in, 92–93; compared with Cairo, 167–172; field research in, 55; historical context of, 68; housing in, 75–82; humanitarian funding for, 118–124; informal settlements in, 83–87; national government and, 24; neighborhoods in, 82–83; Palestinian camps in, 101–104; public infrastructure in, 141–142; smuggling economy in, 155, 157–158; spatial impact of refugees on, 76–93; Special Economic Zone, 140; Syrian refugees in, 15–16, 57–63, 74–93, 244; taxes in, 111; underground economy of, 155–156; unemployment in, 72; waste management in, 138–152
Trump, Donald, 18, 29; administration, 4
Tsing, Anna, 229
Türkiye, xi, 10, 39; humanitarian funding to, 113–114; refugee camps in, 67, 86, 94; refugees in, 53, 58; smuggling and, 154, 159

Uganda, 36, 105, 130; border towns in, 39; census data, 35; external funding for, 17; informal settlements in, 46; Kampala, 17, 146, 147, 257–258
Ukraine: return to, 61; Russian invasion of, 5, 79, 110, 270
Ukrainian refugees, 4–5, 9, 38; humanitarian assistance for, 122; impact of, on housing markets, 79; in Poland, 15; in United States, 18
UN agencies, xv, 10, 24–27; attacks on, 209; donor funding and, 117–120; in Lebanon, 118–119; national hires, 212–213; rents paid by, 123; security at, 209–210; smuggling and, 162–163; staff of, 77, 79, 167–168, 209, 211–213, 216. *See also specific agencies*
underground economy: hawala system and, 236–243; smuggling, 153–164; in Tripoli, 155–156
UN Development Programme, 27, 145
undocumented status, 60–61, 71–72, 102–103, 164, 179, 186–188, 267
unemployment, in Lebanon, 67, 72
UN Environmental Programme (UNEP), 27, 150
UN-Habitat, 92, 150
UNICEF, 25, 117, 119, 120, 136, 257
Unilever, 30
Uniqlo, 30
United Kingdom, 5, 29, 268
United Nations, 112. *See also specific agencies*
United Nations High Commissioner for Refugees (UNHCR), 10, 25–26; in 6th of October City, 208–213; budget of, 25–26, 120; cash assistance by, 128, 131–135; compound buildings of, in Tripoli, 77–78; contributions to, 28–29; data from, 31–34, 64–65; in Egypt, 182, 208–215; funding for, 117, 119, 120, 213–215; in Lebanon, 65, 70–71, 118–119; mission of, 25; national hires, 212–213; operations of, 26; private sector and, 29–30;

329

INDEX

United Nations High Commissioner for Refugees (*cont.*)
  protests at, 209–212; RCOs and, 257–258; refugee camps and, 97–99; registration with, 183–184; resettlement process and, 60, 215–217; security at, 212; staffing and office space, 123, 216; Syrian refugees and, 64; unpopularity of, 212–213
United Nations Relief and Works Agency (UNRWA), 178
United States, xii, 4, 5, 17; aid from, 25, 28–29, 119, 148, 214; asylum seekers in, 60, 185; census data, 35; definition of refugee in, 22; desire to move to, 57; refugees to, 17–18; urban sprawl in, 49
urban agglomeration, 40
urban informality, 45. *See also* informal settlements
urbanization: in Cairo, 190, 192, 197, 199; popular, 51; from refugees, 80–81, 269
urban land grab, 41
urban migration: of displaced people, xiii–xiv; versus humanitarian influxes, 8–12; regular, xiii
urban refugees, research on, xii–xiii, 4
urban renewal, 18
urban sprawl, 41, 49
Urfa, Türkiye, 39
USAID, 28, 29
US State Department, xii, 27–29, 92
Utica, New York, 17–18

Valetta, Malta, 39
Venezuela, 10, 39, 232
violence, against women, 252–255
visa regimes, 57, 154

vocational training, 28
Vodafone Foundation, 30
vouchers, 129, 131, 132, 135

wages, 66, 72, 97, 130; wage discrimination, 14
Warraq Island (Cairo), al-, 50
Warsaw, Poland, 79
waste: management, 138–152; pickers, 141, 147, 149–152
water systems, 15, 81, 86, 131, 141–142, 145, 198
Wendywood (South Africa), x
Western Union, 233, 235
Wilson, Claire, 19
women: protests by, 253–254; refugee, 250–255; violence against, 252–255; women's groups, 256–257
Women in Informal Employment: Globalizing and Organizing (WIEGO), 150
workers: Egyptian, 176, 193; undocumented, 60–61, 102–103, 164
work opportunities, 220–229, 267–268
work permits, 70–72, 126, 157, 159, 183
work policies, 12, 71–72, 183, 218, 267
WorkReady Denver, 267–268
World Bank, xv, 10–11, 27, 28, 30, 66, 112, 120, 124, 132, 230
World Food Programme (WFP), 25, 117, 119, 120, 124, 214, 217
World Health Organization (WHO), 253
World Refugee Forum (WRF), 30
WorldRemit, 235

xawilaad, 236–241
xenophobia, 13, 181, 225

330

INDEX

"yellow card," 183, 185
Yemen, 61, 176
Young, Helen, 41–42
"You Stink" campaign, 143
youth development programs, 131

Zaatari camp, Jordan, 263
Zamalek (Cairo), 168, 189–190, 212, 248
zero-waste society, 150
Zikhali, Whitehead, 243
Zimbabwe, xi, 242–243